BORDERLANDS AND CROSSROADS

Funded by the Government of Canada
Financé par la gouvernement du Canada

Demeter Press
140 Holland Street West
P. O. Box 13022
Bradford, ON L3Z 2Y5
Tel: (905) 775-9089
Email: info@demeterpress.org
Website: www.demeterpress.org

Demeter Press logo based on the sculpture "Demeter" by Maria-Luise Bodirsky <www.keramik-atelier.bodirsky.de>

MIX
Paper from
responsible sources
FSC
www.fsc.org   FSC® C004071

Printed and Bound in Canada

Front cover artwork: Janet Maher, "The Ride," 2015, paper collage, paper ephermera, plastic rings, matboard, coloured pencil, matted and framed, 22 x 17 inches

Library and Archives Canada Cataloguing in Publication

        Borderlands and crossroads : writing the motherland
/ edited by Jane Satterfield and Laurie Kruk.

Includes bibliographical references and index.
ISBN 978-1-77258-024-2 (paperback)

        1. Mothers--Literary collections. 2. Motherhood--Literary collections. 3. Women--Literary collections. I. Kruk, Laurie, 1962-, editor II. Satterfield, Jane, 1964-, editor

PN6071.M7B67 2016   808.8'035252   C2016-905134-X

BORDERLANDS AND CROSSROADS
Writing the Motherland

EDITED BY
Jane Satterfield
and Laurie Kruk

DEMETER

DEMETER PRESS

In memoriam
Rishma Dunlop 1956 – 2016

Table of Contents

Acknowledgements

Thanks to Andrea O'Reilly, publisher of Demeter Press, for encouraging us to think and write about mothers, motherhood, and literature ... and for putting Laurie and Jane together in a fruitful cross-border collaboration and digital dialogue.

Thanks to all at Demeter Press who made production possible, especially Angie Deveau for her work on promotion and distribution.

Special thanks to Janet Maher for cover art.

Thanks to the women of Nipissing's Faculty and Administrative Support Services and Print Plus for generous and timely technical assistance.

For their support and critical commentary, we'd like to express our gratitude to Valerie Miner and to maternal scholars Ruth Panofsky and Sheena Wilson.

Thanks to friends and mentors for conversations that helped inspire this book.

On the home front, thanks are due to our families for cheering us on. Jane's mother and daughter offered inspiration and support. She would also like to thank Ned Balbo, partner in life and art, for unflagging encouragement.

Laurie would like thank her three families—of birth, of love, of chance—for their continued support and inspiration. As a writer, she also valued creative input offered by Janet, Jennifer and Cathy (of "WWW"), and her husband, Ian McCulloch.

Lastly, our gratitude to the talented and accomplished writers included here for sharing the words and vision which made this book possible.

JANE SATTERFIELD

Introduction

The words are maps.
—Adrienne Rich, "Diving into the Wreck"

I have been thinking about a drive I took once, as a passenger in a small car nosing along a rutted road in the English countryside. I had a road atlas or official ordnance survey—a real map, printed on paper—propped open on my lap. The pages laid bare a neural network of routes that could be traced with a finger, visual markers of transit and arrival. That day's designated navigator, I was charged with finding the way back to the main road from an auxiliary road that led to the Neolithic stone circle I'd come to photograph.

It was late summer and a mix-tape spilled indie music from the tape deck. I was humming along until I wasn't. The road tumbled to a swatch of gravel and suddenly gave out, dead-ended. No signs, no clue, no warning on the map. An unmowed field ahead. The only, obvious choice was to reverse course, to re-route.

Much later on, in the hazy post-partum days after my daughter's birth, and on and off throughout her first year, I'd find myself thinking back to that uncanny moment—the car stalled there, the road a blank stitch, a vacancy. I'd debarked in the strange new country of motherhood, and, like generations of mothers before me, had to find my way in a land of shifting borders and vivid transformations.

I'm not the only one. Throughout the poems, essays, and stories collected here, you'll encounter the powerful voices of prize-winning writers who reverse course, re-route, ditch old maps and chart new ones as they travel through maternal landscapes past and present, recovering lost connections and forging new ones. Intimate and disarmingly honest, the poetry and prose selections in *Borderlands and Crossroads* reflect many modes—lyric, narrative, deliberative, elegiac—and reveal, too, the profound connections between private and public life. In the forty years since the publication of Adrienne Rich's *Of Woman Born: Motherhood as Institution and Experience*, much has and hasn't changed. Across the globe, societies still impose powerful proscriptions. The maternal body remains a site of political contention. Religious, social, and economic forces continue to generate obstacles that limit practical support and greater progress. Gratifyingly, the literature of motherhood itself has become a vital force of commemoration and change.

Though the work of writing is often solitary, in long hours spent at the screen or hovering over the page, no writer exists in isolation nor writes without some connection to family, history, and community. If mothers are "the countries we come from," as novelist Rachel Cusk suggests, it's no accident that in our anthology selections, metaphors of travel, exile, and displacement abound. The maternal body is a primal landscape, a space of belonging whose influence reverberates throughout a lifetime, regardless of where our wanderings take us. The poetry and prose collected here reaches us from those front lines. With wistful humor, poet Beth Ann Fennelly offers a vivid dispatch from the front line of new motherhood, where child and mother are "tied to the tides of whimper and milk." The mother's relationship to her former life recedes as the demands of lactation and infant care take over, superseding maternal independence and fulfillment. This brief interval, intense though it may be in the moment, is short-lived, especially in retrospect. As the poet considers the shift in her priorities, she finds a kinship in the "factory-working wives" of another generation who were absolved from wartime duties to return to hearth, home, and soldier-husbands. Eventually, as Fennelly jests, the mother's breasts "resume their lives as glamour girls" and "the motherland recedes on the horizon."

The border between *before* and *after*, so vividly inscribed in maternal memory, is further complicated by the shifting geographies of twenty-first century life. Through the lyrically insistent lines of the *ghazal*, a form of Arabic origin traditionally focused on romantic themes, poet Nicole Cooley circles back through the aftermath of 9/11. As ash-filled smog fills the air of Lower Manhattan, the poet considers the suitcase that her grandmother gave her for childhood sleep-overs: the same suitcase she packed in her third trimester, preparing for her daughter's birth, and the same suitcase she now fills with emergency items in the event of another terrorist attack.

Here, as in other poems we've collected, the borrowed form is an expedient container, lending shapeliness to the chaos of a watershed moment while bearing the weight of elegiac vision—an urgent fusion of tradition and innovation. Woven throughout our collection is a recognition of our migratory past. In the wake of trauma, war, economic or other displacement, how much must be jettisoned, what can possibly be carried, what must be sacrificed—for mere survival, for the preservation of the next generation?

The impulse toward preservation resonates powerfully throughout *Borderlands and Crossroads*. Each contributor offers a unique and unforgettable object lesson; many meditate on souvenirs and other domestic objects that take on talismanic status. Literal reminders of inheritance circulate in the framed photos that family members carry or abandon: the dollhouse lovingly restored, the bread baked, the documents saved. We encounter the heirlooms left behind, the memories that vanish or persist—a slant of light across the cobbled streets, the wind and weather, the life story preserved on an old cassette, corn pollen dusted over a newborn's head, the paper flowers thrown into a funeral pyre, the friends and adversaries, national songs, phrases of the mother tongue.

Here, too, we see that the very act of writing serves as an aide-mémoire and more. Narratives preserve joyful moments and help writers and readers preserve that which might be lost to time. They build kinship, and they shape and store the silences that are painful to recount. Kirun Kapur's "Light" revisits the stories handed down, the clues overheard in women's kitchen conversations that circle around the unspeakable gender violence in the wake of India's Partition. Pimone Triplett's maternal elegy adapts a traditional Thai verse form, grieving a miscarried child even as she recovers a homeland. Penelope Pelizzon's measured verse, with its elegant lines, spools through memory and maternal histories, coming to terms with family, weighing the loss of an unborn child, and confronting the tenderness and cruelties of Neapolitan culture. Pushing past silence, recording and transmitting knowledge in this way, the writers represented in this anthology resist cultural and political limitations in order to stake out geographies of hope.

Transformative and empowering as it may be, motherhood is disruptive; its wisdom often arrives in accidental or piecemeal fashion. This is why I believe that the literature of motherhood shares a kinship with other crisis narratives: disruptions are represented in the form of fragmented and elliptical scenes and in unadorned language that seeks to interrogate and revise assumptions, presumptions, and inherited scripts. This kinship is unmistakable in the essays collected here. By its very nature, nonfiction creates a broader canvas for analysis, meditation, and reflection; whatever their vision, essayists revel in the freedom to trace lines of inquiry wherever they lead.

The pleasure of reading essays is heady. They offer urgency, the intimacy of confession, the delight that comes with an impassioned quest. They make us feel like trusted companions on a perilous journey that careens from certainty to doubt to surprising revelation. In "A Brief History of Near and Actual Losses," Camille Dungy recounts the frustration she felt at her two-year-old daughter's restlessness during a visit to the slave dungeons in Ghana's Cape Coast Castle. The child doesn't want to be carried, wants to be freed from her mother's grasp, permitted to run around, to make contact with ancestral ground. Dungy worries that her child's behavior distracts the other visitors, worries about her daughter's exposure to dirt and grime, worries about this behavior's seeming trespass on sacred ground. Later, while the mother is trying to relax on a coastal beach, her daughter is swept up momentarily in the Atlantic's powerful tide. Dungy's essay forms a powerful meditation on the ways that "the fetid history" of legacy can distract us from present dangers.

The essay is nothing if not capacious, an elastic form that perfectly accommodates the temporal and tonal shifts of contemporary life, as well as questions of allegiance, of transit and arrival. In their explorations of the adoption triad, Jennifer Kwon Dobbs, Emily Hipchen, and Heidi Czerweic consider the social and emotional construction of kinship, imagining and re-imagining choices made by or for biological and adoptive mothers, illuminating the impact of choices that resonate beyond a single moment in time. Elsewhere, in speculating about maternal identity and national belonging, Adrianne Kalfopoulou turns to a literary mother, Hannah Arendt, to conduct a conversation across generations. Kalfopoulou's essay shuttles between present day New York and Greece (the adopted homeland undergoing a tragic economic collapse), the memory of the New York of her youth, and the tensions between herself and the college-aged daughter who wants no border-crossings between the essays that they write: one for reasons of survival, the other for course credit. Michelle Elvy's lyric prose, meanwhile, captures an all-too-brief cross-cultural exchange. In the heat of a park in an ancient colonial outpost, the writer and her daughters encounter a group of women who encourage them to try on the burqa, *hijab*, and *niqāb*. Having raised daughters outside the traditional moorings of gender and nationality, making a home in a sailboat that crosses through international waters, Elvy meditates on the spaces unexpected events open up and the crossroads where lives intersect, even briefly. The essay is a powerful force with which to conjure.

The notion of motherland—as literal landscape, as inheritance, or home—is vast and varied. It's my hope that the work gathered in *Borderlands and Crossroads* will spark further travels, in poetry and prose, in person and in print.

POETRY

BETH ANN FENNELLY

Latching On, Falling Off

I. When She Takes My Body into Her Body

She comes to me squirming in her father's arms,
gumming her fingers, her blanket, or rooting
on his neck, thrashing her mouth from side to side
to raise a nipple among his beard hairs. My shirt sprouts
two dark eyes; for three weeks she's been outside me,
and I cry milk to hear my baby—any baby—cry.

In the night, she smells me. From her bassinet
she wakes with a squall, her mouth impossibly huge,
her tongue aquiver with anger the baby book says
she doesn't have, aquiver like the clapper of a bell.
Her passion I wasn't prepared for, her need
naked as a sturgeon with a rippling, red gill.

Who named this *letdown*, this tingling upswing?
A valve twists, the thin opalescence spurts past the gate,
then comes the hindcream to make my baby creamyfat.
I fumble with one hand at my bra, offer the target
of my darkened nipple, with the other hand steady
her too-heavy head. She clamps on, the wailing ceases.

No one ever mentioned she's out for blood. I wince
as she tugs milk from ducts all the way to my armpits.
It hurts like when an angry sister plaits your hair.

9

It hurts like that, and like that you desire it.
Soon, soon—I am listening—she swallows,
and a layer of pain kicks free like a blanket.

Tethered, my womb spasms, then, lower, something shivers.
Pleasure piggybacks the pain, though it, too,
isn't mentioned, not to the child, now drunk and splayed
like a hobo, not to the sleeping husband, innocent beside us.
Let me get it right so I remember: Once, I bared my chest
and found an animal. Once, I was delicious.

II. First Night Away from Claire

I forget to pack my breast pump,
a novelty not in any novelty shop
here at the beach, just snorkel tubes,
shark teeth, coconut-shell bikini tops.

Should we drive back? I'm near-drunk
from my first beer in months. We've got
a babysitter, a hotel room, and on the horizon
a meteor shower promised. We've planned
slow sex, sky watch, long sleep.
His hand feels good low on my back,
tracing my lizard tattoo. And he can help—
he's had quick sips before—so we stay,
rubbing tongues, butter-dripping shrimp.

Later, he tries gamely, but it's not sexy,
not at all—he'd need to suck a glassful
from each breast. The baby's so much better.
He rests. *It's hot,* he says, and *sweet.*
We're tired. We fall asleep.
I wake predawn from pain.

Those meteors we were too tired to watch—
it will be thirty years
before they pass this way again.

III. After Weaning, My Breasts Resume Their Lives as Glamour Girls

Initially hesitant, yes,
but once called into duty,
they never looked back.

Models-turned-spokeswomen,
they never dreamed they'd have so much to say.
They swelled with purpose,

mastered that underwater tongue,
translating the baby's long-vowel cries
and oozing their answer,

tidal, undeniable, fulfilled.
For a year, they let the child draw forth that
starry river, as my friend Ann has termed it—

then, it was time, they stopped the flow.
They are dry now, smaller, tidy, my nipples again
the lighter, more fetching pink.

The bras ugly as Ace bandages,
thick-strapped, trap-doored,
too busy for beauty—

and the cotton pads lining them
until damp, then yeasting in the hamper—
all have been washed and stored away.

So I'm thinking of how,
when World War II had ended,
the factory-working wives

were fired, sent home
to cook for returning soldier husbands
when my husband enters the bedroom—

Aren't you glad? he asks, glad,
watching me unwrap bras
tissue-thin and decorative

from the tissue of my old life,
watching, worshipfully, the breasts resettle
as I fasten his red favorite-

Aren't you glad? He's walking
toward them, addressing them, it seems—
but, Darling, they can't answer,

poured back into their old mold,
muffled beneath these lovely laces,
relearning how it feels, seen and not heard.

IV. It Was a Strange Country

where I lived with my daughter while I fed her
from my body. It was a small country, an island for two,
and there were things we couldn't bring with us,
like her father. He watched from the far shore,
well-meaning, useless. Sometimes I asked
for a glass of water, so he had something to give.

The weather there was overcast, volatile.
We were tied to the tides of whimper and milk,
the flotsam of spit-up, warm and clotted,
on my neck, my thigh. Strange: I rarely minded,
I liked the yogurt smell trapped beneath her chinfolds.
How soon her breath bloomed sweet again.

She napped, my ducts refilled
like veins of gold that throb though lodged in rock.
When she woke, we amped up our body language.
How many hours did she kiss one breast or the other?
I told her things. She tugged my bottom lip, like
sounds were coins beneath my fascinating tongue.

We didn't get many tourists, much news—
behind the closed curtains, rocking in the chair,
the world was a rumor all summer. All autumn.
All winter, in which she sickened, sucked for comfort,
a cord of snot between her nose, my breast.
Her small pillows of breath. We slept there, single-bodied.

Then came spring and her milk teeth and her bones
longer in my lap, her feet dangling, and, rapt,
she watched me eat, scholar of sandwiches and water.
Well, I knew the signs. I held her tight, I waded out,
I swam us away from that country, swam us back
to my husband pacing the shore, yelling and waving,

in his man fists, baby spoons that flashed, cupping suns.
It was a strange country that we returned to, separately—
strange, but not for long. Soon, the milk stops
simmering and the child forgets the mother's taste,
so the motherland recedes on the horizon,
a kindness—we return to it only at death.

NICOLE COOLEY

Suitcase

Gold-zippered, blue plaid, gilded with initials: suitcase
we were told to pack *in case of a new attack.* Girl's suitcase,

my grandmother's gift for those first sleep-overs.
I fill it with duct tape. *Cipro* hidden in the lining of the suitcase.

The pediatrician refused to give the drug but, yes, I begged, cried,
I demanded. In the *Before,* this would be my daughter's suitcase.

While she slept inside me, I'd pack a silky nightie, toothbrush.
In the third trimester, I'd lie in bed and arrange the suitcase.

Now: Swiss Army knife. Distilled water. *Potassium Iodide*
to carry with us *at all times* when we leave our home. *In case of—*

tablets to *swallow immediately* as the subway fills with smoke.
This city permanently on *Orange Alert,* the ready suitcase

waiting while I nurse my daughter, watch the news.
In the *After,* another day of jewel-blue sky, I pack the suitcase,

seal the windows as we were told against *possible chemical attack,*
but still we breathe in the burning, the ash, the soot.

Plan an evacuation route. With each warning, the city shuts tunnels, cuts us off. We're packed and ready, with our suitcase.

I watch the news. I already know I won't have another child,
not in this city. Packed and ready for the next attack: our suitcase.

Now the baby no longer fits in the circle of my arms. Pregnant,
I'd dreamed the girl I'd birth as safely miniature, kept in a suitcase.

You must be ready, the TV tells us. *To leave your life,
for the safety of your family.* I lay my daughter in the suitcase

stamped with my initials, N.R.C., letters engraved long ago
on a headstone, and now not mine, not hers, no one's suitcase.

MARILYN L. TAYLOR

To the Mother of a Dead Marine

Your boy once touched me, yes. I knew you knew
when your wet, reddened gaze drilled into me,
groped through my clothes for signs, some residue
of him—some lusciousness of mine that he
had craved, that might have driven his desire
for things perilous, poisonous, out-of-bounds.
Could I have been the beast he rode to war?
The battle mounted in his sleep, the rounds
of ammunition draped like unblown blossoms
round his neck? Could I have somehow flung
myself against the wall of his obsessions,
leaving spells and curses on his tongue?
Your fingers tighten, ready to engage
the delicate hair-trigger of your rage.

MARILYN L. TAYLOR

A Commencement Villanelle

I'd like to tell him something he should know
on this momentous day— his graduation.
I don't think he's going to like it, though.

He'll claim he heard that sermon long ago,
why can't I rid myself of my fixation,
quit mouthing things I think he ought to know?

He's certain that I'll tell him Take it slow.
Do all your messing up in moderation.
He's right. And he won't like it much. Although

he'll like it better than the way I'll go
mano a mano, some smooth variation
on all the things he doesn't know I know—

like where he hides his stash from Mexico
and other shortcuts to intoxication
beneath the basement stairs. He'll deny it, though.

Still, I'll avoid that burning down below,
exclude all references to fornication,
even small precautions. (Like he doesn't know?)

And that's my make-believe scenario,

my grand conclusion to his education:
I'll tell him everything he needs to know.
He'll barely listen. That won't stop me, though.

A. V. CHRISTIE

And I Thought of the Bracelet
That Said "Fall Risk"

My daughter is a "fall risk"—
no bad hip or sprain. Hairline fracture to continuing on
so that lack of belief in any future
shows up in the bloodwork.

In her hospital room, nurses in shifts—
Silent or proclaiming—
entrusted to keep watch, we having failed
in the watching.

The pills a flock that took her
to where she was translucent above the branches,
like speech. She was a robin's egg
and still more fragile.

She could not stand, fell forward
on me—I could not hold her.

A friend called to say the Arroyo Creek
had flooded his yard. How simple, I thought,
how one-to-one—*arroyo* meaning creek.

I was at home, then, putting under lock
everything sharp, everything poison.

I saw that everything was
or could be sharp, that even mild things
in abundance, or mixed,
could be toxic

A. V. CHRISTIE

Niagara

She is at the edge of the broken, the smooth, the no-moment-the-same,
the noise, the force, the forced.

She is afraid of analogies: *it could be anything.*
My daughter has started to become alone.
In the mist: cormorants.

Metaphor is one damn flimsy ineffectual barrel off the edge of.
It's got nothing on grief, the sheer scale of it, tumult,
and the going under.

Metaphor pretends to be vast and is an embarrassment.

So many cataclysms
any of which can introduce a double-ness into life.
To make a view larger or smaller.
All the ways to say *Help me, Help me.*

So many syndromes one after the other
Am I alive or dead?
Is this a dream or an afterlife?
Has the blood turned to powder?
No continuing recognition of my face—
no corresponding self.

And, too, I read about the experiential seizure—

always the vision, while convulsing, before going down:
repeatedly, guttering of the city in ruins
or watching people enter the room
with snow on their clothes.

No sense— so that
99¢ dreams are to breathtaking
as again and again is to wind
body is to threshold   as fear not is to torrent
gesture is to disturbance   as imply is to sunset.

Thus it follows, dear one, thus—   and thus—.

Love is this thundering veil, this vast span
with and without precedent.

JENNIFER FRANKLIN

One Photograph

—after *The Last Album: Eyes from the Ashes of Auschwitz-Birkenau*
by Ann Weiss

They hold nothing but each other. Fixed
like this forever, mother and daughter—

their love survives: testament to life before
God's great silence. No one alive knows

their names or will. Maybe it is wrong for me
to mourn them. But I put what remains in a small

pewter frame next to my dead grandmother
and her sister. When you rest your hands

on my shoulders, I think of them—the mother
in her housecoat, blossoming roses, the girl

in her swimsuit, tummy round and innocent.
In the cold cattle car, they had no nest but each

other. Human cries around them drowned out
owls in autumn, smothered everything but

stars that watched them suffer. I hope
they were together when they died—that

their eyes were the last of what they saw
in this fallen world. Even in the thick darkness

of my living room, I see them: embracing,
always almost kissing

JENNIFER FRANKLIN

My Daughter's Body

If you saw her, you would think she was beautiful.
Strangers stop me on the street to say it.

If they talk to her they see that beauty means
nothing. Their sight shifts to pigeons on the sidewalk.

Their eye contact becomes as poor as hers. They
slip away with varying degrees of grace. I never

know how much to say to explain the heartbreak.
As her smile sears me, I hold her hand all the way

home from the swings. The florist hands her
a dying rose and she holds it gently, without

ripping the petals like she does to the tulips
that stare at us with their insipid faces,

pretending that they can hold my sorrow
in their outstretched cups because I knew them

before I knew grief. They do not understand that
they are ruined for me now. I planted five hundred

bulbs as she grew inside of me, her brain already
formed by strands of damaged DNA

or something else the doctors do not understand.
After her bath, she curls up on me for lullabies—

the only time that her small body is still.
As I sing, I breathe in her shampooed hair and think

of the skeletons in the *Musée de Préhistoire*
in Les Eyzies. The bones of the mother and baby

rest in a glass case in the same position we lie
in now. They were buried in that unusual pose,

child curled up in the crook of the mother's arm.
The archaeologists are puzzled by the position.

It doesn't surprise me at all. It would be so easy
to die this way—both of us breathing our last

breaths with nursery rhymes on our open lips,
the promise of peaceful sleep.

BLAS FALCONER

The Annunciation

Whether she lifts a hand to her breast in protest or
surprise, I can't say, though we know how it ends.

He reaches out as if to keep her there, her fingers on
the open book of prayer or song, the cloth draped

across her waist. *Faith*, he might have said, even as
the cells of disbelief began to multiply: a son

who'd face great pain? Certain death? In one account,
she fled. He chased her back into the house—

not as Gabriel but a pull inside the ribs until
she acquiesced, exchanging one loss for another.

X-rays expose a sign of someone else's brush.
Experts doubt the dress or wings are his

but claim the sleeve, the buttoned cuff,
a triumph, young as the artist was, not having found

perspective: the vanishing point too high, one hand
too large, the flaw in her face: a lack of fear or awe.

BLAS FALCONER

Orphan

—after *Nocturnal (Horizon Line)*,
by Teresita Fernandez, graphite, 2010

I'd come to help settle your
mother's affairs. On the last night,

we ate where she worked
all her life. Now that she's gone,

you said, I'll never come back.
Looking out over the dark, you saw

a light in the distance, a boat
crossing the bay, and told

the story of the fisherman
cursed to float adrift

forever. You hadn't thought of it
since you were a child, and held

your hand across the table to
show me how it trembled.

I didn't understand until, alone,

years later, wandering the city where

I was born, I stood before
a black wall, polished to shimmer,

and it looked to me like the sea
at night, hard and endless.

ROBIN CARSTENSEN

Ghazal: The Bystanders

Seven a.m. in the Newark fog, three days after Christmas. You have not grown
tired waiting for your plane, gazing at the watery dust on the runway, at the grown

people carefully choosing their seats for as long as they can, as if building a small fire
between one another. You study a woman studying the horizon. You have not grown

a resolution to be braver next time you fly home to the land time forgot: Fathers
and mothers frozen, sons and daughters shrink-wrapped, petrified, not quite grown.

In Chicago, on a layover to your home, you sense the weight on men drinking in bars.
It wasn't raining that hard, mother had said to you. *I thought you would have grown*

more responsible, and taken the trash to the curb, father had agreed. You love the rain,
you just thought the trash could wait. *I raised a wimp,* mother announced to the grown

guests and your 41-year-old face. You could have shaken her until everything seized,
even the Keininger clock behind its beveled glass box, until she saw you,
a grown

woman, not the girl home from school, leaning in for the tempest, not
the eight-year-
old's failure to understand obedience, like math, its transparent cleanness,
its grown

up logic and flat surface, a glass door that the dreamer, the rogue bird,
smacks into before she hears it—the swift crack against the mouth to
make her see, and the sting, grown-

all over the body. Sometimes blurred images come into focus when we
stand back far enough: how your mouth fell slack when you saw your
mother trapped, not grown

past the girl who can't talk back to history, the way it packs down hard,
how the boulders, unbearable, shift and roll over the bystanders—the
children sooner gone than grown—

you swallowed back the gutted road. Noon at a dark oak bar in O'Hare:
you let the ale
linger on your tongue, trickle all the way down until you are warm again
and grown.

ROBIN CARSTENSEN

Villanelle for the Fearless

Twilit rain is rattling the loose shutter,
slapping and rolling down the windowpane,
soaking the swollen earth in surrender.

I dream of your mouth on mine and whether
you could burst like sun in the harvest grain.
Will the eaves give way like the loose shutter?

In the mist someone looks for her daughter.
Where in Kabul or Okemah has she gone,
soaking the earth overflowing surrender?

The best we can do is touch one another,
stroking the fears from our bodies falling
like rain rattling down a loose shutter.

Come let the rain bear down like a lover
weaving her scarves from the curve-faced moon
pulling the seas over shore, surrender

what you will, beloved balm and fire
cumulous in my arms, unbound, reborn
and soaking my ground. I surrender
like rain pounding loose every shutter.

HEIDI CZERWIEC

A Child of God, Much Like Yourself

I will pioneer a new way, explore unknown powers, and unfold to the world the deepest mysteries of creation.
— Mary Shelley, *Frankenstein*

I.   Wormwood, Gall [Chernobyl, 1986, 2011]

He snatched a fire and cocked it. Bang, he said. First, the face vibrates with stinging pins that pierce the skull with white light. *Stippling against snow, he sparked.* A metallic taste of iron sucked, sickening the tongue. Gag, coughing and vomiting as insides deliquesce, atomic bonds unlocking arms, the way a cold front melts or a Cold War melts down, Soviet states of matter breaking up. *He flailed, faultline, and burned absolute in his innards like saints.*

Children play in Ukrainian rain that turns black and oily. A gentle murder. Each child a lit lantern to be blown out: a toddler whose torso blooms into a tumor, *other self fused in a collision;* abandoned boy, *spraddlelegged and ragged,* slithering on a floormat and lapping oatmeal like a whining pack animal, *laborious gargoyle, unlearned;* a girl radiant in the *frail sheathing* of her throat—*unpinned ribbon of tongues, odd steel of grace tonged to the fire's temper*—until the doctors cut out her thyroid, glowing Chernobyl necklace. *Winter, outraged, cauterized them young.*

The elderly return, following the trails of mushrooms shining in the forest, find their way back by the lights of their own throats. In the Russia under Russia it is daylight all the time now. They prefer to die on familiar contaminated soil than in the anonymity of cities. Around them the forest thrives, crackling alive—the world's background noise increased threefold, *its jaw a galvanized fist chattering*—static hum, hidden in the milk like spilt glitter. They say the lost come back as boars, as luminous deer, as swallows, songs in their scarred throats, *frayed breath a vicious hissing.*

In the zone's irradiated radius, the concrete sarcophagus admits visitors minutes at a time.

II. No Romper Room for Miss Sherri [Germany, 1962]

Little seal, little seed *rutted ill,* you slid through a thalidomide-ridden womb, *homemade jigsaw pieced of slumpshouldered bump,* concealed for days from your mother until your flippers affixed to prosthetics for a gaudy appearance of passing. Beautiful mutant, *nubbin shucked bare, night-damp and humped in a dream-midden,* middle-aged now and what if no one to remind us of this ghostly treason? What then? Body *shucked bare,* the seal the true skin.

III. Theodore Roosevelt Approves this Message [Eugenics, ongoing]

Everywhere mothers spilt their milk, spilt fetuses they feared, fearing that ancient threat: that a woman visited with a corrupt birth be with her brood buried alive, each child a lit lantern to be blown out. *Vicious hammer, springloaded, sprocketing like an uncoiled snare. Slow occlusion rolling her to doom.* A severe doom, you will say, and not to be used among Christians, yet more to be looked into than it is. Keep the life stream pure of *some self-veering mutant, meniscus tilting aswamp.* Cleft Palate. Anencephaly. Feminism. Negro Criminal Youth. Idiot Brain. Asymmetrical Face. *Wrong blood, borne up. I'm supposed to be here, he said.*

IV. Orange Agents, Ready for Round-Up [Red River Valley, 2013]

Closer to home, women miscarry or give birth to genetically-modified organisms near a river whose banks overfloweth with farm runoff, *opaque vitriolic* to prevent more bad biology from breeding in. One baby bleeds out in utero, *blowed tree a shapeless bloom;* another's catastrophic defects cause a cascade of shutdowns, *no way to live in the ordered mistake of his losses. Palmupward, they bore it, crude agrarian figures in a violent mural.* You who have seen death—*a coffin-sized door, canted*—

V. [Fukushima, 2013]

go now, goddamned.

Italicized phrases are lines from an erasure poem I made from Cormac Mc-Carthy's novels Child of God *and* Outer Dark; *also contains riffs on lines from Lucie Brock-Broido.*

REFERENCES

Talbot, Eugene S. "Degeneracy: Its Causes, Signs, and Results" (1898). Online at *Medical History Library.*

Owens-Adair, Bethenia. "Human Sterilization: It's [sic] Social and Legislative Aspects" (1922) *Medical History Library.*

Fusco, Paul. "Chernobyl Legacy" (2010): a photo essay/narrated slideshow online

"Nuclear Nightmares: Twenty Years Since Chernobyl." Photos Robert Knoth; reporting Antoinette DeJong.

NoBody's Perfect (2008) film, dir. Niko von Glasow.

Wikipedia entries on Chernobyl, Thalidomide, Agent Orange, and Round-Up.

PAUL SUTHERLAND

Leaving Canada

The thirties' high-speed locomotive, in stone
relief, headlines the C.N.R. station, now trackless,
where the city slopes towards its long-discoloured bay
where, rucksack and a case underarm, I left my home
mum and my puffy-eyed grandma seeing me off.
We must've taken a twilight cab as none of us drove,
neither of them anticipating I might never return.

In semidarkness, we waited on the hardest bench
my escorts' hands folded in mine soft as a pudding
with their spring-scented wrists and lipstick smiles.
The Atlantic-bound was late. After months and years
of planning, for a moment, it seemed I might not leave.
Then a gust of air whistled; couplings flexed into place:
from the pull-down window waved a wave I can't retract.

KATHLEEN MCGOOKEY

Thank You for Your Question

I was unprepared for the sacrifice and noise. What did I know about earwax and antibiotics, car seats, or lost blankets with yellow stars? Caden from preschool had not yet chased my son with the potty plunger. Noah had not yet chewed with his mouth open at snack time. Freddie had not pinched Carson. Halle had not asked to sit in my lap. To say whether I enjoyed it? I liked rocking in 4 a.m. darkness, sleepy and afraid a face would appear at the window. Or that I'd hear, over the monitor, a stranger in the baby's room. But days full of obvious work, nowhere to be, alone with the baby, I would not have believed.

KATHLEEN MCGOOKEY

The Long Silence

When I told my children they could no longer speak, immediately they closed their mouths. They wanted to ask how long, and I wanted to say years, but I showed them the window where the mountain hid in fog. I held out a fossil they'd pulled from the creek. Soon it snowed. Years did pass. In that long silence, I washed dishes. I peeled beets. We forgot we had ever spoken and what we had spoken about. Folding their clothes was like saying prayers. I set out bowls of soup, and while the children ate, a forest rose up. Spiders spun silver hammocks where the children swayed, petting pearl-colored kittens that had dropped from the trees. If they fought, they rolled their eyes and pinched each other and then their fights were done. My daughter sewed dresses of leaves. Green snakes curled around my son's shoulders if he napped outside. When he woke, he built cage after cage of twigs. Soon hundreds of parrots flew in front of the sun, then circled and landed in the trees. They were hungry and lonely. They had traveled a long way to reach us. And then they opened their mouths.

V. PENELOPE PELIZZON

Blood Memory

Hunched in the bath, four ibuprofen gulped
        Too late to dull the muscle cramping
                To sate a god who thirsts
        Monthly for his slake of iron,
I am just a body bleeding in bad light.

But after an hour, as the wrenching wanes,
I run more water in, remembering
        When I was a girl my mother knew
                        One cure for this pain
                And, while I cried,
        Carried me mugs of tea and whiskey
                Clouded with sugar cubes.

In a palm of pinkish water, I scoop up
        A burl of my flesh, almond-sized.
                The tissues settle, livid
Red to nearly black as I tilt my hand
                Against the light to see it
Glistening like a ruby cabochon,
                Appealing as it appalls,
        Recalling one future, years ago,
        That would have borne itself on my blood
                        Had I allowed.
                The question swims into view:
Would I harbor another life now?

39

Last spring, I sat above the harbor in Naples
        With three friends whose children,
    After a week's vacation, were all
Safely back at school. Palpable,
           The holiday mood
    A morning freed from offspring brought!
(I'd felt a guilty pleasure I'd go home
        Not to cook someone's lunch,
        But to read.)
Still, it wasn't long before our talk's
        Compass needle trembled North
         Toward the Motherland:
Soccer games in the Flegrean fields,
         Ancient sun
    Reborn and swaddled putto-pink
In mist above the fumaroles;
        Rococo
    Messes of gelato;
First words, whose honeyed gravity
         Weighed on me
         Like a toddler's head
Snugged below my chin in sleep.

        Then, Serena described
    Troubles at her daughter's school.
Their new principal refused to pay
        The local gang's protection money.
         And so, the teachers
    Arrived at work one day to find
    The hutches where the children kept
Rabbits and a little clutch of chicks
        Overturned.
    From the playground swings
    The throat-cut animals hung.
Next time we come for you
Someone had written across the door in blood.
    Now parents wanted
    The principal to pay;

That was how these things were done.
                Screw her ideals,
                Serena heard.
That bitch is going to get our children killed.

                A blade bossed with oyster floats,
The harbor glinted below Serena's voice.
                Into that water, Apicius wrote,
                        The Romans tossed slaves
                To glut the eels they'd later eat
With *tits and vulvae, succulently cooked,*
                        Of sows who'd aborted their litters.

                        And from that water,
                Fishermen pulled a girl
                        Who'd been under
                        At least a week.
                She may have been the missing one
                The papers were reporting on,
                        Whose photo showed her
                Lippy, grinning, seventeen.
                        A week in that wake.
                She was scoured of identity.

                Water's thick in Naples
                        As martyr's blood
                Rusting in ampoules in the cathedral,
Where it liquefies on schedule
                        – And it *does;*
                I've seen the miracle —
                        To show the city's
                Still protected by the saint.

                I can't remember, six months later,
                Loggy in my cooling bath,
If some net had hauled these images
                Writhing up at me that morning
                        As we sat together

41

Near the harbor,
Or if they'd tangled in my thoughts
That same evening after Serena's dinner
Honoring Women's Day.
Across Europe
Lapels flickered yellow wicks of mimosa,
Marking the feast.
And in Naples
Flowers fumed for women
Burned on the flank of Mt. Vesuvius,
Where they'd been sewing
Sweatshop zippers on fake designer bags.

But as it did with everything,
The city managed to transubstantiate
Horror into carnival.
With Theresa and Ellie
I'd walked home late along the harbor.
Fireworks seethed above the bobbing masts.
Mirroring those harrier stars
The water seemed to flame, while
Drowned in lights
The lungomare phosphoresced.
Scooters rippled through
Reefs of cars,
Barely slowing for schools of boys
And women in flocks,
Stiletto-heeled, who stalked
Screeching over the cobblestones.
From an alley's mouth
A gobbet of men disgorged.
One, drunker than the others, loomed
Over and bent his face to mine.
Where are your babies? he hissed,
Spit pricking my skin.
Get home to your babies.
Not just drunk but whetted, his glare
Stropped beyond seeing and testing its edge.

You're over the hill
For trolling – is that what he meant?
Or was he putting all women away,
Including the vampire-
Lipsticked teens?
Whatever he meant, he meant to make us bleed.

I wince, drain chill water out,
Drizzle in a little
More of the hot,
And wonder at this habit
Of holding others' words as worry stones
To fidget absentmindedly
When thought goes slack.
Agates of fury, quartzes of scorn.
Cold in my ear's palm
The hematite heaviness of a final *no*.

And I still turn over my mother's words,
Costly pearls
Handed me years ago
In a college project on oral history.
She took my assignment seriously,
Agreeing to an interview
As if it would allow
Her, too, to wash
Through the wrack of half-forgotten truths.
Painstakingly on tape
She recorded her life,
Lapped by sluices and hesitations.
Her years in the Women's Army Corps,
Screening films on safety and hygiene
To bored enlisted men.
Her depression.
Decades as a secretary. Marriage.

Until, near side B's close, there gathered
A final, muscled wave:

43

How, when she was well past forty,
                    Her bleeding stopped.
At first she thought it was her age.
Then, slowly, sickly,
                    She understood.

                    She'd tried to find
A doctor who would help her, but
                    (Her voice cresting, breaking)
Five months along, it was too late,
Even if she'd had the money.
The tape's hiss like receding surf.

        So here I am, at daybreak,
                Adjusting the taps with my toes.

    I think we are shelled animals,
Hauled at by tides, sleeking invasive grit
                With our nacre. I think of her
Hiding in the tub for half an hour
                To read; think how pleased
I was, finding her, to pull her
                Back to me.

Little plumes of my flesh rock in the swells
                But my body is bland now,
                    Yielding as kelp,
And with my toes I pull the plug.

Drained, I need a couple hours of sleep,
        Then I'll start the day again.
    And maybe, if I'm sleeping late,
                The dream will come,
            One that intrigues me almost
More than it disturbs, in which
                I'm falling, bound,
Into a bay of blood-threshed water.
            Fear ties me; brine

44

Bites my lungs and I can't breathe.
Then, with a clarity I mistake
          For waking, I wake
Below trees, at a table laid
        Variously with meats –
        Meats I realize,
From a shudder in the grove's air,
            Are human.
It should be awful; it *is* awful.
          But with a calm
Familiar only here, a calm
I've never known in any other place,
I find myself longing to taste
         The dish's savor,
Braised and stuffed, as Apicius writes,
        With larks' tongues.

LAURA DA'

Vantage

Driving past Vantage:
    damp sign proclaiming ginkgo fossils
and iron sculpture of wild horses on the ridge.

At the turn of the last century,
Cayuse ponies were bred with European draft horses.
    A leaner, tougher work animal for the logging fields.

Trumpeter swans stitch
    the sallow slab of sky.
        Two birds swap point position
        to cut the air's polarity.

Path that pulls the taste
of mixed blood into my mouth.
Late February
and I am three weeks pregnant. I drive
    and the Columbia loosens
        my dad's easy silence.
He talks about his grandfather:
star musician of the Haskell Indian School Marching Band,
        telegraph operator, rodeo cowboy?
Tracking his family across
three states to hunt for big game
was habitual.

My grandfather,
dead within a week of my birth;
    I am told
        he looked at a Polaroid
        and proclaimed me an angry little Indian.

Late August in a post-depression labor camp
in the Mojave desert.
      My dad was born; he might have been premature,
         covered with dark hair and sick enough to die?

Terraced sun shower wading through the cloudbank.
      Recollection becomes embrace?

At twenty-nine weeks,
the doctor's chart advises me—
      my child is two and a half pounds, like a Chinese cabbage.

Blinking heavy eyes and fluttering his newly formed lashes.
My hair still damp from swimming laps.
      Warning signs:
         severe headaches, excessive nausea, a change in reflexes.
Feel of the doctor's hand pushing me back onto the table.

In the hospital, I ask for books.
      Posters from old rodeos.
A photo of a Mimbres pot
from southern New Mexico
black and white line figures—
      a woman dusting corn pollen over a baby's head
      during a naming ceremony.
Medieval women
    ingested apples
        with the skins incised with hymns and verses
as a portent against death in childbirth.

Heparin sodium

injected daily and nightly
        in a slow abdominal arc
incising my skin
        like a creation spiral; my hope apple.

Say splitting the rails of the body
to lay down a fence
between harm and one's young.

Terraced sun shower wading through the cloudbank.
My son at ten months
staring calmly at morning stars
during his naming.
The faint trail of corn pollen suspended
        in his fine, dark hair.

EMILY HIPCHEN

Leavings

I.

In the courtyard below, snow crowns
Our Lady of Victory, her orb like a frozen heart,
the bronze image of Jesus still in her arms.
Another unmarried girl with a baby
looks out her dark window into the whiteness.

My almost-mother draws her drapes instead.
She sits down in the dark with her red suitcase open
and slides her pageant dress over her head.
It pools above her swollen belly, the spangles flashing
like a school of minnows, ripples of silk cool as a wedding gown,
and all at once, she's home riding the Christmas float—
still Miss Somewhere, still a beauty queen
upright in a froth of white carnations,
one gloved arm waving, the other cradling the scepter.
She dreams of that life, her slippers lost
over the horizon of her stomach,
her nightgown tight like her squirming skin.

Come Valentine's Day, the snow erases her footsteps,
the taxi door a crust of ice breaking open.
Behind her the adoption papers with her blocky
signature tap-tap to line up with the edges of my file.

II.

Pomona, painted goddess of this hotel lobby, scatters apples
across the canvas and clutches a veil, her sisters in bronze
frozen in dance. The concierge takes our picture.
This is reunion. We stand, awkward as children
though none of us is young anymore.

In the hallway my mother clings like a dandelion seed
to the green of my coat, her pale yellow hair
fanned out on my neck like a seine. *I held you once,*
she says in my ear, like a lover. *I stole a photo of us.*
In the elevator, she pushes my bangs back, then her own.
Look, she says to my father. Widow's peaks.
Just the same as me, only she's dark. See?
And we three inspect our foreheads in the mirrored wall
as the lights number the floors to the lobby.
She calls sometimes afterwards, her voice drowning in distance.
Your birthday, your birthday, she cries, at sea in her memory.

III.

Her heart stops on my birthday, ticking down like a cooling engine.
The call comes, my sister phoning from the side of some road,
Dead, she says, she's dead.
At the funeral, my mother's picture watches everyone the same way.
Her flowers spend themselves in patterns on the carpet
in the hot light that spills through the plain-glass windows
and lights the candles redder than their own fire.
Outside the plane the clouds rise
rough and cold, the snow coming for sure.

IV.

I live in all of her I have left.
Except this: A hair I find months later
nearly woven into the lapel of my winter coat.
It pulls free full of static, electric as if it lived.

When I was born, my mother was a Breck girl,
her shining flip perfect in every picture.
This strand seems like a lost lover glimpsed in a crowd,
like a half-sleeping eye just opening,
like a phrase stuck on the tip of the tongue.
It means remember, it means gone.
I twist it tight around my finger, like a band.

CHARLOTTE PENCE

How to Measure Distance*

I. *Only Use Light Years When Talking to the General Public*

or to squirrels testing spring between two
branches. Or to a new mother saddened
by thoughts of earth and its death; sun's death;
her death. She watches her husband leave
the room for a burp cloth, wonders, could she
do it without him? What's the measurement
of distance between two people growing
too close, too quickly?

II. *The Measures We Use Depend on What We Are Measuring*

Distance between parents? Hills? Rogue comets?
Within our solar system, distance is
measured in Astronomical Units.
Or "A.U.," an abbreviation that
sounds similar to the "ow" of a toe
stub. Or similar to the sound of a mother
teaching the beginning of all sound. "Ah,
eh, ee, oo, uu." Watch her mouth widen,
purr, and close. This is the measurement
for what we call breath.

III. *For Most Everything Else—Stars, Galaxies, Etc.... —the Distance Unit Is the Parsec (pc). This Is a Convenient Unit*

for gathering groceries, grains in silos,
gasses we cannot package and discount.

This is convenient, too, when measuring
stars' distances by triangulation.
1 pc = 3.26 light years =
about the distance to the nearest star.

An equal sign leading to an "about."

An estimate. A close enough.

Close enough feels safer than being wrong.
Or exact. "Close enough," we say of that
asteroid skimming past our atmosphere's skin.
"Close enough," we say when he returns
with a guest towel.

IV. *For Distances Within our Galaxy or Other Galaxies, It Is Kiloparsecs*

She is unsure what fatherhood will do
to him. Accurate measurements require
one to know where one stands, where one belongs,
where one imagines going. Rub the toe
of the blue shoe into the dust. See how
the dust is not a bit bluer. The shoe,
a bit browner. Distance = a thing
between and against.

V. *The Exception to These Units Is When One is Studying a Smaller Object*

Father to mother to early zygote.
Branch to squirrel to tail-twitch and release.

53

Knee to toe to spring mud too soft to flake.
No units for these.

VI. *One Might Say, "Its Radius Is 5 Solar Radii", Meaning It Is 5 Times*
   the Size of our Sun

Her fear is five times the size of sun, five
times the hours of sleep or lack thereof.
Five times the huddle of father, mother,
child. Five times the energy created
for one nap as opposed to the distance
of that nap, that leap.

VII. She Wants Answers

but is realizing that won't happen.
She fears the truth that nothing stays the same.
Rashes fade, yet skin will prickle again.
Cries will quiet, yet the quiet will cry.
The man will leave, yet the same man will leave
again. That's why eyes are bloodshot, why she
answers questions as if she doesn't care.
All answers are "almost" or "about"—
everything moving. And this thing called light
years is a distance she can't comprehend,
yet somewhere she squirms at one forever-
changing end of it.

*Note: Italics indicate lines are from NASA's Goddard Space Flight Center
website written by Jonathan Keohane.*

LEONARD NEUFELDT

Addendum Filed with the Medical History

The chair was too far from the telephone
and your hearing aid's off; that's why your hip
shattered without a sound, you said, startled
by all those wheelchairs in the foyer
gathered in gossipy, desolate queues
but not by the death of your few remaining
friends or the sudden coming on of blindness,
the nakedness of your white stick.
You agreed with your sister's *too often*
there's hell to pay between points
A and B, the sister who had helped you
give up on hell, a space too large for
anyone's need or bequest and laid out entirely
in a single pattern like the village
when night swallows street corners

The right hemisphere's first bleed
rearranged its loyalties on what to keep
and what to let go: why regret the certainties
your husband salvaged from ancestral
wreckage and left for you as a tidy
inheritance. Why cherish grievances
instead of a reading machine, or your new
immigrant friend who painted the colours
of her veneration and with simplest words
helped you see how they worked together?

Her voice is a kind of seeing: your chin over
your dinner tray as you wiped your mouth
with the back of your good hand,
a tribute to fine flavour and God's refusal
to confiscate small pleasures or curiosities
insubordinate as your epidemiologic theory
of the chapel's singing groups

But another hemorrhage can eat its way
like miles of fire before the chill
sets in and leaches the need to hold years
and place together, memory slow
and gentle, a thin clear stream seeping
through a bog, small recognitions bubbling
like the dark water of winter under sunlit ice,
and you stared at the wheelchaired painter,
who couldn't remember the brush strokes
of rehab, who saw you as mere detail
unthreatening as a stranger far off
or the gravelly spatter of the sprinkler
loud against the hospice window,
your eyes empty except for the small smiles
drawn in, given back

ANDREA ZAWINSKI

Women of the Fields

for Dolores Huerta

The women of the fields clip red bunches of grapes
in patches of neatly tilled farmland in the San Joaquin,
clip sweet globes they can no longer stand to taste
just twenty miles shy of Santa Cruz beach babies
in thongs, Pleasure Beach surfers on longboards,
all the cool convertibles speeding Cabrillo Highway
women line as pickers, back bent over summer's harvest.

The *campesinas* labor without shade tents or water buffalos,
shrouded in oversized shirts and baggie work pants, disguised
as what they are not, faces masked in bandanas under cowboy hats
in *fils de calzón*

> the young one named Ester taken in the onion patch
> with the field boss' gardening shears at her throat,
> the older one called Felicia isolated in the almond orchard
> and pushed down into a doghouse. The pretty one, Linda
> without work papers, asked to bear a son in trade
> for a room and a job in the pumpkin patch,
> Isabel, ravaged napping under a tree at the end of a dream
> after a long morning picking pomegranates, *violación de un sueño.*
> Salome on the apple ranch forced up against the fence
> as the boss bellowed his ecstatic Ave, Ave Maria.

The *promotoras* flex muscle in words, steal off into night
to meet face-to-face to talk health care, pesticides, heatstroke, rape,
meet to tally accounts — forced to exchange panties for paychecks
in orchards, on ranches, in fields, in truck beds — to speak out to face
joblessness and deportation to an old country, a new foreign soil.

Women of the fields, like those before them, like those
who will trail after — *las Chinas, Japonesas, Filipinas* —
to slave for frozen food empires in pesticide drift,
residue crawling along the skin, creeping into the nostrils
and pregnancies it ends as they hide from La Migra
in vines soaked in toxins or crawl through sewer tunnels,
across railroad tracks, through fences to pick strawberries,
for this, this: *la fruta del diablo.*

ANDREA ZAWINSKI

It Was Then I Kissed Her

The sky a flutter of birds
just before the day turned dark,
    she sometimes might be sitting,
    sometimes might be reading something,
    a Conrad or Faulkner novel, something
    she salvaged from thrift shop stacks.

The night a clamor of crickets
rubbing their wings in early dark,
    she sometimes might be sitting,
    sometimes writing something,
    long letters in fine points of memory
    traveling short distances, just across town.

The nightbirds rioting the green of trees,
a cacophony of crickets under an indigo sky,
    she sometimes might be complaining
    about something, those next door kids
    out too late, the plot of grass she paid
    to have mowed turned a dried mud patch.

The crickets almost a deadening drone,
Nightbirds a mutter settling into the trees,
    I sometimes might be leaning into her then
    to kiss her quickly on her cheek,

she most times pulling back, shooing me off
like some unexpected junebug grazing the face.

All night birds would flutter the trees,
and crickets would rub in the dark,
and kids would go in for their beds,
and the book would close on its leaves,
and letters would be licked shut,
and she would frown when she thought
I wasn't paying attention to something.

And neither of us would ever admit
it was not much longer for this kind of living,
and then when the sky went really dark,
and the birds were really quieted,
and the crickets stopped their wild song,
    then, for the first time,
    in her casket,
    I kissed her hard
    and on the mouth.

KELLY NELSON

The Practice of Female Dispersal

Abstract
Two million years ago, males stayed close to home, females radiated.

Methodology
Find nineteen skulls in a cave in South Africa, relatives
we barely know. Test their fossil teeth for traces
of minerals from the soil where their childhood food
had grown. Test if those minerals match the minerals
in the soil where their bones, unburied, were
found.

Findings
Males died close by to where they'd grown up,
while females, most of them, had left their first
homes.

Discussion
When I die, my teeth will tell of Hostess
Cupcakes, Frosted Flakes, chicken pot pies,
Butterball turkeys, frozen fish from a bay I've never seen.

No trace will tell that I moved six hundred miles
before I had any teeth. Or that I moved five hundred

miles more before my second teeth pushed
through. I was set in motion, like my mother
and her mother and hers again — we all left
home.

TANYA GRAE

Matryoshka

My life circles within a tight radius,
                                                the spiraling, the groove.
I wake early to have the house to myself for hours,
until everyone is up & milling, the routine of breakfast
& getting ready & out the door.
                                        And one by one, they go
as I head to work & then repeat the reverse.
                                                My mother made me
mise en abyme, standing between two mirrors. I see ripples
in the pool. Spilling out, every choice goes on forever, notes
recorded in the vinyl record, this galaxy carousel.
                                                I need to feel
unique & responsible & alone.
                                        In the car last week, my teenager said
it doesn't matter what I do & she will be okay & whatever
I choose, whatever I want—I raised her strong.
                                                Déjà vu,
she repeated all the same words I told my mother
at almost the same age & my mother hers.
                                        This, Fibonacci's parlor trick:
the object depicted within itself, again & again,
a strange loop of self-referential, the vortex seen from above,
a cut tree, layers & layers of ringing —
                                        Don't be me.
Otherwise, what have I given?

Dolls

nested one within the other, in nature & craft, recursive
conversations with an innermost child.
                                        My daughter
wraps her arms around me & says good morning
before she makes herself eggs.
                                Somewhere inside I am fetal
                                                & we all are
proof enough, my mother inside me & hers,
                                        & the day goes on.

MARTHA SILANO

At the Zoo

among the Chilean flamingos, there was always one lone swan.
What were its days? What was it like to be dressed in white

when all the rest decked out in creamy coral? Laughing at the antics
of the thick-kneed squawkers, their skirmishes and scuffles, but then

the solitary like the Earth only whiter, only winged, and whether
it had a mother and a father, and if so where, and did the tapirs

have parents? They don't have mothers anymore, I could've said.
Or *Their mother is at the store, buying krill and grasshoppers,*

said it in a high-pitched voice I can't remember when I invented
to laugh off helplessness, morbidity, dread, for when the children's

moon doesn't shine down on a mother and child, on a stroller,
here down the path past the pink stuffed birds I keep my daughter

from wanting by explaining whoever made them was color blind,
here with Ginger and Lucy, sister hippos sprawled on the stubby grass

like slabs of slick brown rock. And lucky us, while we're discussing
the lives of caged tigers, the two gals come waddling toward us for a soak,

ladies without much need for air—sometimes down under so long
it's like they're dead, and then a bubbly *spppppppprrrrrrrrrrr.*

MARTHA SILANO

Not Exactly Meditating
at Lake Sammamish Park

not mourning the loss of believing I can, with words,
describe these many-lumped fruits, these brambles

and branches, these toothy stalks, these grabby
leaves on this semi-contemplative August morning,

so what am I doing? Reaching out with magenta fingers.
Plunking berries into a bucket tied around my neck.

Noting that for every drupe I manage to keep,
several fall to the dead-leaved dark. Talking

into the night, Hass discovered *everything
dissolves,* like dropping Alka-Seltzer into water,

but here in this prickered, decaying thicket,
in shorts when I should be wearing pants, the insides

of my arms scattered with constellation-y scrapes,
dissolve feels sterile, medicinal for what's going on

in these woods, for what my daughter's calling
a caterpillar when it's not on its way to becoming

regal, ethereal — Blue Morpho, Goliath Birdwing —
but a maggot, larva of a beetle or fly sent down

to devour the diminished. Hass says *a word*
is elegy to what it signifies because there's no specific

utterance to describe a child whining *stop,*
don't pick enough for a pie, skip the swim in the lake.

It's not the imprecision of language eating me—
bucket, bramble, branch—but the worms

I've been eating all morning, *thin wires of grief,*
my body not exactly numinous but embodying

what tenderly dismantles all that is falling
more quickly than anyone can gather.

LESLEY WHEELER

Abortion Radio

God told me and I did not listen, the tinny
speakers lament. Outside the car, ghost boles
of oaks float by. Brown leaves jump up
from the mountain road, swirl down again. *I felt
something pass, I caught it, my baby. Tiny
hands, skin translucent.* Every stump resembles
a deer that's poised to leap. My friend just hit
a doe last night, driving home from a conference,
having missed her son's bedtime for three
nights running. Her first thought: *I killed a baby.*
She stood in my office door to tell the story,
her eyes pinking up as she laughed at herself.
Shortwave talk refracts through me while I
tune in a stronger signal. A spouse has put
the kettle on, and children sleep in nests
of pastel belief. The deer my friend struck
lay down by the faded line at the verge of the road.
Its sides fluttered fast and then it died.
It went somewhere. Everyone goes somewhere.

JANUARY GILL O'NEIL

Zebra

for my son

You are not who they say you are.
You are Nubian with white stripes

and sport a Mohawk for a mane.
Once hunted to extinction,

your deafening bray is a song for the fallen.
Some might even say you are God's mistake.

But how ordinary the world would be without you.
They will say stay in your herd, stick close to your mother's side.

Remember, you are all equine.
Put another way, you are a wild ass.

Raise those ears. Kick your legs.
Gaze that impenetrable stare.

Your forefathers once grazed on African grasses.
Your place in this world is the one you claim.

PIMONE TRIPLETT

Family Spirits, with
Voice of One Child Miscarried (Thailand)

Come in. Everyone does. This is the house of our name,
a tourist destination. Here, the legendary general,
        father-spawn, travels forever
            his flame of fluorescents
                and burning incense. Also we've got the World

        Bank posters for sale, servants humming
to pop tunes a-tonal, suffering the street's
        traffic blather. We've got boas
            below the driveway.
                A blue coral in the toilet bowl.

    As for the others,
the blind- and sunbeam,
        the pipe- and whip-snake,
            the dog-eared or dwarf—
                when someone rattles at a lily's foot, we listen.

Oh but you can't be   *always, you see, in residence,*

can't hide behind the fence   *of your city forever.*

Why should more souls come   *down, in sum, in sever,*

be whomsoever   *accident makes of skin?*

70

Child, our sleep is your dream
danced open each morning by the girls
selling fruit and rice.
There's a spank
of hammers on tin, a clank of constant

construction,
sprouting capillary action,
heavy electrical veins.
Born into the trade, for money and motive we love
anyone long time, each of us all together.

To be poured over   *the stone, for the repose*

of flesh and its closed   *riddles? But not to give,*

as if wrong, a stroke   *of soul, joke that still lives*

like a fugitive,   *spirit thus being broken.*

Built by a man in love
with change, this house of our name.
Yesterday the seer, the one with the hole, the mole,
on his face, told us how grandfather comes
back to this place often. He sits in the gold-flecked

pagoda, picking beige leaves from the money tree, eating
one apple after another. Planned the fall of a king, ruled this city
by charging for water. In this family we sigh,
if only he'd been corrupt,
we could have been really rich.

Please, give more detail.   *Things sexual come mostly*

unclear. Who's the host,   *what's below wet groundswell?*

This taste of salt is   *a business. Say you sell*

the heart on faretheewells.   *Then best is not to be born.*

        But also there is kindness. My cousin
carries the torch
     at our grandfather's cremation, bowing
          in uniform, jaw braced above his bright gold
             buttons, head bent, fingers splayed.

        Later he commands all
paper flowers thrown
     into the fire. Here's yours.
          Let it go. The smoke alone helps the spirit
            to rise.

        Coming back
with ashes in his hands, later he tells us
     because of the scent
          of burning body and his love
            he'll never eat bread again.

Shadow falls on rock.   *Aftershock. Refusal.*

There's the first canal,   *birth and the other than.*

If unborn, the stain   *can remain so within,*

so wedded to thin   *shadow it still goes to speak—*

        Child, I don't know how else
to get at this. Goes the rumor, this life,
     a space-for-rent, as we own a corner of land
          that used to be slum, that's called the place
            of snakes. As for this being poured into

space, name, body, the era someone oh
so subtly plots you unto, maybe it's
side winding, maybe it's serpent. The skin
comes off. Once I stood by a river watching
the skin come off. Membrane of how

we wanted you, which was not enough
to keep you from turning back.
Behind, along the path the snake had come,
dirt, combed loosely,
showing its tracks for a while.

"Family Spirits, With Voice of One Child Miscarried"—the voice of the unborn spirit enters in the traditional Thai form of khap yanii. In it the lines of four are broken into two parts consisting of five and six syllables each. The fifth syllable must rhyme with the eighth syllable of the first line. The last syllable of the first line must also rhyme with the fifth of the second, while the second line's final syllable must rhyme again with the last syllable of the third line, and so on, repeating the internal fifth and eighth syllable pattern as well.

KIRUN KAPUR

Light

The only aunt I know would tell me,
This is how you knead the dough.
I don't remember the old stories—
Make sure it doesn't get too tough!

Knead carefully to make the *atta*.
Good girls know how to make good *puris*.
Make sure the gluten doesn't toughen,
A *puri* should be light and golden.

Good girls know how to make good *puris*.
They don't ask for the old stories.
A puri should be light and golden,
Like your cousin's and your cousin's cousin's.

I overheard the stories
When all the women shared a bed.
My cousins and my cousin's cousins—
The older women slept still dressed in saris.

When all the women shared a bed
The fan chuffed through a cloud of talcum powder.
Still fully dressed in saris,
They whispered names I'd never heard before.

When the fan chuffed sandalwood and roses,
I raised my arm above my head.
They named lost aunts and daughters.
I caught hold of my cousin's hand.

I raised my arm up in the dark.
There was a niece who could have been recovered.
I held my favorite cousin's hand.
Her name meant *light,* like mine does.

There was one niece who could have been recovered.
My grandfather had her traced.
Her name meant *light,* as mine does.
I've tried not to imagine her face.

Somehow my grandfather found her,
But her brothers refused to take her back.
I imagine the row of our faces,
Women in bed in the dark.

Her brothers refused to reclaim her.
This was after the riots and trains.
In bed, in the dark they could say it:
This is what broke us apart.

After the riot of years,
How should we remember the old stories?
What will break and what will toughen—
The only aunt I know will tell me.

JUDITH BAUMEL

Class Roster As Sicilian Atlas Index PS 97, Mace Avenue, The Bronx, 1964
A Reverse Ovidian Meditation

Belice
Brancaccio
Brucoli
Buscemi
Ciminna
Ferla
Gangi
Mineo
Messina
Modica
Mondello
Pantelleria
Partinico
Paterno
Provenzano
Ragusa
Salemi
Sciacca
Terranova

The above-named changed from earthly towns to American children as Jupiter and Juno made concessions to the fleeting urges of the other gods, to squabbling in the extended family, to their own dim-minded mistakes, and thus brought chance and change to these *disgraziati*. Locations to locutions. Sing a song of heavenly glittering.

ANJOLI ROY

Baby Bodhi

It was a cold night, but not as cold as the rest. The moon a jaunty half-full. We walked in the neighbor's dye garden as gentle trespassers, and he held your hand, a blanket around your shoulders. When you stopped to lean and breathe-breathe-breathe, your belly opened your sweater like curtains on a blustery night, your head down as you held his hips, his hand on your low back. You knew the baby would come on its own time, in the water (and at home, of course) as had your last two. I watched you breathe and counted seconds (poorly) but scribbled on a little pad each time the pain hit, his hand at your back always-always with all those pretty words, pressing and holding those points that you needed pressed and held. Those waves came slowly at first, then in quick succession, a rising tide not to be messed with. We were home when the baby was low and ready, and you both were in the water. I fumbled with the camera I couldn't get working, and then I saw in place of a head little legs between yours in the water, which set mine wobbling. It didn't help that I'd seen this in a dream, and that it was all okay then. I said prayers, quickly, and felt that some place in me, some place primal and deep, I knew how to reach in those waters and help you twist and free and guide that small form coming out of you, those pale legs in dark water, but I was thankful that he would do it, he the papa, that he wouldn't answer your question on the sex of the baby (though I think he smiled when you asked) but instead said we should focus on getting the head out, then assisted with his big hands, listening to your patient, slow-worded instructions as if wobbly-legged nervousness was for suckers. This was all normal. In that way that birth was all normal and cosmic and every day and world-shattering, just as it is the purple center of the core of every bit of this bright universe. And then you two lifted the baby out of the water and she looked at you with impossibly wise, quiet eyes that told you all those things promised and yet to be had and it wasn't until she had seen into you that she yowled at last, ringing in her place in the world.

RISHMA DUNLOP

Adagio

When father dies,
mother packs up the moon and stars.
She commits to the task of grief,
paces the half-dreamt rooms,
continues to punch the clock at the public library—lost in books and sounds
of silence.

Outside in the garden of flowers
father named, spring's plaque of blooms, maimed birches.
I clip rain-battered stalks
of white lilacs and iris.
I climb a tree like I did as a girl. Perched in the weeping willow,
I dream of waking
in the wood of true stories.

Meanwhile, in the rubble
of the burned library in Sarajevo,
the cellist plays Albinoni's "Adagio in G Minor"
for twenty two days, for twenty-two
killed waiting in a breadline.

The scroll of his cello
is a fist shaken in the face of death.

RISHMA DUNLOP

Somewhere, a woman is writing a poem

Somewhere, a woman is writing a poem
as time spills over. The young woman I was climbs the
moonlit stairs. She tucks her child into
bed, bends over her desk in the yellow lamplight, frees her hand
to write, breaking through the page like that Dorothea Tanning
painting where the artist's hand gashes through the canvas, fingers
and wrist plunged to the bone. She writes a dark, erotic psalm, an elegy,
a poem to die in, a poem to grow old in.

Somewhere, a woman is writing a poem,
as she gives away the clothes of her dead loved ones,
stretching crumpled wings. Her words rise liquid in the air,
rosaries of prayer for the dying children, for the ones who
have disappeared, the *desaparecido*, and for the ones who
have been murdered. She writes through the taste of fear and
rage and fury. She writes in milk and blood, her ink fierce
and iridescent. Somewhere, a woman who thought
she could say nothing is writing a poem.

PROSE

JANE SATTERFIELD

Daughters of Empire

Mothers are the countries we come from.
—Rachel Cusk

During the year I lived in Newcastle-under-Lyme, the borough adjoining the Six Towns of the English pottery empire, I never drove. Instead, I made my way around in the stuttering red buses run by the Potteries Metropolitan Transit, dubbed by commuters to firms in Manchester—those who drove to work in Fiats, Volvos, and Vauxhall estate wagons—"the public muck truck." Heading to town, I'd hand my pound coin to the "good morning, love" drivers, saying in an audible whisper, "Newcastle return, please," trying to blunt any trace of the outsider's colonial twang, then quickly moving on to a free seat.

Among single mothers, black-garbed unemployed youths, and old age pensioners, I'd pass through worn lanes lined with rows of dilapidated council houses, feeling on one hand that I was a tourist, and on another, completely at home, a constant ricochet between two opposed sensations. My EU passport, muted wardrobe, and calculated way of speaking afforded assimilation: access to the library, the Job Centre, and, unlike my husband, a nonjudgmental welcome. Settling into a slower pace, I browsed in shops and at the library, reading two newspapers a day to get the pulse of British culture. Unstrung from the American workweek's familiar rhythms, I began to pursue simple pleasures—wandering the market or Sainsbury's aisles, frequenting the bakery in the hour that it opened because the bread would be sold out by noon. At the coffee bar, I'd catch the chat of the sixth form college students around me, smoking and sipping pints of the foamy "cream of Manchester," their laughter rising over the pounding rain. But as the bus lurched its way through a wall of lashing weather, I'd feel surprised at times to long for a familiar face—for sunlight to throw its scrim of lace across an expansive sky. Far from family and friends, I found myself, perhaps for the first time, thinking fondly of America as home.

As far back as I remember, England, land of hope and glory, home, as my mother called it, was a constant presence in her conversation; the culture of suburban Maryland where she resided after marriage was always judged, in comparison, as wanting. Halloween hysteria and the intricacies of home-made costumes; fast-food joints and supermarkets full of packaged food, cheerleading and American football; the lack of public transportation which forced her, reluctantly, to drive; endless, unasked for self-disclosure—all these struck her as indulgent, mystifying, and subversive.

The youthful, smiling Ellen McCartin was the only daughter of emi-grants: parents who'd once left a provincial Scottish town for the English steel town Corby, almost equally provincial. Ellen, too, sought a better future, leaving Corby on the verge of what would become the Swinging Sixties with my father, an American serviceman: though he enjoyed his stay, John was relieved to have finished his overseas assignment and return proudly to the States with his "English" wife and daughter. I doubt my mother would consider me British, as she even now still sees herself. By the mid-'80s, my father's need for high-security clearance (he worked on data security for the EEOC and later, the IRS) had compelled his wife to become a naturalized U.S. citizen; besides, she'd wanted to vote, and had borne four sons in the U.S. Still, her emigrant grief impressed itself upon me, an only daughter, too. Landscapes, letters, framed postcards, travel prints, old cosmetic tubes, King George VI coins, and most of all, family photos of relatives I'd never known were scattered throughout the house, each an urgent *aide mémoire*.

Even now, decades later, my mother's Christmas shopping centres on visits to "the British store" for overpriced sweets and biscuits, British ba-con, packets of tea. I go along happily, my daughter Catherine between us, all of us enjoying this seeming exercise in nostalgia. Like all daughters of empire, my mother absorbed the implicit lesson, and then passed it on to us: England was, in Jamaica Kincaid's words, "the source" that gave "our sense of reality, our sense of what was meaningful, our sense of what was meaningless."

So, for me too, England's meaning accrued over the years. Thanks to my grandfather's airmailed parcels, I acquired royal wedding booklets and other souvenirs, commemorative coins, a Silver Jubilee medallion; at the same time, I internalized a map of Ellen's beloved Britain from the classics she nudged me to read: *Sense and Sensibility, Wuthering Heights*. Day after day, I'd heard of England; talked and read about England, inhabiting a space where British superiority—in character, music, fashion, schooling, TV, and even chocolate—was, maddeningly to my poor father and American-born brothers, beyond debate. American vulgarity and self-centredness; the puritanical hypocrisy from which Hawthorne had recoiled; the reflexive right-wing patriotism that would one day capture Ellen—I, too, noted these flaws and dismissed American "ideals." Besides, the notion of England still retained, in those post-British Invasion years, a certain cultural cachet: the Beatles (together or solo) still ruled popular radio, there were Monkees reruns, and so I treasured Britain's paraphernalia, my favorite being a pair of Union Jack dungarees which I wore the one summer I spent in Corby. Little wonder I grew to envision exile from the U.S. as a necessity for self-invention: to paraphrase the Beatles, with a simple transatlantic move, I'd get back to where I'd not once, but always belonged.

One day, in the steadfast grime of Stoke-on-Trent—the federation that, in 1910, had united the Six Towns—I showed my visiting mother around: she was home again, or close to it, in the country that she loved. Corby is in the East Midlands, two hours from Newcastle-under-Lyme, and before my father had left for America, they'd found time for a short visit, my mother saddened not to find the neighbors she often spoke of, in a town that now seemed smaller, dirtier, backward, rather than forward-looking. It was May, and my life, too, had changed. Now, ten months after my arrival, Rob's Fulbright teacher exchange nearly concluded, our future was more unsure than ever: I was the mother of his daughter, a child I loved with all my heart, but whose existence tied me painfully to a past I couldn't escape. What lay ahead I couldn't know, though Catherine would be part of it—the part for which I could be thankful—though I'd be saying goodbye to England once again.

Stepping up to pay for groceries at Tesco's, the British supermarket chain established during my mother's absence, Catherine dozing in my arms, I paused to look at wall-sized photos of nineteenth-century pottery workers (Rob had dropped us off earlier and continued his own errands). In these images of Stoke-on-Trent's past, women stencil china tea sets with floral borders and bands of gold, their brushes poised in the air, white dresses and pinafores spotlessly clean. The concentrated looks and half smiles of these artisans, most of them surely mothers, betray a certain pride: their decorative art graced unknown tables near and far. Theirs was the refined end of factory work, and the extra pennies they earned for their skills added up. But to what? A future dimmed by blindness or other occupational diseases? Each time they'd stencil another filigree or refine the petals of a rose, they'd taper brushes stained with lead paint to a point upon their tongues.

Hours earlier, we'd visited the Gladstone Pottery Museum, a popular tourist site in a neighboring district. Replaced in the early 1970s by modern technological methods, the original bank ovens survive in one exemplary row—tapered like bottles, as large as houses, each constructed of bricks and mortar—preserved to commemorate Staffordshire's pre-eminence in the pottery trade. No cloud escapes the smokestacks as local schoolchildren and tourists view the emptied factory room lined with museum cases and photographic texts; there's a café, a souvenir shop, and basement space for hands-on activities: there, university students, their aprons stained with mud and clay, take breaks from demonstrating the trade, drinking tea from porcelain cups. Mum tried her hand at the potter's wheel, beside a wall of wages and health stats, struggling at the task beneath the collage of photographs and signs. One quoted a factory inspector who'd toured Stoke in 1844 and declared that the advantage of relying on women workers was that "Their labour is cheaper and they are far more easily induced to undergo severe bodily fatigue than men."

The seemingly endless queue at Tesco's began to test our patience. My mother soon saw how much she'd become Americanized: frustrated that no managers offered extra help, that cashiers chatted too long with customers, my mother had rifled through her handbag—where were her traveler's checks? Ellen's mother had died of breast cancer in 1962, mere months after the dance at Alconbury Air Base where Ellen had met John, the striking G.I. whom she'd marry and for whose sake she'd move across the Atlantic. A mere traveler in her own country, she rummaged now through memories: the war-time Red Cross parcels and ration books; being woken near midnight to taste a melted chocolate bar, a perk her father had saved from his shift at the steelworks; the long ride to Sunday mass across Tyrone's rock-ridden roads, bouncing in her grandfather's donkey-driven cart.

In the rented second hand Metro, my mother's purchases stacked up: a breadboard, sultanas, soupspoons, boxes and boxes of tea. A tureen and soup plates covered with scenes of old Staffordshire, another of many recently discontinued English product lines. Exiting the shop, my mother sighed, adding up what she'd spent. I bundled a sleeping Catherine into her car seat.

***

In my mother's day, teachers named forms (the British equivalent of "home-rooms") for Curie, Pankhurst, and others; but this proto- feminist gesture must have been lost on most of the girls, consigned as they were to the rudiments of housekeeping—ironing, hospital corners, pastry-making— that were part of the school curriculum. In a place and time sanctified by pre-Vatican II Catholicism, youth's trajectories were defined by traditional gender roles. At sixteen, boys went off to the steel works, the girls to some office or trade until they could make a suitable marriage. Then ... child-birth, and being "churched," a Hiberno-English ritual derived from ancient purification rites: entering through the side door, a new mother accepted the priest's blessing, welcomed again to join the parish congregation. For the young women in that displaced Scots and Irish community, Saturday mornings meant Mass and a meeting of Legion of Mary, regardless of how late you'd been up the night before, downing small blue bottles of "baby cham" (a Prosecco-like drink socially acceptable for single women), dancing your heart out to skiffle or rock.

Such small rebellions aside, Ellen's concept of womanhood met the conventions of her time, deriving from the domestic spheres of home and parish. At five, she'd slacked off learning French, stubbornly determined to become a cleaning woman—as my mother put it, a "lady for scrubbing"—a goal which rankled the good sisters at the Ursuline convent school where a charge's sights were expected to rise beyond her humble background. Later, at her all-girl secondary school, Ellen's main interests were dancing and attracting beaus, one of whom was the son of Latvian refugees and front man for The Hep Cats, Corby's legendary (and largely unrecorded) skiffle band. But her father, Peter McCartin, forbade her to see Ilmar Zacks— known as "Cru" to the fans for his G.I. haircut. Peter hoped for a better match for his only daughter—a professional perhaps, not a steelworker or a musician whose family weren't even English. Ellen had no head for figures, yet the reigns of England's monarchs and Shakespeare's sonnets struck a chord, and she easily earned outstanding grades in history and literature. But what could these subjects offer, when a woman's place was in the kitchen? In the end, the choices were these: spinsterhood, a life in the church, or a husband and home—a lesson not lost on most women of Ellen's generation.

Today, my daughter Catherine is already thirteen years old, her American father's German background mixing with our line. What will her inheritance be? A dual national like me, she's grown up an American kid, each morning standing with her classmates, hand over heart, pledging allegiance. One day, maybe, remembering that she's British, too, Catherine will find a realization hitting home, her double citizenship a gift she'll want to make use of or explore. For now, however, she makes her own way as she did in the days after the Twin Towers fell, happily wrapping her ponytails in ribbons of red, white, and blue—the colors of both flags—then, with little understanding, scribbling the anti-war slogan "no blood for oil" on her notebook. Sometimes, caught up in conversation, I miss my chance to get away and watch the morning Pledge—usually silent, hands at my side. The children, every one of them, are gathered on the playground, one student holding the flag while the principal speaks through a megaphone. I watch my daughter as she recites, her face serious, committed, one of many voices swearing to a nation under God.

I'll think about the chill I felt traveling in London where tube station warnings like "Bombs – Be Alert" were posted fairly frequently—visual reminders of the IRA's mainland campaign. The morning papers, slapped on the step, offered up gleeful English youths waving the Union Jack in Irish soccer stadiums, even flinging uprooted benches at Irish players on the field. Meanwhile, each night, the BBC brought to my borrowed house the bombed-out ruins of Bosnia, or the bloodstained face of a Chechnyan girl, the roof of her house blown open, or reports of genocide in Rwanda. No wonder Jorge Semprun, Resistance fighter and Dachau survivor, wrote in *Literature or Life* that nationality is the "thing which least belongs to you," the most "accidental" and, therefore, most "dangerous" part of identity. As the principal called the students in by grade, Catherine turned back once to wave before blending into the crowd.

Except for a half dozen visits to England and the year I lived in the West Midlands, I've resided my whole life in the U.S., thinking what? That living elsewhere would erase any trace of American influence? Recently, a colleague pressed me, implying my favored metaphor—that I was an exile—was highly contrived. He wondered how someone who'd lived in Baltimore for most of the last decade could really feel so disconnected from the country where she grew up. I watched his eyebrows rise above professorial wire-frames, as if to suggest this troubling "exile" is little more than baggage, a romanticized longing that it's time to put aside. At that moment I saw my cherished "difference" exposed as a stubborn hangover of my upbringing, a literary affectation.

And yet. Memory crosses great distance. It makes nationality something more than mere geographic convention—part of the sum of who we are: an identity forged of feeling, custom, and blood. An identity that mothers and daughters labour to keep alive.

REFERENCES

Cusk, Rachel. *A Life's Work: On Becoming a Mother.* New York: Picador USA, 2002. Print.

Kincaid, Jamaica. "On Seeing England for the First Time." *Best American Essays: College Edition.* Ed. Robert Atwan. New York: Houghton Mifflin, 1998. Print.

Semprun, Jorge. *Literature or Life.* New York: Viking, 1997. Print.

CAMILLE T. DUNGY

A Brief History of Near and Actual Losses

All the new thinking is about loss.
In this it resembles all the old thinking.

—Robert Hass

We are at Cape Coast Castle, and Callie refuses to be held. She won't let me carry her in my arms. She won't let me put her in the cloth carrier on my back. She won't ride on her father's shoulders. She won't sit astride my hip. She wants to be in charge of exactly where her body goes. She wants both feet on the ground.

I don't want her feet on the ground. The floors of the slave dungeons are caked five to seven inches deep with centuries of hard-packed dirt and sweat and human waste. In one chamber, a drainage canal has been dug to reveal the brick half a foot below. This way, visitors to the former slave-trading outpost on the west coast of Ghana can more fully visualize what constitutes the floor under our feet. What kind of mother would freely let her child walk on such filth? I try to hold her off of the floor, but Callie wiggles out of my arms and runs in circles around her father, our guide, and me, giving the soles of her tiny Keens maximum exposure to the nasty ground. Again and again I try to pick up my daughter. Again and again, she makes it clear she will not be carried anywhere against her will.

It is the middle of May 2013. It is three weeks before my daughter's third birthday and 206 years since the British Parliament passed the Abolition of the Slave Trade Act, March 1807. The dungeons are museum installations now, part of a series of UNESCO World Heritage Sites dotting the Ghanaian coast. Our guide tells us the castle serves, today, to remind people of the horrors of the Atlantic slave trade and to caution us to treat one another better this time around. To never let slavery happen again. I can't find the energy to remind him that people are still at risk, still being shipped away for profit, every minute, every day. My daughter, running circles around me in her babyGap shorts, is driving me to distraction.

The exterior walls of Cape Coast Castle are brightly whitewashed, so when we walk out of the tropical sun into the male slave dungeons—chambers that are essentially windowless and purposefully dank—we are blinded by the darkness of the place. For extra shock value, our guide turns off a chamber's one dim bulb. This is to help us imagine something even more horrible than what we can already see.

"I don't like it here," Callie says. "I want to get out of this place."

Our guide turns the light back on, acknowledges how uncomfortable these dungeons are. My family is alone with him in this room, having chosen to pay more for a private tour. The guide assigned to us has been leading these tours for many years and is personable and quietly authoritative. He understands what we want from this experience. He asks us to imagine being packed in here with two hundred men, shackled and naked. He asks us to imagine the stench, the vomit, the sounds of writhing bodies, chains drawn against chains. Callie wiggles out of my arms and nearly evades me, but I grip her hand and keep her near. "Shh," I say. "This is a sacred space. Be still."

My husband and I flew from California to Ghana so I could speak at a conference for pan-African women writers, but also so he could visit Africa for the first time. I wanted to make sure Ray's first trip to the motherland was memorable, and so I'd carefully planned our stay. After several days in the capital city, Accra, we'd ventured to Cape Coast to visit the historic sites where Old World Africans were converted into New World slaves. Cape Coast Castle hosted more than one hundred thousand visitors in 2012, more than eighty thousand of whom were from outside of Ghana. New World Africans are drawn to this site of rupture, curious to stand on the soil where sometime someone who was somehow related to us last took a breath of African air.

The walls of the chamber where we are standing are lined with memorial wreaths, candles, and bottles for libations. Callie runs toward these memorials, then circles back toward us. "She's disrupting the tour," I whisper to Ray as I tug on her arm, trying to curtail her frenzied circle. "She's herding us like some sort of border collie."

This is Callie's forty-sixth airplane trip, so though Ghana is the farthest she's ever been from home, she knows the protocols of travel. On the eleven-hour, overnight flight from JFK to Accra, she ate her dinner, watched the first movie, then crawled into her father's lap and slept until we landed. She knows how to behave. She is no stranger to museums, historical sites, shrines, and churches. She has visited dozens in her short life, and never have I known her to act like she's acting today. She knows she needs to stay near so I don't lose track of her in this strange and crowded place. She knows I would prefer to wear her on my back as we move from one unknown destination to another. She knows how to be quiet on a tour, how to wait patiently next to me while I read informational placards. She knows, in short, how to be the kind of child who causes adults to say, "What a great little traveler you are!" These circles she is running, her refusal to let me carry her, are out of character. After three years of moving around the world in basically the way I've asked of her, Callie is asserting her independence. I do not like it one bit.

I grab her again. She squirms and pushes away.

"She's reclaiming the space," my husband says. "Let her be." Then he turns back to our waiting guide. "Go on," he tells the guide, and on the guide does go, describing chambers that led to other chambers that led to other chambers that led to a tunnel that led to the Door of No Return, where boats waited to carry human cargo over the shore-hugging waves and into the holds of transatlantic slave ships.

Cape Coast Castle was occupied over several centuries, first by the Swedes and then by the Danes, the Dutch, and then by the British. Between 1665 and 1807, the building was constructed, reconstructed, repurposed, and reinforced numerous times, used as an outpost for trading first timber and gold and blankets and spices and then, most lucratively and for the longest duration, human beings. The upper levels of the castle once served as the colonial government headquarters for the British on the western coast of what was then called the Gold Coast but would come to be known as Ghana. There was a church, a customs house, an open courtyard for military parades. There were eighteen-foot walls to protect the castle from the onslaught of the rough Atlantic surf, and lookout posts and cannon mounts to protect the fortification from the onslaught of competing military (and financial) forces. Over time, the castle's stewards built quarters for the colonial governor, quarters for colonial soldiers, and holding rooms for African men and women awaiting shipment to the New World. Up to a thousand men could be held in the male dungeons at any given time, divided among five different chambers. In a different part of the castle, there were chambers for the five hundred African women who, our guide points out, added their monthly blood to the filth that soiled their chambers' floors.

Cape Coast Castle prepared fifteen hundred African men and women at a time for transit to colonies in the New World. Men, women, and children from throughout the interior and the coast. Men, women, and children from many tribes and nations, many language groups. Fifteen hundred, and then another fifteen hundred, and then another fifteen hundred, and another, month after month, year after year, decade after decade, for more than 150 years. Most of the West Africans who ended up in the British colonies in the Americas passed through the castle at Cape Coast. Millions of Africans who ended up in the Americas passed through these dungeons. Visiting Cape Coast Castle, for a New World African, is, in a most distressing way, like coming home.

I have been here once before, in 2003. After that visit to Cape Coast and Elmina, the coast's original slave castle farther west, I had lunch with Ama Ata Aidoo, one of Ghana's leading writers. "Tell me," she asked, "what did you think?"

I remember being quiet for longer than seemed polite. I was trying to formulate an answer to her question. "Honestly," I told her finally, "I don't know what to think. It was all so overwhelming."

"Good," she said. "That's good. I've lived in the shadow of those castles my whole life, and I still don't know what to think about them. If you had words already, I'd say you weren't thinking hard enough."

I didn't feel Ray should travel to Ghana without visiting the castles, and I didn't want him to have to go alone. So the whole family went together. I had been curious to see if the castles would be different the second time around, but nothing had changed since I'd visited them a decade ago. I am still awed by the experience of standing on this polluted ground.

This time, though, I have my daughter with me. I am trying to make sure she behaves like a civilized girl, and I am also trying to push back waves of terror that overcome me when I think about what it would have been like to be a mother here, terrified not only for my own life, but also, I understand palpably now, for my child's.

In Elmina, the day before, Callie first demonstrated her refusal to be carried. The pan-African women's conference had arranged a tour of the Portuguese stronghold as an extension of the week's historic and literary explorations. When the thirty-person group we were part of stopped in the women's holding pen, Callie ran in circles around everyone. Some women appeared not to notice her at all, some actively ignored her, but a few women smiled and held out their hands for Callie to slap as she neared them.

Part of me welcomed my daughter's wild behavior. My reactions to Elmina were muted because I was focused on Callie, trying to rein her in, trying to keep her from infringing on the other travelers' experiences.

The tour of Elmina progressed from one horror to the next. Our group stood in the courtyard in front of the women's holding pen learning about the well that held disease-laced water in which particular women were made to bathe before they were sent up to the governor's quarters where they could be used by any man whose path they crossed. I was busy keeping my daughter from the well's open pit. All my attention was focused on her body. Though I heard what the guide was saying about all the other bodies that had been in jeopardy right where I was standing, I also couldn't really hear him because I was too busy worrying about what might happen to my girl.

She and I split from the group and climbed the stairs to the governor's chambers. Callie has always loved stairs, and letting her climb them was the best diversion I could come up with. Outside of the castle would be worse than inside. Hawkers and grifters patrolled the exterior courtyard waiting to beg money from foreigners whose wealth, even when meager, was exponentially more than theirs would likely ever be. The taxi we'd hired to ferry us between our resort hotel and Elmina was parked some distance away, and walking into those crowds to find it would mean fending off dozens of men, women, and children practiced in the art of extracting money through guilt and manipulation. My husband was still on the tour and would be for some time. Since nothing was air-conditioned in that part of the country, including our taxi, the coolest, most comfortable place to wait for him was inside the castle. Upstairs, in a room with walls yellow as a child's painting of the sun, Callie could move freely. In the governor's quarters, she ran circles around the site that would have held the governor's bed, a bed into which centuries of African women were forced for the pleasure of the men in charge.

"This is really out of character for Callie. She doesn't usually run around like this," I said to a woman who'd broken from the larger group and joined us upstairs. She was a poet from Harlem. Callie and I frequently spend time with her when I travel to New York for speaking engagements.

I said, as much to convince myself as to remind my friend LaTasha, "She's usually incredibly well behaved."

Callie ran in circles and circles and circles around the room, and when she finished her circles she ran to the big window that looked out over the exterior courtyard and down to the sea. "There!" she said, pointing to our taxi driver. He was standing just apart from a crowd of local men, watching fishermen paddle their boats toward the shore.

"That's right, mamí," LaTasha told Callie, using the Harlem endearment acquired from neighbors who came to New York from stops on the diaspora like Puerto Rico, the Dominican Republic, and Cuba. "It's never too early to plan your escape."

"There," Callie said, pointing toward the ocean and our driver once more.

Later that morning, our guide walked us to Elmina's interior courtyard. He was going on about military exercises and other late colonial uses for the space when Callie broke free from my grip and ran toward a set of stairs on which an elder member from our group sat. She was an African-American woman who spent half of each year living in the Republic of Benin, 280 miles northeast on the old Slave Coast. She was wearing a dress and head wrap made from West African wax-print cloth. Callie sat beside the woman with her feet together. She placed her hands, palms up and open, on her lap. "Auntie," my daughter said, though we'd not directly taught her to use that honorific with a stranger, "I'm hungry. Do you have any food?"

Callie had been asking me for food since we arrived at Elmina, but I'd brought no snacks, thinking it would be disrespectful to eat in a place where so many people were tortured, some unto death. I had a lot of ideas about propriety, and Callie was resisting nearly all of them. Auntie dug in her purse and came up with a toffee, which she taught Callie how to suck without swallowing and which stemmed my girl's hunger and her wandering focus until I could get her back to the hotel for a proper meal.

"This one knows how to take care of herself," the woman said to me. "She'll be okay, no matter what happens." Then she pressed her cane against the castle steps, strained into a standing position, and walked away.

I think of these words now, in one of the men's dungeons in Cape Coast Castle, Callie primed to run circles around her parents and our guide. Maybe my husband was right: she is reclaiming the space. Maybe Auntie was right: Callie is taking care of herself. I decide to let her go, to let her direct her own movements. She circles the three of us, and I falter in my certainty. I look at our guide to see if I should do something to stop her.

"She's not bothering me," says the guide.

"Let her be," says my husband.

We are in the last accessible male dungeon. The guide is orienting us, pointing out the gateways between chambers, and then making sure we see the wall on the ocean side of this chamber that interrupts these connections. In front of that wall is an altar on which a priest is quietly seated. After all the wreaths and offerings, I am not particularly surprised to see a priest waiting on an altar. "There used to be a tunnel there," says the guide, pointing to the blocked-off area behind the altar. This history lesson will go on, the guide's uninterrupted speech indicates, regardless of my concerns about my daughter, regardless of the presence of a priest. "That tunnel led to other chambers and eventually to the Door of No Return. The British sealed that tunnel in 1807 to symbolize the end of the slave trade. Never again would a person have to walk through that tunnel to the waiting ships," he says. Callie circles and circles and circles. Then she stops.

She stands in front of me now, watching the priest. The priest is dressed in a traditional manner, a cloth draped over one shoulder. He is holding something in one hand that looks like a feather-tipped wand. His sandals are at the foot of the altar. His feet are bare. He has his back to the sealed tunnel and is facing in the direction of the chambers through which we've come. He does not seem to be looking at anything at all. The wall opposite him, maybe. Maybe something inside the wall, or something beyond it, but nothing I can discern.

Now our guide is nearly finished in this room. "People leave offerings here," he tells us, acknowledging for the first time the wreaths and flowers and bottles we've seen lining the walls. Then he is quiet, as if he expects us to make an offering as well.

"Thank the man for his important work," I tell Callie, because I think the priest's important work is to absolve the horrors of slavery. I should thank him myself but choose, instead, to send Callie. I will wonder, later, if this was a mistake or a godsend. I know there is very little I can do to change the course of history, but later I will reflect on all the decisions I made while I was on that coast. I will wonder if I made a huge mistake going to that coast at all. Right now, though, all I do is ask her to thank the man for his important work.

Rather than muffling her thank-you in her shoulder, as young children often do when asked to acknowledge strange adults, Callie stands up straight, looks directly at the priest, bows, and says, "Thank you." Crisply, cleanly, loudly. I think she repeated this seven times, but when I tell the story to my mother on our cheap international cell phone later that night, Callie will correct me. "No, Mommy, five times." She will say this with authority, though she will not dwell on the issue any longer than required. "I did it five times."

As we leave the dank confines of the chamber and walk out into the Atlantic coastal air, our guide will tell us the priest back in the dungeon serves a local god. The castle and its dungeons were built over the place where the god lives, but the god did not move, even after all the things that happened here. Now that the castle is open to the public, a local priest has set up his altar. He returns, regularly, to honor the god, and people come for blessings and to give offerings.

When Callie says her five thank-yous, I watch the priest, who watches my girl. When she is finished, he gives her a nearly imperceptible nod. I will wonder about this later, but at the moment I am simply amazed.

***

Three days later, we are staying in the African Rainbow Resort at Busua Beach, seventy miles southwest of Cape Coast. The shore is shallow here, the currents calmer.

The night after Cape Coast Castle, Ray and I ask Callie to tell us her favorite thing about the day. We ask this of her nearly every day, so we don't think about how difficult a question it might be after a day spent in a 350-year-old dungeon. Callie doesn't hesitate, though, to describe her favorite thing. "Visiting my imaginary castle that wasn't scary," she says.

"Yes," I say. "I guess the real castle we visited was pretty scary, wasn't it?"

"Mmm hmm." We are at dinner. She is eating french fries.

After a moment's hesitation, she puts down her fry so she can say the rest of what she needs to say. Her hands fly up as if she is holding scales of justice, one palm up to the right of her head, one palm up to the left. Between each clause she pauses, as if considering her options. She shrugs her shoulders, lifting both hands simultaneously, before continuing. "There are only a few things you can do when you are someplace really scary," she says. "You can play or ... be confused or ... do something.... Or read a book." Then she drops her hands and focuses on her fries.

This girl is three weeks shy of her third birthday, and already she knows how to address priests of the ancient order. She knows that a sacred number in Ifá, a dominant religious tradition of West Africa, is five, not seven, the sacred number of Christianity I'd attempted to impose upon her. I hadn't explained slavery to her, could not explain slavery to her, but she knew how to deal with the stress of being asked to thank a priest who may or may not have been cleansing a site of centuries of trauma. We put her in positions where she had to take care of herself despite, and sometimes because of, our well-laid plans. I feel awful that I put my baby girl in a situation where she had to define her coping strategies so specifically. Ray and I determine, immediately, that the history portion of our Ghanaian tour is over. We are finished with slave castles and slave forts and slave dungeons and trading ports where the commodities of trade were human beings. We are going to relax on the beach.

At Busua, the beach extends a long way out, maybe a hundred yards, with hardly any increase in depth. This means that even at high tide my husband and I can safely walk out quite a distance. The waves come in sets of two. One wave takes the water level from waist-high to shoulder height, then seven or eight beats of calm, a slight undertow, nothing too dramatic, then another wave takes the water level from waist-high to shoulder height. Perfect bobbing conditions.

At other beaches on the Ghanaian coast, I kept a firm grip on Callie's arm, but here we frolic. I am not scared. Ray's got our daughter on his back. He's holding her with one arm, and she's holding him around the neck. Callie has finally agreed to be carried. She is going where she wants to go and how.

We bob when the swells come; we're a good twenty feet from where the waves are breaking. We are laughing. We are not thinking about any of the horrible things we've been thinking about for the last several days. One wave takes the water from waist-high to shoulder height, then seven or eight beats of calm, a slight undertow, then the water swells from waist-high to shoulder-height. We come together again as a family. We are all laughing and happy. We are feeling clean, finally, in this warm water. Callie is on her father's back, and I am beside the two people I love most. One swell takes the water level from waist-high to shoulder height, a slight undertow, then I look up at the twelve-foot wave that is breaking over our heads.

When I come up for air, I look immediately for Ray. He does not have our daughter on his back, or in his arms, or anywhere near.

"Where's the girl?" I shout. I am so frightened I can't remember the name we chose for her.

"I'm looking for her!" my husband shouts back. I am swimming toward where he's standing, and we both see her, then, sinking just under the surface, legs toward the ocean floor, arms floating out to her side, like she's been crucified in the water, chin tucked into her chest.

He grabs her out of the ocean, and we head toward the shore. Callie is coughing now, thank all the gods. No one says anything. We are just listening to the sound of the air coming in and out of her lungs.

We reach the beach and collapse on the wet red sand. Callie looks around and stands up. She walks higher up the beach to where the sand isn't wet anymore, and then she sits, her legs planted firmly on the ground, running her fingers through the dry sand, staring at the ocean she narrowly escaped.

I pride myself on being a California girl, the sort of girl who has mastered knowledge of the ocean. I am used to gleaning meanings from the patterns of waves. I counted the sets and trusted, from this history, that I could predict the future, forgetting what a longer view of history could teach me.

When we leave Busua and travel back to Accra, we stay a few nights with a woman who lived for years in the city of Cape Coast. We tell her what happened to Callie in the water, and she is horrified. "You have to be very careful swimming in those waters," she tells us. "All the time people are lost to the Atlantic. All the time."

Of course. Of course. We know this. How many centuries of parents have lost their children along that voracious coast? São Jorge da Mina Castle, the first of the castles, was built by the Portuguese in 1482, first for the extraction of gold and then for the extraction of human beings. By late 1637, St. Georges of the Mine Castle, or Elmina, as it came to be known, was under the control of the Dutch West India Company, one of the most rapacious slave-trading outfits in the world. Elmina, Cape Coast Castle, Fort Metal Cross. Fort Amsterdam is in the same village as the resort where we stayed while we visited Cape Coast and Elmina. Fort Christiansborg, now known as Osu Castle, has served as the seat of government in Ghana in recent years. Fort Santo Antonio, Fort Vredenburgh, Fort San Sebastian, Fort Batenstein, Fort Patience, Fort William, Fort Orange, Fort Apollonia, Fort Good Hope. We could have visited more than twenty-eight slave castles and forts along the coast of Ghana, but we'd thought for a few days we could get away from all that fetid history and play, carefree, in the ocean.

At Busua, just out of sight of Fort Metal Cross, we sit with Callie and watch the water for a good five minutes until she finally breaks the silence, says, "That was a really big wave," and we feel, again, the coastal African sun as it beats on us, warming and also darkening our skin.

AMINA GAUTIER

Taste of Dust

She has come to be rocked in the cradle of mankind.

Through doors open to the sun and the heat, she has come knocking, shouting hodi into the shadows. From the shadows emerge a chorus of *karibous*, inviting her to enter. Gleaned from a pocket-sized traveler's guide replete with explanations of indigenous customs and idiomatic phrases, her manners are impeccable. She uses her adherence to the guidebook to set her apart from the other five with whom she has come, to declare that she isn't like *them*. No, nothing like them at all.

She has come to East Africa, to the place the British, the Germans and the Italians all scrambled to claim. She has come to the land of *homo habilis* and *homo erectus*, to the land that has lured many. Here had come Hemingway, seeking to define his masculinity. Here had come President Roosevelt, slaughtering in the name of science, salting skins to send the Smithsonian. Here a princess became queen, inheriting an empire while away on a royal visit, when back in England her father breathed his last.

She has studied her travel guidebooks like the Bible and learned both language and custom. She can ask for the restroom and inquire after price. She knows the exchange rate for dollars into Kenyan shillings and she has a suitcase filled with Imodium A-D, Pepto-Bismol tablets and hand sanitizer. She knows better than to take offense at the intrusive and chauvinistic nature of the questions to which the Africans frequently subject her; she fends off questions about husbands and children, and ignores the pitiful looks Kenyans reserve for women traveling alone.

With five other university faculty and staff members she has come to a manmade village in the Kitui district. Funded by the university, this working pilgrimage in Kenya is meant to enrich her understanding of the university's mission and its commitment to service. The promotional pamphlet calls it top-down experiential learning. What she learns will infuse and inform her classes. She will imbue her students with the essence of her experience. The experience will help her solidify her tenure case by strengthening her service column and it will improve her teaching by allowing her to bring innovation into the classroom. At least this is what she wrote in her application essay as she competed for the chance to travel to the birthplace of civilization. There were other locations to choose from. The university offered a trip to Europe and one to an orphanage it sponsored in South America, but it was Africa she wanted. Craving the place she has been taught to pity rather than revere, she has come across the Atlantic Ocean on a journey that is the reverse of the one her ancestors took. She has come willingly, without chains, without beatings, without starvation. She has connected in Paris, flown to Nairobi and then traveled hours in a rickety van just to get here. Now that she is here, she wants just to be one with them, one of them, until it is time to go.

In the guest house kitchen three women prepare a lunchtime meal of chapatis, lentils and rice. Meat is saved for Fridays when the nun—a woman more dead than alive— comes down from Nairobi to check and make sure all is well.

She greets the women, practicing her fledgling Kiswahili. "*Habari za leo?*"

Three heads nod and three voices murmur, "*Nzuri.*"

She has practiced with them before. Through conversations riddled with hand gestures and basic vocabulary, she has learned their names and their number of offspring. She can see that they are busy today. Opting out of pleasantries, she holds two lamps aloft. "The lamps have lost their charge. Where should I leave them?" She asks this in English; the question has not been covered in the guidebook or in her English-Swahili dictionary. Uncomprehending, the women merely nod at her and smile.

He always knows where she is. He can hear her from a distance of several meters. She's taken the few words she knows and made conversation, trailing greetings behind her, walking in a wake of *nzuris*. As she greets the villagers, she asks his whereabouts and it is the sound of his name in her mouth that announces her arrival.

Nicholas is in his office tabulating the last donation of new shoes that have come for the children when she appears in his doorway. She raps her knuckles twice against the open door. "Hodi? Nicholas?"

Only his wife pronounces his name correctly. The others—all volunteers and in Kenya only temporarily—do not drop their accents long enough to do it justice. They do not attempt to pick up any Kiswahili or make an effort to pronounce things the African way. Mostly, they have British tongues, quick and tripping, and when they say his name they rush through it so that it sounds more like *necklace* than Nicholas. This American black, or black American—he is not sure what they call themselves—gives his name its full three syllables, but still does not get it right. Coming from her mouth, it sounds like *nickel-less*. Only his wife, his Naomi, raises the last syllable from the dust, makes it sound like loss.

Two days more before Kilonzo brings the van to take him back to the city. Two more days before he can see Naomi. Two more days before he makes the van trip on dusty roads past Kwa Vonza, past Machakos, past Wamunyu just to make it to Nairobi before Juma and Adija go to bed and he loses one more day with them. Two days more before Naomi can make him forget all about the black American woman.

"Karibou." He welcomes her. "Come in."

The black American woman comes with a group from a Catholic university. There are six in all, and only two are not white. She is many shades lighter than him, much too fair to be African. Whenever he sees her standing beside her colleagues, she seems to blend right in before his eyes until he can no longer tell where their white bodies end and her own begins.

"You look busy," she says. "Am I interrupting?"

Yes. She is. Days with the volunteers are always wasted ones. They arrive in the village dressed for the beach with arms and calves bared and heads covered in big floppy hats. Slung over their shoulders they carry bags stuffed with precautionary measures, bottled water, sunscreen, umbrellas, hand sanitizer, baby wipes, and digital cameras. They come prepared for any emergency they think might befall them during the short two-mile walk from their guest house to the fields. The arrival of volunteers always sped everything up and slowed everything down all at the same time. After the first few days spent with them, Nicholas handed them over to his foreman and retreated to his office in hopes of salvaging some of the remaining week.

He waves the question off, invites her to sit across from him. He is Kenyan; he is always polite.

"What are you doing?" she asks. She scans the room, taking in the large generator, the sumptuous drapes, the tidy desk.

"I must double check the last donation to make sure there are enough pairs of shoes in enough sizes so that all of the children receive one pair. They go through them very fast."

"What if there aren't?"

"Then we'll wait until more arrive so they can be distributed equally. We never know which items will arrive in a given week."

"It's so much for you to do," she says.

"It is nothing. What can I do for you?"

She trails her fingers over the tops of two framed pictures on his desk. "I left the lamps in the guest house kitchen," she says. "We've finished our two."

"You and your roommates must be staying up very late." The battery-operated lamps are meant to provide enough light to last six hours before recharging. "Are you teaching them Kiswahili?"

"I don't know enough to teach anyone." She takes a seat.

"No, your Kiswahili is very good. Many have said so. You fit in like you were born here." He places two fresh lamps on the desk before her.

She brightens at this. Since being here, she has seen so many faces which mirror the ones she left at home. She could have been born here—she wishes she was—wishes she had a tribe to claim, a language that dated back hundreds and thousands of years in a single unbroken line rather than a sliver fragmented by slavery. "*Asante sana,*" she says. She selects one of the picture frames and turns its glass face towards her. Two young boys with solemn eyes stand on either side of a tall and serious-eyed woman. "None of the others bothered to learn any Swahili."

"Kiswahili is very difficult to pick up in only a few days," he says. "Especially if you don't know any other African languages."

"We've known about this trip since mid-semester. We all had more than enough time," she says.

Her colleagues had just not bothered. How quickly they changed their tune once they arrived and discovered that they could only communicate with the staff members because none of the villagers spoke English. She won't label them racist—she doesn't know any of them well enough to judge—but, certainly, they exhibit a latent indifference to anything lying outside the pale of western civilization. She doubts they would have been so cavalier about preparing for a trip to Paris. Prior to this trip, she had not known any of the five with whom she has come. She had never seen any of them anywhere on campus—never run into any of them at Faculty Senate meetings nor seen them in the cafeteria. Upon return she will be expected to share her experiences. The alumni magazine will feature an article on the trip to show the university's graduates what lengths faculty will go to in order to get new material for their courses and better serve their students. "I wasn't up late teaching them any words. We leave tomorrow afternoon. There's no longer any point."

Nicholas has been pleased with her linguistic efforts. Many of the volunteers who came for less than a month did not bother and students studying Kiswahili were usually encouraged to go to Tanzania, where the language was believed to be purer. "Was it research that kept you up?" he asks. She has told him that she teaches literature back in the United States and is paid to do research, which is her word for reading and writing. It seems the most wonderful job to him. How different his life would be if he were compensated for reading books. As it is, he and his staff members were already overeducated and underpaid. The men and women who worked for him had advanced degrees in agricultural science, but were barely paid enough to subsist.

"No, not research," she says. "I was up all night thinking about something I need to—"

"—Hodi!" Hasani knocks and enters Nicholas's office.

"Sasa!" she says to the foreman.

"Fit," Hasani answers.

"Yes?" Nicholas asks his foreman, wondering where and when the black American woman picked up Sheng and learned to speak the slang of Nairobi's youth.

"Bwana, I have the report."

Each day Hasani reports on the activities of the volunteers. They are assigned different tasks depending on their age, the purpose of their visit and the length of their stay. The Australian couple who have been in the village for three months and intend to stay a full year have been given the responsibility of erecting the schoolhouse. The husband works the construction site, leading the men in installing solar panels onto the rooftops. His wife works with the staff and the nuns to prepare the schoolroom's interior and make ready the classrooms. Student and short-term volunteers are sent to the fields to plant and cultivate. Nicholas has Hasani rotate the Americans among the light tasks, planting beans and watering acacia saplings.

She rises from her seat. "I can see you're busy. I'll leave," she says. "Will it be all right if I come back later? I have a favor, something I need to ask of you."

"Of course," Nicholas says.

She takes the two lamps in hand. "I'll come back in two hours. Will that be all right?"

"That will be fine. My work for the day will have ended by then. Tutuonana," he says, believing he can guess, believing he knows what it is she wishes to ask.

She wants him to make love to her. He is sure of it. Until now, he has not flattered himself. He is accustomed to being the one the volunteers seek out; the manager and the go-to. He speaks the necessary three languages, English, Kikamba and Kiswahili, and thus can talk to anyone and everyone in the village. They are always most comfortable in his company. He never lets his popularity with the volunteers go to his head. Though their trip is special in their eyes, a life-defining moment for many—volunteering in Africa—two weeks later when these volunteers have departed, the village will once again fill with new volunteers and new life-defining moments. It is his job to keep everything going, to keep the work done. This village is a manmade one, made possible by a gift of land from a brotherhood of priests, erected to shelter children orphaned by the AIDS epidemic. The village is the product of volunteerism and sponsorship. Slowly, it is coming together.

There are always more volunteers. Several come from the United States, but most come from Britain, Australia, Italy, Germany and New Zealand. Those that come are mostly wazungu; hardly ever are they black. The volunteers come to serve their god, to evangelize, to get college credit, to practice their language skills, to build, to construct, to get away, to beautify the land, to save the savage, to assuage guilt. Until now, none have ever come to lay claim to him. For the past ten days, she has found him at some point or another, but never before by special request. She has passed by his office and stopped on her way from the fields, the shantytown, the artisan's cooperative. She has knocked, called hodi, entered and plied him with questions, all professedly in an attempt to better learn and understand the people around her.

Hasani reports on what the volunteers have accomplished and Nicholas tries not to think of making love to the black American woman. Where before only his wife's image ever rose before him, this American black woman makes him think of her instead. Will he make love to her, if she asks? For he has no doubt that she will. A favor to ask of him. She has said that she would come to him this night, has made sure he would be free from administrative duties. What else could she want? After Hasani has gone, she will return and offer herself, a parting gift before her departure. Indeed, had she not been building toward it the past ten days? Had not the questions, the lengthy conversations, been her method of working up to it?

When she returns, he will wait for her to make an advance. He will let her make the first move. He will await her signal.

Like any other African man, he has heard how forward and easy American women are. He expects little from women who refer to their unborn children as bumps, who bond over exploits of promiscuity, and who use the terms chick and slut as endearments when addressing one another. He excuses the American black woman as a product of her culture. She hails from a country that celebrates the drug dealer-turned music mogul-turned entrepreneur and accepts the sex scandal as a legitimate form of résumé building. He has seen their movies and has read their newspapers and he knows the antics of their public officials, their businessmen, their recording artists, their actors, their athletes—all the figures they look up to. He has seen their music videos—women portrayed as prostitutes and strippers. How else is she to behave? Her American-ness pearls her skin like beads of sweat; entitlement and privilege perfume her. She has never had to think of water and thus has never had to think of drought.

Two hours later she knocks and enters. "Hodi. Are you free?"

"Quite."

She collapses into the seat opposite him. "I've loved it here," she says, meaning it. Prepared to live in squalor for ten days, she has found herself happily disappointed. Built with international donations, the village houses and guesthouses all boast gold plaques bearing the names of their generous benefactors and are designed to closely resemble each other. Constructed of a reddish-gold brick the same color as the dry and dusty ground, the guesthouses have two to three bedrooms with metal bunk beds and a large living room area with wooden tables and chairs. Unlike the village houses, there are no kitchen areas in the guest houses. All of the guests and staff take their meals in the main guest house. Though the guest house has a bathroom with only a stall for bucket showers and a hole in the ground called an eco-toilet, the rest of its accommodations far surpass her expectations.

"Everyone will miss you. You must write them once you have left. You will always be welcomed back. Many will be sad to see you go. In a short time, you have become one of us."

"I'm going to miss it all. Especially tea time. Especially the maandazi," she says, lifting the bottle of orange Fanta he has set on the desk for her. She hands it to him and he opens it for her. "Back at home, a Fanta wouldn't get me any favors." Quickly had she learned the value of sugar and of bottle redemption fees. The present of a Fanta and the promise of the empty glass bottle opened doors, procured favors, gained her entry into homes.

"You were not so brown when you first arrived," he says. "Working in the sun all day has made you resemble a true Kenyan."

"I like it," she says, lifting her arm, smiling. He is unsure if she is referring to the work or her skin color.

"The work has not been too difficult?" he asks.

"It's fine," she says. She drinks from her soda and sets it back down. "Sawa sawa. Back at home, I go to the gym all the time. I'm used to lifting weights." She lifts her right arm and makes a muscle, proudly displaying a small but well-defined bicep.

"You are very strong," he says, wondering if the baring of her arm is the signal. No, Americans are not so subtle.

"Thank you."

The ten days have made her tougher. She has seen the poverty of shantytowns, has clashed with Indian merchants who mistook her for a Kenyan and treated her shabbily, has shopped in Kwa Vonza at the peddler's stalls and picked among rows of tables piled and crowded with flip flops and fabric, batteries and fans which made her nostalgic for the makeshift stalls on Fulton Street and Pitkin Avenue. She has squatted, has taken malaria pills, has sprayed herself sticky each night with insect repellent. She has endured roads made dangerous by the congestion of pedestrians, cyclers, and fearless drivers. She has sat in open-aired vans and breathed the dust that comes in from all sides. She has made do without refrigeration, consuming mostly starches, eating only non-perishable items and forgoing eggs and dairy products. She has risen with the sun to wash her clothing in cold water in an outdoor concrete basin. Alongside the village's women and children, she has rubbed her clothing with the same bar of soap she uses to wash her body, wrung her items out and draped them along the guesthouse fence, knowing that by the end of day her clothing would all be dry. She has gone two weeks without the use of hot water upon her person. Cautioned against drinking the well water, she has rinsed her toothbrush with bottled water, and guzzled more Fanta and hot chai than she cares to think about. She has followed the orders imposed upon her group before they left the U.S. She has deceived none of the children with false affection, tricking them into getting attached to her only to have her leave soon after. She has given no hugs, no kisses. She has touched no one since her arrival. She has done all that she has been asked and now she wants this one thing.

She stands. She believes she has indulged in enough small talk. "Please," she says, holding out her hand, asking permission. "Would it be all right if I touch you?"

Yes. Not so subtle at all. "Pardon?"

"Tafadhali, Nicholas," she says. "Please."

Before he can answer, the American black woman kneels beside his chair and presses her palm to his cheek and cups his chin with her fingers. She takes the smile from his lips, tracing it with two fingers, erasing it with the fleshy pad of her thumb. She doesn't mention what she has left on the other end of the middle passage—a job that saps her and offers little recompense, students who feel no guilt at plagiarizing the work of others, who believe they can negotiate for higher grades, parents who hover and little understand the difference between high school and college, who believe their tuition payments entitle them to access the records and grades of children legally recognized as adults. It seems so much simpler here. There are meals to prepare, fields to tend, children to watch, scold, and love. Here there are no pressures to publish, no committees to serve upon, no undergraduate majors to advise, no struggle to balance the three. There is no research agenda, no idea to invest two years of her life into, only to discover someone else already has a book on the same topic in the pipeline, only to find herself beaten out and back at the starting line with two years of her tenure clock irretrievable. Here there is no one to make her feel less than. There is no culture to proclaim she is lacking. Here she feels beautiful. More important than what she has left is what she seeks—some sense of self, some part of her that she believes can only be found here, can only be claimed in the presence of this man, one she believes has never felt inferior.

Her touch is pressing and insistent. "Coconut grove. Cinnamon tree," she croons. "What is Africa to me?"

"What is it you are saying?" he asks.

"A poem."

"Yours?"

"Countee Cullen's."

"Your husband?"

She laughs. "He's a famous poet who died long before I was ever born."

"He is an American black man?"

"Yes," she says. "He wrote during the Harlem Renaissance."

This is a new thought to him, black Americans immortalizing Africans into poetry. Was she memorizing him to take back with her? Was he the poem now beneath her touch? "Will you answer his question?"

"You mean, what is this to me?" she removes her hand and waves it widely, to take in the well-appointed room and the hot, dry, dusty and bare ground surrounding it outside. "I don't think I can explain what it means for me to be here."

Her hand returns to him, gliding from temple to brow. The guidebooks have taught her well. She knows what to expect from the locals; she has been cautioned to protect her person and her health. She knows how to keep her money from being stolen, and how to keep herself from looking like an easy target, how not to contract malaria and how to bypass diarrhea, but none of the books prepared her for the way she would feel, flying on a plane staffed only by Africans, seeing only black pilots, only black flight attendants, landing in a country of black faces, seeing black skin everywhere she turned—for once— not being the minority. Nothing—neither guidebook nor dictionary—has prepared her for the feeling of coming home.

She lifts her fingers into his hair. "If any one did this to me back home, I'd be offended." She pushes her fingers against his scalp, working to plow small rows through his thick and impenetrable hair. How strong the kink, how fragile the fiber, how thick the strand.

"No," Nicholas says. "I am not offended." Far from it, his skin tingles in the places she has touched.

She scratches a memory she has thought long forgotten from his hair, finding it in a patch of smooth uncovered scalp. "When I was in seventh grade, my class went on an overnight trip to Washington, DC, and stayed in a hotel, four girls to a room. That night, we all went downstairs and jumped into the hotel's pool. I was the only black girl in the class and when I got into the water, my hair shrank, reverting to its natural texture.

When I emerged, the girls in my class all gathered around me, wanting to know why it looked so crinkly. They kept touching and patting my hair. They made me feel like a trained dog. I've never felt so ugly."

Her upturned face, unlined and smooth, unmarred by sun or wind, is lovely. Nicholas takes her hand, places it back on his cheek. He cannot imagine being the only black person anywhere. "I am not offended. Please, continue," he says. The urge to be touched by her, to feel her hands upon him is great. She has worked alongside the others without complaint, doing far more than her share. He has seen her high up on the ridge working with the men, pushing heavy wheelbarrows, overturning hers more than once, but never surrendering nor taking the easy way out and joining the other women who waited for the wheelbarrows to come to them. The hands which touch him have wrapped schoolbooks, planted trees, held a machete and planted castor beans. He'd thought her hands would be calloused by now, but when they touch him they are lotion soft.

"As soon as we left DC, I begged my mother to take me in for a perm. I've worn it straight ever since then." Her other hand comes to rest once more in his hair. Her fingers press against his scalp and Nicholas closes his eyes. "No one ever told me this was beautiful," she says. "And I was too young to know any better." The hand on his cheek frames his brow. The air in the room is now charged with her.

She has come past the manmade dam, past fields of castor beans and rows of guest houses, past children playing soccer to find him and enslave him to her fingers. With just one touch, she takes away all the years of his schooling, his advanced education—he is far too educated for his current position— takes away the meager shillings they call his pay and in their place immortalizes him, turns him into poetry. Until now his face has been just a face, not the long lost face for which someone has been searching, for which fingers express their joy in having finally found.

Back in the city, a life awaits him which is as metropolitan as any the black American woman has known—teeming streets, hurrying people, speeding cars, street vendors, homeless persons, beggars, orphans, and addicts—and the safe haven of his wife and nephews amid the bustle.

Forgive me Naomi, he thinks. The entire time the American black woman touches him, he sits with his hands by his sides. He has not touched her in return, he has not made love to her, yet he has been unfaithful. Beneath the American black woman's hands, he has allowed himself to become her poem, he has become all of Africa to her and there is no way to tell this to Naomi in any way she can understand. Whenever the black American woman thinks of Africa, of Kenya, she will think of the touch of his face, his skin beneath her palms and he will be there with her, conjured at will. He is something of a souvenir, a keepsake of her visit. Now he will always belong to her and this his Naomi can never know. Each time now with Naomi, there will be some part of him missing, some small part his wife will never notice, but some part nonetheless and this American black woman would have it just as she now controls his whole body with the whim of her touch, with thumbs gliding down the sides of his face, index and middle fingers gently tracing his lip and jaw. With just the touch of the ragged edge of her fingernail, her pinky's nail scratching the edge of his ear lobe, desire shudders through him. All that lies within him rises to meet her.

Two more days before he can see Naomi. In two days he will return to Nairobi and spend the weekend with his wife. He thinks of all of the ways he will love Naomi when he sees her, all of the ways he knows she likes, all of the touches he knows she prefers. Thoughts of Naomi are meant to steel him against the lure of this American black woman's touch.

Two nights from now, he will see his wife. He will push Kilonzo to make the trip in record time. He will wash off the layer of dust he always seems to carry with him from the village to the city and he will get there in time to see his nephews tucked in. He will tell Naomi how great his need for her has been. He will prepare his words ahead of time and keep thoughts of the black American woman from getting in the way.

He has two lives, one here as the manager of this manmade village in the Kitui district, and another life in the city with his wife and two nephews. It is because of Naomi that he can have both lives. Were it not for Naomi, his nephews would be lost to the streets of Nairobi, intoxicated by glue. It is because of Naomi that his two nephews now have a home and now have himself and his wife for parents. Normally, he returns home at the end of the week, but because of the schoolhouse construction, he has had to remain. It is only that he has not lain with Naomi in many weeks, enough time to make any sane man randy. He is convinced that it is only this pileup of weeks without Naomi that makes him susceptible to the black American woman. Surely it is not that he enjoys her company, nor that he has been wooed by her many questions. None of the other volunteers have ever asked as much as she has. The Europeans that come are professional volunteers. They've devoted their lives to volunteering in Africa.

They have served in South Africa, in Lesotho, in Ethiopia and Eritrea, in Somalia. Kenya is nothing special to them. They ask no questions. They've been through it all already, but the American black woman's questions never cease. She comes with a litany, asking about the purpose of the sand dam, unable to understand the concept of a manmade village, wanting to know if Africans use deodorant, curious as to why African men wore long sleeves and long pants rather than tee shirts and shorts in such heat. It is the weeks of abstinence that make him vulnerable. It is not that he enjoys her company, nor the way her questions elevate him. Posed to him as if he is an expert authority, her questions put him on a pedestal, make him feel special, a completely different feeling than that which Naomi inspires. Always with his wife— a Kikuyu from a wealthy family of wabenzi—he feels unworthy. Naomi's people run the capital city. She could have done so much better.

Her hands relinquish him. "Thank you Nicholas. Asante sana. I didn't think there was anyone else who would let me," she says.

Until she speaks, Nicholas doesn't realize he has been holding his breath. "No," he says, exhaling. "Few would understand."

"I'm glad that you do."

She rises to leave without offering to make love to him.

He understands the error of his assumption and feels but little disappointment. Tomorrow this American black woman would be leaving and memories of squatting above concrete toilet pits, of washing with cold water would soon be forgotten. She will return to her country, to her city, to her home and regale her friends and colleagues with the quaintness of this village and her magnanimous nature in volunteering. The children whose books she covered in protective wrapping to make them last that much longer, the women who wave from their work in the fields, the saplings she helped to plant will all become anecdotal, stories to be told over lunch, recounted on a first date to break the ice, these people and these sights so real to her right now will be memories conjured only by looking at the pictures and the hand-carved elephant paperweights she will take back with her, by a stamp in her passport only will they be recalled. But he—he will be forever, the touch of her hands upon his skin told him so. Never before has he been a poem. He wishes to tell her all that he understands, but his tongue lies thick in his mouth and between his tongue and teeth he finds only the taste of dust.

JOY CASTRO

Grip

Over the crib in the tiny apartment, there hung a bullet-holed paper target, the size and dark shape of a man—its heart zone, head zone, perforated where my aim had torn through: thirty-six little rips, no strays, centered on spots that would make a man die.

Beginner's luck, said the guys at the shooting range, at first. Little lady, they'd said, until the silhouette slid back and farther back. They'd cleared their throats, fallen silent.

A bad neighborhood. An infant child. A Ruger GP .357 with speed-loader.

It's not as morbid as it sounds, a target pinned above a crib: the place was small, the walls already plastered full with paintings, sketches, pretty leaves, hand- illuminated psychedelic broadsides of poems by my friends. I masking-taped my paper massacre to the only empty space, a door I'd closed to form a wall.

When my stepfather got out of prison, he tracked my mother down. He found the city where she'd moved. He broke a basement window and crawled in. She never saw his car, halfway up the dark block, stuffed behind a bush.

My mother lived. She wouldn't say what happened in the house that night. Cops came: that's what I know. Silent, she hung a screen between that scene and me. It's what a mother does.

She lived—as lived the violence of our years with him, knifed into us like scrimshaw cut in living bone.

Carved but alive, we learned to hold our breath, dive deep, bear our teeth to what fed us.

When I was twenty-one, my son slept under the outline of what I could do, a death I could hold in my hands.

At the time, I'd have denied its locale any meaning, called its placement coincidence, pointing to walls crowded with other kinds of dreams.

But that dark, torn thing did hang there, its lower edge obscured behind the wooden slats, the flannel duck, the stuffed white bear.

It hung there like a promise, like a headboard, like a No, like a terrible poem, like these lines I will never show you, shielding you from the fear I carry—like a sort of oath I swore over your quiet sleep.

RACHEL HALL

Heirlooms

They left behind furniture. Of course, it was too bulky, too big to bring to America. Out of the question—the armoire, the walnut dining table with feet like claws, though it was at this table their destination was decided, their future set in motion. And it was here the child, Eugénie, did her schoolwork each night, its surface pocked with her efforts, the indentations testament to her diligence and precision. They left marble-topped dressers, bookshelves with glass doors, a settee covered in a geometrical print, Eugénie's bed where she had cried at night, thinking her sobs private.

Her Aunt Lise and Uncle Jean's bed had been his parents', its headboard painted with posies by his mother. This they left for a friend, but when he came to retrieve it later that week (petrol being hard to come by still) it was gone, stolen by the landlord's son and installed in the apartment of his mistress on rue Vincennes.

They left family. Lise's brother, in a mass grave in Poland, in a town with a name like a howl. Her sister-in-law, the child's mother, buried in Saint-Malo. They left a trunk of the tiny embroidered dresses she'd made Eugénie, and bloomers, smocks with scalloped hems, the stitches so small they were nearly invisible. One or two of these garments might have been saved, so small they wouldn't take up much space. No, it is better not to think in this way, Lise decided. Better to think instead "useful," "necessary," "indispensable."

They left Jean's mother in Montpon, the village where she was born. She, in black since the previous war, in the back garden, bent over her lilies. "Go on, then," she had said. "Go!" She hadn't wanted to cry. Afterwards she prayed the rosary for them, her only son, his Jewish wife and the child who wasn't theirs.

They left the bakery Jean's father had left him. They left the wicker baskets of breads, the glass shelves in the front windows lined with tartes and cakes, the air heavy with sugar. Jean kept the recipes in his head, but in America they will fail. Cakes are soggy, soufflés fall, meringues don't harden. Later they will learn that the bakery became Montpon's first modern laundromat.

They left friends like the Laurys, the Gelas, the Moreaus. People who knew them before the war, knew Jean's *gateaux* when flour was plentiful, remembered Lise's laugh, the surprising way it started out loud and then simmered on. When the child was ill, Monsieur Gela had driven his bicycle into the country and come back with black market eggs. Madame Laury played the piano in her parlor and they all sang "The Marseillaise" though it was forbidden and "Au Clair de la Lune." Their voices rose together, Jean's hearty baritone guiding them. There are photographs from these times—the girls smiling despite their many layers, their knees knobby in too-short dresses, the women's lips heavy with red. The men are all handsome, hair slicked back, clean-shaven. The word that comes to mind is dapper. They seem not to make men like these anymore.

They left words, phrases, a sureness with language. Their mother tongue. They left their names because they proved difficult for Americans. Jean became John; Lise became Liz; and Eugénie, a name like a brook flowing, became Genny.

In America, they will speak French together in their home, but in this confined space, the language turns reedy and thin, a plant growing without light. The child is glad after only a year to shrug off the last of her accent. She can, after much practice, manipulate her tongue to form "*th*." "*The th*eater is closed *Th*ursday," she can say, "due to *th*e *th*reat of *th*understorms." She is an American girl now, walking to Thomas Jefferson Elementary School with her hair in long braids, penny loafers on her feet. She passes the cemetery gate of their new city with hardly a thought.

The new language makes them miss their old friends, people who laughed at their jokes. In the new language, it turns out, they are not funny, only odd. There are other problems too. The American habit of concluding a meal by saying "I am full," which in French means "I am pregnant."

They left money—only a small amount—in a bank in Saint-Malo. They meant to close the account on numerous occasions, but it was in the child's mother's name. They had her death certificate, but not the proper guardianship papers to prove they were adopting the child. So many papers after a war! Is the money there still, accruing interest? Perhaps they are rich. The child thinks of this money for many years, thinks of what it could buy her—crinolines like those of her classmates, a stucco house with an oval swimming pool, a sister.

They left books about history and politics, songbooks, novels, several journals containing sketches and notes. They left the child's schoolbooks and report cards, a book she won for high marks—about the Queen of England, of all things. They left an old address book filled with the names of people they realized they never really knew.

They left the sound of cathedral bells and their reverberations through the narrow cobblestone streets. They left the chants of schoolgirls skipping rope outside their window, of mothers calling into the dark, "*A table maintenant!*" They left the thunder of boots stomping up stairs, loud knocks, shouts, and then pleas. They left this, but not their fear of the night, and an attentiveness, even in sleep, to the possibility of loss.

For a long time, the child will look at any new place with an eye to hiding. Under the kitchen sink? The narrow cupboard by the stairs? Behind the thick bushes in the park? One day she realizes this habit has left her. It, too, is gone. Still, when she looks at photographs from before the war, she can't believe she is that grinning girl, can't remember what it was like to feel such joy.

"Sometimes," Lise will say, "I find myself wondering where something is—an owl brooch set with turquoise eyes or a particular square platter. And then I know: it is gone." She shakes her head, laughs at her forgetfulness.

It turns out there are things that cannot be left. The very nature of secrets, for instance, insists that they be kept. The child savors hers like a smooth candy in her mouth. She believes her father is alive somewhere, hiding still. Perhaps no one has told him the war is over. Perhaps his journey home has been long and difficult. Perhaps he is already waiting for them in America, his arms extended in welcome. Sometimes she is certain she sees him turning the corner, exiting the Metro, but it is some other man who only resembles her father. He takes the arm of the woman beside him, pulls their child into an embrace.

Lise cannot leave her desire to have a child. It will dog her onto the ocean liner and across the Atlantic, on the long train ride, and from one airless apartment to another. All her life holding other women's babies, her eyes tear up, her throat tightens.

Walking home early one afternoon, days before they are scheduled to leave, Jean smokes an American cigarette and wonders how he will ever learn to like their paltry flavor. He is alone on the street at this hour, the businesses closed for lunch and rest. His eye is drawn to a dark alley where papers flutter in a down draft. As he gets nearer, he sees that the paper is money. The wind makes it lift and soar, spiraling back down to rest near his feet. He scoops it up, stuffs it in his pockets, but can't fit it all in—There is so much! He isn't far from home, and he runs there to get a box or a bag. Inside, he pulls the money from his pockets, starts to call for Lise and the child. The bills, he sees now, are old and funny looking. He looks carefully and sees that it is money printed during the French Revolution. The edges are crumbled and torn. He can buy nothing with this. Later, he will take the bills to an antique shop and find they are worth little; they are not even pretty to look at, printed as they were in accordance with the revolutionaries' utilitarian ideas.

It is a silly thing to take when so much else has been discarded or given away or sold. What will he ever do with it? Still, he cannot forget the way the bills sailed in the wind, how he felt running toward them, hope lodged in his throat.

EMILY HIPCHEN

Ybabruopeek

The Conversation. Aunt Beth calls it The Conversation.

It is not, as so much of this experience is not—it is not at all what I imagined happened. There is no office, no desk, no background of books, nothing official. My destiny is sealed in the Delanys' front room, on impeccably clean couches and chairs above short-shorn carpets, twelve neat-shod feet in even neater rows, twelve hands in various attitudes from clenched to gripping, six oval faces in a single row, curved together, facing each other, facing the problem. The Conversation. She calls it that.

Aunt Beth says it happened while she was babysitting down the street from the house, that her boyfriend at the time came over, burst in the front door and told her that the Baris and the Delanys were sitting down together, talking together, in a kind of truce. Or rather more like two sets of generals, like statesmen for the victorious offering terms.

It is 1963. I imagine the decor in that living room, the colors, the fabrics, green and that orangey-red and plastic everywhere, some glass pieces on shelves not a bit dusty and drapes rich and heavy, hanging from careful pinch-pleats over windows on louvers looking out into the street. The sound passing cars make is embraced in them, stopped dead and suffocated; it is their sole purpose, since they are not and do not pretend to be beautiful. Until tonight nothing untoward has come into that room, nothing unwanted, nothing that would ruin the implications of it, make it less than what it is intended to be: nothing less than an empty, precise place only the rich can afford, a space filled with what is uncomfortable and has no practical use, arranged like a photograph from a magazine. Tonight, in glacial immobility, it is outraged as only such a room can be.

119

Tonight Anna and Joe and the parents sit in it in those torturous chairs, looking at the writhing bits of glass and the chloroform-gauze drapes and not at each other. Tonight they must have a conversation and this is the only place fitting in the house to have it, the only place that makes clear in its formality, in its high-chinned mortification, the impact of the children's behavior. The Conversation, like the room in which it takes place, is not intended to welcome comment, to foster discussion among equals: The Conversation consists of options which are not options really, choices which do not allow anyone to choose.

They are seated, hands and feet neatly arranged, symmetrical and controlled. Then Anna is confronted, Joe is confronted. This is the lever under the world, this is the attitude the Delany and Bari parents assume. It is designed to cow and control. The Delanys become outraged parents of a debauched daughter; the Baris play the parents of a son who has embarrassed and disappointed them because he has debauched the young Delany. Thus The Conversation begins, as all such things must, with posturing and displays of power; it begins with what the adults can do to the minors. What lawyers properly engaged would make of Anna and Joe's relationship (no one has to say "statutory rape," though the phrase hangs there in the air, like a safe on a slim cord, echoing and echoing in all their heads). What the rich man can do to the poor one if the latter proves obstinate, what the old can do to the young, what the man can do to his daughter if she will not obey.

And perhaps these threats are all just implied, not stated. Perhaps they sound in the back of what passes for bare pleasantries in that room, sounds unspoken but heard like the faraway pounding of guns whose purpose everyone knows but no one talks about, no one needs to say anything about. Perhaps they are only suggested in the way each participant in The Conversation sits, how much space each takes up, the position of legs, face, arms, hands. Stated baldly or not, it must have been there; the power is first, in coercion it is always and must be.

And then there are the options. "Here is what must be done," Anna's father, my grandfather, says finally. Broaching the subject. He looks straight at his daughter, straight over her belly and into her face, not acknowledging the belly, not acknowledging the man beside her who made it. "Here is what we will do. If you keep it, you are entirely on your own. You must feed and clothe yourselves and it, must house and drive and pay for yourselves. If you keep it, you lose us. You lose your family and your futures.

If you keep it." And here I imagine he pauses, waiting for that to sink in properly like a fisherman sets a barb in a bass's mouth, waiting carefully until it has swallowed so deeply that the hook catches something vital.

And then he says, "But you can, if you decide not to keep it, you can give it up for adoption. There are places you can go. It doesn't need to be difficult. You can have it, give it away, then go on with your lives as if it never were. Your separate lives, of course. As if it never were."

There is a lamp on a small table beside him, its shade a pale-pinkish cream. The light shines through it onto his shoulder, his lap, shading his face, making the reddish hair on his arms glint like mica in granite, edges catching light. He watches her, watches them, knowing what they will choose. Everyone knows what the options are, everyone knows what they mean, that there is really no option. It will happen as the four parents have planned it, the mistake rectified and no one the worse for it, since it will be gone, the evidence, the proof and the product out of the way.

Aunt Beth is wrong. It was never a conversation.

Joe tells me that his mother and father, when they found out about the baby, told him and Anna that they would help them, that the three of us could live in the attic room that had become Joe's once he grew older. That they would help with the baby, help the couple, let them become a family as they so wanted. I imagine Anna and Joe heard this with a certain sense of relief, believing that there was finally a choice, that they had, after all, been given some control over their lives and mine. That they could choose, really choose, even if they eventually chose to give me up for adoption. But then, at some point, Joe's parents changed their minds. It's tempting to imagine money and power, to imagine them overpowered and overawed by the Delanys, to imagine a second conversation that perhaps never really happened but happened anyway, one in which it was made clear that the Delanys would not allow Anna and Joe to have options, in which it was made clear what would happen to them, and to me. And fighting it was immaterial, would be ineffectual and wasteful and wrong.

But however tempting it is to believe this, it's far too simple. More likely the Baris began to see it as the Delanys did, as a mistake that did not need to cause permanent damage, need not be permanently binding. They began to see it as the best way to help their most promising son, and so took it, encouraged and enforced it, made it so that there was again no choice. None at all. And in that front room they all sat that night, Anna and her belly, both sets of parents, and Joe, his hands big and brown-fingered, lying flat on the black pants he wore, the creases passing just under his palms like two edges to balance upon.

***

There was, I understand, a rescue attempt. Joe found out where Anna, now Marilyn, was and went to save her, to save us.

I understand that, at that time, he did not have a car. He was a freshman on an athletic scholarship at Seton Hall and didn't need one, I guess. And yet, somehow, in this crisis he scraped together enough money, somehow he found the cash to buy a car to bring Anna back in. I imagine it was an old one, maybe from the late 1950s, more than a little decrepit. I imagine its whiteness, since all such steeds are supposed to be pale and pure—probably it was black or brown, though. The nuns, had they seen it, would have found its color symbolic, a sign, a spot in the white snow that certainly lay all around that cold January day in upstate New York.

I am told that Joe and a friend left Long Island on the day Joe decided to free Anna. Probably he followed the same route she and her father or mother had taken some days earlier, in hot silence the whole way, the rise of her belly between them choking off anything they might say. Joe smoked then, and this was a two-pack trip, a cigarette always between his lips, and the next on the seat beside him, waiting to be lit from the red end of the last. After dark, the cigarettes made bright arcs to the pavement, skittering away in sparks when he flipped them out the window he opened for that purpose.

Anna tells me that The Immaculate Conception Infant Home had a prison regime. The women were indoors all day, in lock-down in their cells. They were allowed only a few minutes a day outdoors, to walk in the garden on the grounds. Joe waited in his car nearby for one of these small liberties. I don't know how he figured out that she would be there. I don't know if he waited and watched or if somehow, in a way that seems impossible to imagine if Anna's described the place accurately, they actually exchanged messages. All I know is that Anna walked, and Joe waited.

And this is what I imagine happened next: it's winter, a New York winter. Accustomed as I now am to Northern cold, to Northern Januaries, it seems improbable that there would be this phalanx of uniformed and dark-coated women walking there, bundled closely against the cold, the scarves and sweaters making them look lumpy but not disguising the reason they walked there in that dead cold garden. And yet Anna says they did this, this walking in the iciness. The trees are surely bare, blackened, stick-filled, the ivy on the blood-red brick has died and left only its stems to show where it will come again, but not soon, in a flush of heart-shaped greenness, a spring opening upwards past windows that glitter coldly, vacantly, upwards to the slate-colored roof. Everywhere in January, in Syracuse, there is snow, probably a lot of it, piled beside the path there in the garden, shoveled and dark with treacherous slicks of ice that the women walking there sometimes briefly slip on, though they seldom fall. The low yew bushes are their winter green, blackened with frostbite. As all boxwood does, they still smell sharply of urine, but the chill air subdues its summer pungency—in June and July, that scent mingles with stronger smelling marigolds and flashy gladiolas, and the women walking there then turn away from such profusions of odor and color. The garden is cared for, when it needs caring for, by a church guild. I imagine the women forbidden to touch the soil for fear they might eat it, for fear they might extend the contagion digestively, for fear they will forget what they are and what they are doing there—perhaps because the nuns understand metaphors and are afraid of them.

When Joe's white car (I won't, you see, give up my visionary vehicle lightly), when Joe's white car noses its way into Anna's consciousness, when she sees the round, familiar, beloved face behind the dark windshield glinting the light in lancet patches back into the garden, her heart lifts, I imagine, feels lighter than it has since spring. The women are watched, of course, in their walking. But ones so huge and ungainly, so far advanced in their sin as Anna is now, these are considered too little nimble for real restriction. Even an old nun with prayer-stiffened knees can catch an eight-months pregnant woman waddling to freedom. I wonder how many tried, and if Anna was the first that month, that year. She certainly wasn't the first ever; the closeness of the rules implies her predecessors too strongly.

When she sees Joe's car, Joe in the driver's seat, I imagine she extends the circle of her path carefully, subtly, spiraling outward slowly so as not to raise the alarm. She knows the last bit must be a dash and that given she is big and front-heavy, that dash must be short. She is assiduous. The car creeps closer. Each step she takes moves out and out and away.

And then she is in the back seat somehow, lying down with me humped above her hipbones. I have, I am sure, imbibed the adrenaline that brings her breath in small gasps and makes the wash of her heart quicken in my ears. I turn and turn in my small space, excited, my legs pumping as she wishes hers could again, running in a dream into paradise. Joe drives, but he reaches back once to lay his hand on the mound of me. I, an ingrate, an early Morse-coder, kick it. It is the first contact we have, through the medium of her skin.

And then they are off, fast as they can drive, fast as the poor, one-horse car can carry them.

I don't know why—perhaps they were pursued, perhaps it's just that they saw the recklessness and sheer impracticality of stealing Anna from The Immaculate Conception Infant Home—I don't know why. But after a little while, they turned around and went back.

When Anna got out of the car, she shut the back door solidly, creaking it into place, then pushing hard. She didn't see Joe again until after I was born, until after I had been delivered, like a package. I imagine that in some ways, that first meeting of theirs was one between strangers.

***

There is something sad in misdirected letters, in envelopes that never get posted, or that end up on the post office floor, kicked under a bench somewhere accidentally. Letters written to sit in desk drawers like plain girls waiting for a phone call or an invitation to dance. There is something forlorn in letters like this. Dead letters, long dead.

I am standing in the dark, in October, outside my grandmother's house on Long Island. Beside and above us, the trees whisper in the night, the air not crisp, not balmy precisely, the breeze like the tickle of a forgotten word on the tongue, there and not there quite. The dark moon wheels above, taking its time across the sky, through stars that never change, or never seem to, anyway. On the main road, two blocks away, the cars pass, their headlights dimming on and off slowly. On this street, no one passes. It's too late for that. Everyone is sleeping or watching the news, doing something inside all these little houses, the same ones, precisely the same ones, my father grew up among, on whose lawns he tumbled, in whose backyards he played catch or dodge-ball, in whose kitchens he played other games with his friends under the feet of, under the watching eyes of, women who were not his mother. When I shift my eyes to the right, I can see the ball field over my uncle's shoulder, the one where my father played on Saturdays, I imagine, his uniform always too short in the arms and legs just a little, or too long, for growing into.

I am talking with my uncle about my father and mother, what he thinks of them, what he thought of them, what happened almost four decades ago now, as best he can remember it. We are discussing my adoption again, he is filling in details I never knew (as they all do when they see me, a sort of reflex, knowing that I crave the stories, seeing how open-mouthed I am with hunger to know), details he says my speaking and writing about my experience have recalled to him. He looks so much like my father I want to cry, to tell him everything I have ever felt and done, how much I've missed him, how much I am afraid I will miss him. But I don't. I can't tell him these things and I would never say them to my father in any case.

There was, my uncle says, a letter. From my father to my mother. I don't remember if he says he discovered it during the time she was away at the Infant Home, or if it was before that, before she came home for Christmas that year, before anyone had made a decision because they didn't know (did they?) that there was a decision to make. But it is clear the letter was meant for her, left in the bedroom he and my father shared. I have been in this bedroom, up the carpeted stairs that jog to the left after the landing, filled now with odds and ends my grandmother doesn't use regularly—with boxes of Christmas ornaments, old furniture, that sort of thing. The twin beds are still there, right and left, small window in between, blue corded bedspreads and pillows as if the occupants, now men in their fifties and much too large for such Lilliputian mattresses, might be back to lie down any minute. To turn over and whisper in the dark to one another, though I don't know if they ever did this. The ceiling arches up on both sides, meets in the middle. The room is bare, otherwise.

In this room they shared, my uncle once found the letter my father had written to my mother. I don't know where he found it, perhaps under the bed, under the pillow, on the desk under a piece of paper, some homework, an open book, a glove with a baseball cradled inside. I don't know when he found it, though I imagine it could not have been earlier than fall, later than Easter. It was most likely winter, cold and dank and dark, brightened only with Christmas and the promise of spring eventually. Winter was when they had to decide, as much as they ever could decide, and so I imagine my uncle in this room, in winter, bundled in clothes, holding the envelope that holds a letter to my mother, a white envelope probably, blue ink I think, though it could have been anything from black to pencil. On the outside of the envelope my father in his eighteen-year-old script had written "ybabruopeek." Uncle George says it this way, "Eebahb. RooOh. Peek." Has to spell it, interpret it: *Keep our baby.*

I remember watching *Amadeus*, watching the actor in the beginning of the film speak English backwards extempore. I thought at the time it was clever, difficult to do, that it sounded like Danish or what I might imagine an Asian language would sound like, Chinese or Korean maybe—wholly foreign, wrongly rhythmic, the stresses in none of the expected places, the music all indecipherable. I laughed at the movie, at the vulgarity of a Mozart who could talk about love in a sophisticated pig-Latin all the while visibly itching with desire for his busty girlfriend.

But this was different. Ybabruopeek is as close as I've ever heard to the sound of something broken, something breaking that hurts in a way I can't understand any more than I understood the syllables the first time I heard them. It's all backwards, out of sync, wrong wrong wrong. Was the envelope empty? I can't imagine what my father could possibly have said when everything there was to say was in the corner somewhere, on the back, encoded like one of those childish languages meant to deceive adults, meant to be fun. Ones you used to say things like "My sister smells" or "Your mother wears army boots," and then everyone falls over in the grass giggling mercilessly under a cloudless summer sky. Not one meant for "Keep our baby." Not one meant for "I love you," or "Don't leave me," or "Never give up."

Neither Joe nor Anna tells me about the letter. Perhaps they've forgotten. Perhaps they think it's a detail that wouldn't interest me. Perhaps Anna never knew, Joe never sent the letter, preferring instead not to use language this way, to say what he wanted and couldn't have.

***

There is a picture, somewhere, taken surreptitiously, of me in Anna's arms, a stolen embrace one week after I was born. Anna's ward-mates were not all women destined to give up their children. Some, the lucky ones, would have them there and keep them, walk out those oak doors, over the porch with its white, white pillars, rigid and pale against the blood-red brick, walk down the path and step into waiting cars, each woman with her arms full of baby, fair and dark, pink and blue blanketed. All walked out gingerly, their heads bobbing from blanket to car, all smiling broadly, the red of their lipstick making their faces paler ovals than they really were. These were the lucky ones, the envied ones.

These women, Anna tells me, were actually allowed to touch the babies, to cradle, to rock, to feed, to sing to—to handle them. They could have photographs made, as mothers always do, their babies in their arms. In these pictures, the child usually lay across the mother's body, head dark against the pale blanket on the right edge of the photo, body only imagined, running southwest into equally suppositious feet. And the mother's face, usually looking into the camera, eyes open, lips parted—"Here, I have done *this*"—that look.

The photos were probably Kodachrome by 1964, but I imagine the one that Anna had made is black and white. One of the lucky snuck me in, put me in Anna's arms, and quickly, quickly took the picture, then whisked me away again. Anna tells me as her arms weigh down with me, warm and damp, a little asleep, milky scented, my eyes hazel then and unfocused, rolling some—she tells me she will never let me go. In the photo I imagine this moment caught, her lips, pale and unlipsticked, bent down to my still-crinkled ear, her arms like a box convulsing.

It could not have taken more than a few moments, a pause in my infant life as immeasurable as a blink or a summer's afternoon, and yet no time at all, before I lay again as if it hadn't happened at all, in the bassinet with my name on it. My other name.

ELIZABETH EDELGLASS

As Abraham to Isaac, Bilhah to Benjamin

Abe didn't want Misha to grow up so fast. Be a boy a little longer. As if it's so easy to be a man? But with no school, what else for him to do but work alongside Abe at the sewing machine?

And now the baby was coming. And the midwife already gone, one of those possibly not coming back. And the orders for Jews to stay in their houses, soldiers goose-stepping past day and night. Abe heard, even in his sleep, the crack of boot steps. Every now and then a different crack, something worse than boots. And then, sometimes, a scream.

Today, no screams, not outside and also not inside, where who would have guessed Abe would have welcomed a scream, prayed for a scream. With his Manya on the bed, Manya who never screamed like the other wives, not when Misha was born, not when the twins came. And not screaming now, but moaning, her face red with pain and something more, writhing on the damp bedding, gripping her belly with both hands, holding tight to the child inside.

"*Nit itst*," she groaned. "Not now." A child shouldn't come into this world, not now, not here, not in this place. Maybe later, some other day, some better day. But a child doesn't know to listen.

So Abe sent the twins upstairs with bread and cheese and, for toys, wooden spools from his sewing table. But every time he looked up, there they were on the landing, the twins, not playing, but watching. He had to shake a hand, send them back to their room. Should he move a bureau to block their bedroom door? Which was worse, let them see or lock them in like prison? Manya would never forgive if he locked them in. Not now. Not with prison a word that hung in the air outside, threatened to seep under the door like smoke. Prison, or something worse.

And Misha? "Boil water," Abe said. "Mama's soup pot." And Misha did as he was told. Misha, not yet Bar Mitzvah, dragging the heavy pot from the pump to the stove, stronger than Abe remembered, or maybe arms get strong as needed.

When Misha was coming, Manya had walked the floor with the midwife. So strong she was, that first time, too strong to scream. The midwife had sent Abe for wood for the stove, never mind they had already enough wood for ten days, ten babies. By the time Abe had returned, there was Manya, stooping, pushing down with both hands on top of her belly, gloriously naked below her shirtwaist. The midwife reached between Manya's legs, her hands easing, stretching, touching. And, God forbid, it was as if the midwife was stroking between Abe's legs. The sight of it. When Manya pushed, Abe had to push, too, could not hold back, running outside, ripping at buttons, swollen, bursting, pumping seed into the dirt. Thank God he wasn't Catholic like the Poles in town, he'd have had to run straight to confession. Lucky Jew, instead of looking on a punishing priest, he got to kiss his Manya and look on the innocent face of his son, wrinkled, like an old man already wise.

With the twins, not so easy, but the midwife knew what to do. Manya on the bed that time, like now, too weak to walk the floor, too weak to scream. Two days moaning, whimpering. The midwife again with the hands, stroking and prodding Manya's belly. How she knew there were two in there? By the feel of it, here a hand, there a knee. And that belly, so huge and white and frightening, no wonder the midwife sent Misha down the street to Rivka the baker's wife. Abe would have liked also to go, like a scared boy, let Rivka take care of him too. But he stayed, boiled the water, handed over clean bed linen as needed, new sheets that Abe had stitched and Manya herself had bleached and washed and pressed, then folded and stacked in joyous preparation.

After two days, Manya had stopped moaning, which Abe had thought was good. Finally, a rest, two days nobody had slept. But the midwife was suddenly wide-awake, all urgent business, once again with her hands between Manya's legs, this time not just to catch. This time reaching in to pull, actually in, where once Abe had wanted only to be, his private place, now the midwife's place, her fingers, her hand, her wrist. Abe not swollen this time, but shriveled like one of Manya's dried plums, if a plum could feel fright. Then came the water and the blood and the girl and the boy.

Yetta and Yisroel, but not yet, bad luck to name a baby just born. For the girl would come later a quick prayer in shul and a name. For the boy, a bris on the eighth day. Before that, no guarantee the baby would live. But on the eighth day it was safe; the *moyl* would cut the boy's foreskin and give him a name, like every Jewish son and father and grandfather all the way back to Abraham the Patriarch.

The midwife didn't need names, cooed at the babies, gave a bath, the babies and Manya, too, with a cloth dipped in warm water, finally some use for that water Abe had been heating for two days in Manya's big pot. Then she dressed the babies in soft gowns stitched by Abe, set one on each of Manya's breasts, and took that pot back to the kitchen to scrub it out and cook up a fat chicken for some soup. Manya held one tiny head in each hand—the boy on the right, and on the left the girl, with her startling fringe of red hair, no need to open diapers to tell sister from brother—and guided open mouths to suckle, nourishment only she could give. A miracle.

Where was the midwife now, when Abe needed her? Where was a miracle now?

Twice Abe had seen, and he knew Manya was not doing it right this time. Arching backward instead of bending forward, grasping and pulling up on her belly with both hands from below, when she should be pushing down from above. "*Nit,*" she insisted through clenched teeth. "No, no, no."

Even when the water gushed out onto the bed, a sign, Abe knew, that soon would follow the baby, she refused to take off her skirt, her undergarments. Not from modesty, Abe understood, despite Misha's wide, watchful eyes. Manya crossed her legs and held tight. As if keeping her underpants on would keep the child safe.

But it could not be done.

"Quick, Mishky, a clean sheet," Abe shouted as the fluid continued to gush and soak. Together, he and Misha rolled Manya to one side then the other, stripped off the wet sheet and lay down the dry, not new this time, but Abe had patched and laundered, Manya having refused any part in these preparations.

"My scissors," Abe demanded, and Misha ran to fetch them from the sewing table. Then Abe was cutting off Manya's underwear, and already he could see the head bulging between her legs. The red hair, like Yetta's, slick and dark but undeniably red against a tender pink scalp, thanks God, must be another sweet baby girl.

"Push, Manya, push." But she refused to help. Closed her eyes and gritted her teeth. Might have refused to breathe if she could.

Nevermind determined mother and inept father. This baby would come on its own. On his own. Another boy in Abe's surprised hands. A strong boy, opening his mouth to give a lusty *geshrei*.

"Here, boil," Abe said, thrusting the scissors into Misha's hands. And then he was cutting the cord with the clean, hot blades, then pushing on Manya's belly the way he'd seen the midwife do, pushing and catching the bloody mess that came after. Then it was Misha, poor Misha, dipping cloths into the pot for Abe to clean the baby, to clean Manya. Misha, watching Abe wipe Manya's face, Manya's bottom, parts of his mama that a boy should never have to see.

The last thing that needed to be done, Abe had never seen firsthand, the father always sent straight outside after the birth, as if an entire forest must be chopped for a baby, some things a man should not see. That's when the midwife would scald a sharp sewing needle, measure a length of strong silk thread—maybe, for Manya, from Abe's own sewing table—then stitch up the new mother's torn flesh down there, as easy as Abe might tat together a torn lace collar. He'd never seen it done, but he didn't have to see to know. First time after childbirth, when he tried to be with Manya, then he saw, with his fingers if not his eyes, the midwife's fine needlework. Abe also was handy with a needle, but not like that. He pulled down Manya's nightgown, covered up the flesh that needed mending. Would be all right. Would have to be all right.

One more time Misha helped, rolling Manya this way and that, pulling out soiled bedclothes, spreading the last clean sheet. She would not look at Abe, would not look at Misha, hardly looked at the baby, guiding its mouth to her nipple only by instinct. Now Misha looked away, never mind all he had seen today, still a boy suddenly embarrassed by the sight of suckling at the breast.

"So go," Abe said, "bring the children." And Misha charged up the stairs. How easily he carried down the twins, Yetta with one thin arm around his neck, Yisroel sucking a thumb, not even holding on. They knew Misha would not drop them. A good strong boy.

This time, Abe had been hoping for a girl.

A boy needs a bris in eight days. But Reb Shmuel the *moyl* was like the midwife, one of the gone. Reb Shmuel had circumcised Misha and Yisroel. Each time, a big party, friends and relatives and even the hungry young learners from shul. Abe had bought herring and schnapps. Manya's mother and sisters had baked pastries rich with butter and cream. For Misha, Abe's father held the baby as Reb Shmuel brandished his knife for the ritual cutting. Manya's father had to wait until Yisroel for his turn to hold. For a bris, everyone knew, the father's father came first, that invisible thread of covenant tethering son to father to father, through all the generations of Jews.

This time, there would be no party, not with Jews forbidden to walk the streets, and besides, who was left? Grandparents gone with the gone. Aunts run off to the forest with the last of the young learners, cake pans abandoned in kitchens, prayer books scattered on study tables in the empty shul. Abe might have taken Manya and the children to the forest, too, if they hadn't been trapped waiting for this baby. Now the baby was here. And the bris was a commandment, could not be skipped or postponed. Who would take a knife to this nameless little one's penis eight days from now?

Abe's hands trembled just to think about it. Literally, they shook at his sides. Those hands so steady near the flying needle of any sewing machine. Give those hands a scissors, they would cut fabric for a pair of trousers in one cut, never once needing to fix a mistake. With a baby, no mistakes allowed. It was supposed to be a mitzvah to cut your own son, ever since God commanded Abraham to circumcise his son Isaac. Of course later, that same God commanded Abraham to take a knife to Isaac's neck, then changed His mind. A test. Life isn't hard enough, a father needs such a test?

It was dark out, long past suppertime, and the twins were whining what's to eat. Manya needed meat, on account of the blood she had lost, but there hadn't been meat for weeks, her soup pot still red from her own blood, no chicken on hand for a soup. Abe would pour everyone a glass of milk, slice more bread and the last of the cheese.

He pulled a knife from the dairy drawer, wondered which knife would he use for the bris. Meat or dairy? What would God have to say about this, God and His rules about keeping kosher? Such a question, Abe must be crazy. But what choice did he have? Eight days from now, he would pick the sharpest, finest blade he could find, hone it on the stone he used to sharpen his sewing scissors, boil it in Manya's soup pot like today. Then he would say the blessings and give his new son a name, make him a Jew, as Abraham to Isaac.

***

The day they were called out, Manya was still bleeding. The baby, too, its cord, which Abe had tied with strong coat thread, still raw and pulsing. Its penis, on the other hand, like new, uncut, unbloodied. Five days young.

Red was the color of that day in Abe's mind. The red blood of childbirth still draining from Manya's womb, the red of the rags to stanch the bleeding between her legs, the red of the soldiers' armbands. Also the fresh red blood of those who objected, who talked back, who didn't move fast enough, and those who were simply too old, too crippled, too sick. Abe would not allow Manya to be one of those.

She had insisted on packing, bundling their life like the baby bundled in a sling to her chest—warm coats, never mind it was May, Misha's schoolbooks, her mother's candlesticks, her soup pot literally filled with soup boiled from an actual chicken. Abe should have taken as a warning that someone had left behind a chicken. Mishky was strong to help carry, but not that strong. They left the soup, a mistake.

But not the first mistake.

There had been already opportunity missed, not running with Manya's sisters last month when they came with their plan. A plan and a boy they had hiding in their root cellar, a boy with friends in the forest.

But Manya had heard there'd be work where they were sending the Jews, had believed. And food. She'd looked at Abe, one hand massaging her belly, so full from baby and at the same time so empty. Food. As if she'd wanted to be sent, hoped to be sent.

So the sisters had kissed everyone on both cheeks, and the next night there'd been the sound of running footsteps in the street, and then the deafening sound that wasn't boot steps. Since then, no word. Mistake or escape? Abe would maybe never know.

Even that was not the first mistake. First was the mistake of getting pregnant, thinking to bring a new life into this world. Conception, that's what it meant, first, the beginning, nothing before Genesis. There were ways to prevent a new life, Abe knew. Self-control, obviously, plus other ways, if unable to control. And if those ways failed? Still there were things to be done, woman things. Three children weren't enough, Misha and the twins? Enough to replace himself and Manya and even one extra, the tribe of Jews should increase. Who was he, such a big shot thinking he ought to have more? Pride, *feh* on pride, that was the first mistake.

So that's how they came to be on the train, from pride. Left behind on the siding: the soup pot, the schoolbooks, the pride. Whips whipping, dogs snarling, *schnell, schnell, leave it, hurry,* one red-banded arm reaching into the pile, Manya's candlesticks stuffed into someone's deep German coat pockets.

And, speaking of coats, the whole family each wearing two or three layers of clothes, plus on top a winter coat, they should have clothing when they got to where they were going. Never mind the valises and bundles left by the tracks. They would fool those Germans, think they're so smart.

So, who fooled who? Who counted on the train being so hot and the ride so long and the bodies so close, nobody could lift an arm to take off that damn coat? No room even to sit, not even the twins, one hanging onto Abe's left leg, one onto his right, he could not even look down to see which was which, after two days he would have fallen down from the weight of them, if there had been room to fall. No room even to breathe.

Thirsty, Papa, thirsty. How many times he had to hear this cry, one or the other, until they became one voice. *One drink, Papa. We'll be good.*

Manya would bare her breast to them if she could. *Please, Abe,* her eyes begged. *Lift them up. Yisroel is strong, but lift up my Yetta, I will give her a drink.* But here there was no bending, no lifting.

Thank God at least the baby was safely buttoned inside Manya's coat, never mind the heat of two bodies inside that coat, just the top buttons opened, red hair peaking out. The baby wrapped tight to her breast with a sling like a shroud, the baby's mouth to her nipple, sucking life out of Manya's breast. Also out of Manya came blood, dripping down her legs, then at some point more than dripping, she didn't say, but Abe could tell by the color of her face, first flushed red from the heat, then pale, then ghostly white from the blood draining down, down, down, and out.

How many days on that train? Long days, eternity. Nothing is longer than eternity.

And Misha, where was Misha during all that eternity? Abe could not lay his eyes on Misha, somehow separated. In the same car, Abe was sure, had to be sure, calling his name whenever he could snatch enough space to expand his chest to call. And sometimes he maybe heard Misha call back. *Papa.* That was Misha, yes? He looked to Manya to confirm. But Manya's eyes stared without seeing, no answer there.

Abe's eyes, on the other hand, strained to look, to catch a glimpse of Misha, almost Bar Mitzvah. If only a few more months taller, surely his head would rise above the rest, if only the Germans had given them a few more months. So long on the train maybe Misha would grow that extra inch. Abe looked and looked, never mind what his eyes were seeing. Here a dead man, choked on his own vomit, so long since food, yet just enough left in his stomach to choke away his life. And red, more red, blood from heads gashed by whips and truncheons back on the railroad siding, and blood from noses and mouths with no visible wounds, the pressure of the crowd squeezing out the lifeblood through whatever bodily opening was available. Abe must concentrate on expanding his chest just to breathe.

"Breathe," he told Manya. "Please Manya, breathe."

***

Before the train got to wherever it was going, Manya was dead. Still standing upright in the packed crowd, but dead.

The baby, on the other hand, not dead, possibly the healthiest of everyone crammed into that boxcar, still tied to Manya's body, pink lips still circling Manya's nipple. Manya's breast, that's all the baby needed. Such simple needs for a baby: a mama and a breast.

Who knew how long that breast would give milk once Manya was gone. It couldn't just dry up, all that milk, could it? In an instant? Abe had seen it with Mishky and the twins when they were babies, Manya's milk leaking, pouring, spurting. Sometimes ... him and Manya in bed together as God commanded, as Abraham with Sarah ... better not to think on that ... how could a man feel stirrings, even here, even now?

No, all that milk could not just disappear, could it? Not like a person, one minute here, next minute gone. Not like his Manya, *olev-hasholem,* she should be in a better place. There had to be a few drops of milk still left in her breast. But after that? The body makes milk when the mother is dead? Another question nobody should have to ask.

When the train finally screeched to a stop, Abe wasn't so happy as he expected to be. After all these days, too much time to think, and now suddenly no time at all. Again with the dogs barking and the soldiers yelling, *schnell, schnell!* Forcing people out from the car, people who for days had wanted only to get out, now too tired, too sick, too dead to move. So the soldiers were beating, whipping, screaming, forcing everyone off, same as how they'd been forced on. You might think from the sound of it that after all that riding they were back where they had started. But they were not back.

The people in front of Abe poured out the door that finally opened, stumbled out, were pushed out, thrown out. Behind Abe, more people pushed towards the daylight, climbed over the dead, and over the living if you weren't careful. Somehow, with the slightest easing of the crowd, there was Manya slipping to the floor, his Manya, and with her, if Abe didn't act fast, the baby also, the living baby about to be trampled under the feet of the half-dead.

No time for goodbyes, no time for kisses, no time for tears, no time for prayers. Just grab at the baby, rip it out from inside Manya's coat, buttons flying. But careful, don't forget it's not an *it*. It's a boy, a live baby boy, now in Abe's arms. Binyamin. Abe had named him Binyamin. On the train. Some time back, when Abe thought enough days had passed. Hard to tell on the train, in the dark, day from night. Abe lost count, could never be sure. But he had thought it was time, the right day, the eighth day. The bris would have to wait, God would have to forgive, but not the name. Binyamin, a name Abe had chosen himself, because for nine months Manya had refused to discuss. Binyamin, after Manya's grandfather, a name he had chosen to please her. A name Abe should not have chosen, should have known better. Hadn't Benjamin's mother Rachel, in the Bible, died in childbirth? Another mistake.

Now Abe was moving forward, the boxcar vomiting him to the ground, him and the baby, and the twins, Yetta and Yisroel somehow still clinging to his legs. The bark and growl of the soldiers mixed with the bark and growl of the dogs. The twins were afraid of dogs, especially Yetta. Good, their arms stayed wrapped around Abe's legs, tight, like they would never let go. Abe could take a chance, look up for a moment, crane for a sight of Misha.

The soldiers shouted orders in German that might as well have been Chinese to Abe, never mind his own Yiddish, a marriage between Hebrew and German, ha-ha to the Germans. But in this place, these words were totally foreign, crashed against Abe's ears and bounced off.

So who needed words? Anyone could see what was happening, the chaos of Jews being sorted. To the right, the fathers; to the left, mothers and children. Suddenly, a soldier trying to send Yetta and Yisroel to the left. A beady-eyed soldier with ruddy cheeks flaming, he poked at the twins with his whip handle, thank God just the handle, they should follow the other children.

And don't forget the baby in Abe's arms. Binyamin, hot and damp in his arms, how many days he'd been in the same soiled diaper, in his own filth, like the rest of them, even parents reduced to babies? How could Abe hold tight to Binyamin and also grab for the twins and at the same time try to find Misha? The baby crying, the twins crying, and Abe practically crying himself.

Showers. The word poured through the crowd. The mothers and the children would have a shower.

Maybe from the pleasant sound of the word *shower* on her ears, Yetta relaxed, just the tiniest bit, her grip. The soldier finished the job with his whip, the sharp tail this time, broke open her petrified arms from around Abe's leg and dragged her off to the left, to the women and children, all the while Yetta shrieking the shriek of the damned. And here he came again, that soldier, back with his whip for Yisroel. His whip and also, on the hip, his pistol.

Never mind. Abe would bring the twins himself to the left. He would go, too. The other children had at least their mothers for comfort, his would have their father. And showers meant water, no? Abe would lift the children to the faucet, they would all take a drink. Surely hot water, for showers, but water. At last, a drink.

He would have to be careful with the baby, of course. The baby could drown in the force of a shower. Certainly one of the mothers would help, hold Binyamin while Abe lifted the twins. When they'd drunk their fill, he would gently clean the soil from his children, scrub himself with soap, there was sure to be soap. Once clean, he would give Binyamin to suck on his own wet finger, drop by drop, water from his finger to his baby. Not as good as mother's milk, but would have to be good enough, for now.

The soldier had hold of Yisroel, dragging him to Yetta, the soldier's body grown big and solid as one of those ancient trees in the forest, blocking the way of the children trying to run back to Abe, blocking the way of Abe trying to follow the children. How come he cared so much, this soldier, for these two little children in this whole giant stew of people? Just as Abe tried to dodge around him to the left, to follow the twins, here came Misha. At last, Misha, tugging at his elbow, yanking so hard on his arm he might drop the baby.

"This way, Papa, this way." Misha pulled to the right.

"The children," Abe shouted, the twins being pushed forward with the crowd to the left. "Showers. Water."

"No, Papa, this way. You have to come this way."

The twins calling one way, Misha pulling the other. And in between, the nasty soldier with his whip and his pistol and his sharp eyes homing in on Binyamin in Abe's arms. Then, a commotion up ahead, a greater commotion, even the soldier turned to look. Another soldier, another baby wrested from amongst the men, this soldier tall, with long arms, lifting the baby up high, like some kind of offering to God. *Careful,* Abe thought, *don't drop.*

And the soldier did not drop. No. He did not drop. He swung this baby through the air, with all the force of his two long arms. Up, up. And then down, down, down. The crowd backing away, parting, so all could see. The baby's head smashing on the ground. Brains on the ground. Blood in the dirt. An offering to God? Ha. A lamb to be sacrificed, like in the Temple of Biblical days, like Abraham called to almost sacrifice Isaac.

It was Misha who took that moment, Abe's soldier distracted, to grab Binyamin from Abe's arms. Strong Misha, all of a sudden tall Misha, maybe on the train he did grow those extra Bar Mitzvah inches. It was Misha who thrust Binyamin into the arms of a woman passing to the left, another mother also carrying a babe of her own.

It was Misha who pulled Abe to the right, to the men. Misha, who put his hand over Abe's eyes, while the twins and now Binyamin disappeared to the left, out of sight, if Abe could have opened his eyes to see.

"A wet-nurse," Misha whispered into Abe's ear. "Like Bilhah, in the Bible, like you taught me, Papa. Remember?" Bilhah, who mothered Benjamin after Rachel died in childbirth on the trip from Mesopotamia to Canaan, that trip, unlike this one, a trip home. Jacob, Benjamin's father, named his son and placed a stone on his wife's grave and continued on along the road to Hebron, to be reunited with his own father, Isaac, that very same Isaac whose near sacrifice had sorely tested his father Abraham.

***

They were moving again, the mass of them somehow herded into rows, past the ones in striped pajamas with scissors hacking away beards and, for the religious ones, side-curls. Thank God Abe wasn't one of the religious, weeping over his side-curls—but the absurdity, thanking God for *not* being religious. Then stripped naked, all those layers of clothes so carefully planned by Manya now cast aside. Then doused with cold water that somebody actually called showers, Misha scrubbing Abe's skin like just a few days ago Abe had washed Manya and the baby, but here with something sharp, like pumice, that somebody actually called soap. Then striped pajamas of their own, then the numbers tattooed by needles rusty and jagged, Abe would have been ashamed to have such needles on his sewing table back home.

Home, not at all like the shelves of straw pallets where Abe found himself squeezed to the edge, once again in the dark. Against the wall, some fat stranger, where should be Manya. And in the middle, where should be the new baby, Misha, holding tight to Abe, he shouldn't fall over the edge, four shelves up from the floor.

In this place, there would be no mothers. In this place, there would be no babies. Maybe for the first time since Misha was old enough to speak, Abe did not remind him to say the bedtime Shema. In this place there would be no tether of covenant from God to patriarchs to father to son. In this place, there would be no prayers.

ADRIANNE KALFOPOULOU

With my Daughter, Hannah Arendt, and the City of Futures

An individual is no match for history.
　　　　　　　—Roberto Bolaño, *By Night in Chile*

One night after teaching class I go to my daughter's apartment in Brooklyn. Next to the floor mattress that is her bed are several of Hannah Arendt's books. I pick up *Essays in Understanding 1930-1954*, a posthumous collection. I like this French verb, *essayer* (*j'essaie or j'essaye*), "to try." I am trying to understand what it means to be in New York in January 2011, a city very different from what it was in 1984 when I moved to Greece. I've come back to New York City to get away (once again) from Athens. The future that felt so hopeful in 2004 when Athens hosted the Olympics is now in shambles. I am moved by this passage in *The Human Condition* on worldlessness: a shared principle that transcends the world—"a group of saints or a group of criminals." This resonates: "What makes mass society so difficult to bear is not the number of people involved ... but the fact that the world between them has lost its power to gather them together...."

When George Papandreou came into power as Greece's prime minister at the end of 2009 after the myriad financial scandals of the previous government, everyone was hopeful. It was comparable to Obama's election after the fiascoes of the Bush administrations. But when he walked into the White House and said, as the prime minister of Greece, "I feel like I'm at home" Greeks were crestfallen at his all-too-obvious familiarity; he spoke in fluent, unaccented English, unlike so many prime ministers before him, Greek-Canadian-American that he is. And, to Greeks, remains not quite familiar for that fact. I am intrigued by his desire "to get the house in order" as he phrases it in Greek and as my friend Alexandra, a sociologist, notes, "genders" these efforts to make national, political issues more familial, to gather his people.

Yet, despite George Papandreou's efforts, Athens has not stopped seething. Riots, thrown Molotovs, transportation and public sector strikes make Papandreou's measures to control the public debt impossible to ignore. I think that had *Nea Democratia* not lost the last election to PASOK Athens would have erupted into something comparable to Tunisia, Egypt, Libya, and now Syria. The exploding Middle East and the rebelling Greeks, outraged at those who have mortgaged their futures, want more than "economic measures." It is suddenly strange to be in New York, a city without the paralyzing conditions of Athens. Everywhere here ads promise to solve problems from snoring to pet traumas. A business ad catches my eye: "GLOBAL: We make complications simple."

Before going into my class, I read on the New Athenian blog: "The government wants to secure a level of funding from its shrinking tax base that will persuade the troika to release vital loan installments. But its tax measures are becoming increasingly shrill and desperate. While it has refrained from raising income tax, its capitulation to higher consumer taxes (VAT has gone from 19 percent to 23 percent) penalizes the poor." Measures such as these are part of what is disappointing about the current government. Jerome Kohn, in his preface to Arendt's *Essays in Understanding*, notes: "She is uncompromisingly critical of secular bourgeois society, of its deadly conventionality and alert to its tendency to rob man of his spontaneity and change him into a 'function of society.'" The Arab uprisings have been stunning in their spontaneity, though I am feeling as if it would be hard for anyone to erupt spontaneously in this city; I want, for example, to laugh out loud when I hear the PA system's announcement on the subway to Brooklyn: "Ladies and Gentlemen, this is a public announcement, please note that a crowded subway is no excuse for sexual misconduct."

A march in the West Village made up of a scraggly group protesting issues from Nuclear power, cuts in Medicare, to Israel's settlements, are ushered through traffic by armed police, the young robust officers next to the older protestors with their polite "Excuse mes" keep moving people out of the way. What would happen then if the protestors spilled into the day's traffic, or there was a spontaneous swell in their numbers? There is a palpable tension, but it is not from the demonstrating citizens who blend into the city quite harmlessly. There is a certain policed politeness here: "Ladies and Gentleman if you see an elderly, pregnant or disabled person next to you, please give them your seat," the PA voice announces, adding, as if the lesson needs learning: "Stand up for what's right. Courtesy is Contagious." Some ads even suggest that the simplest (spontaneous?) action might be a life threat: "SNORING is no joke! It can kill you! Call 1-888-SNOREGO."

***

There's been snow all month. I walk past a group of the homeless huddled in a corner of Penn Station. The scents of perspiration and dank wool waft by as I pass. It is a good thing that they have these corners to themselves. When I get to the building where I have class, I log into the New Athenian blog again. I do it every time I have a few minutes, and read about what's happening in Athens. More talk about the government's effort to collect outstanding taxes. It has sent out notices on what have been calculated as back-owed debts, taxes on independent businesses, apparent culprits of the black market economy. The scandalous thefts are in professions like medicine and law; doctors and lawyers who ask up front whether you want a receipt or not before naming their fee. An email from a friend describes getting a notice for back-taxes on his deceased sister's free-lance music business: "What do you mean you want me to pay taxes on my sister's business? I told the guy it hasn't existed since she died 8 years ago. The government employee insisted the next surviving relative inherit the debt."

I open another email from Athens: "Terrible things are happening here." There's an attached image of a policeman in flames. Today's national strike is the latest in a series that has brought the city to its knees. I have to get to class so I log off. I am in New York after all, and my students are earnest and disciplined. Elizabeth, who asked me the first day of class if she could record our workshop discussions because she had the beginnings of MS, can't write without pain. Something in my face must have said what I was not saying because Elizabeth smiled a wondrous smile, and said, "I know it's sad." I had more conversations with Elizabeth during the weeks of the semester. We drank coffee together before classes. She is from Alabama, and plans on going back after graduating this year, but is concerned that she has outgrown her town. I suggest a move to another city, talk about it being okay to find new friends, a new hometown, but the doctors in New York, she says, "don't know what they're talking about." She is going to have surgery once she gets back to Alabama. I remember this from one of her poems: "my hand's life-line is in the anatomical vortex of my life."

Elizabeth is hoping to get a job and live to sixty. Like the old who stay close to the sides of streets, gliding shadow-like and grabbing at railings next to steps, Elizabeth reminds me of what happens to the weak, and how easy it is to slip.

After class I log back on to read more of what is happening in Athens. The policeman, who was burning on the street from a thrown Molotov, had been extinguished by another policeman. I log off and decide to pick up some groceries for my daughter at Trader Joe's. Outside there is still snow on the ground. Pools of slush gather around the curbs. I step into one up to my ankles. Trader Joe's is mobbed, and I am quietly frantic, overly concerned with getting soy milk, juice, vegetables, toilet paper; how will I carry it all to Brooklyn, along with binders of student portfolios, books? I am unable to control a surge of panic. The Trader Joe's employees are holding up cheerful bobbing signs, telling people: "THE LINE ENDS HERE." Space is tight; people like me are trying to reach the cheeses and broccoli. A young woman in black leggings leaves the line to pick up something from another part of the store; a space floats between me and the next person. People wait patiently. I move ahead. It's ridiculous to be standing with that open space the woman in the black leggings left in front of me. I'm almost at the cashier when she returns with her basket and looks at me like I should have known better. I roll my eyes. She is about to say something then thinks otherwise, moves back in front of me. I know in Greece there would have been an argument. Here the spaces of protocol are quietly assumed. I could have spontaneously refused to let her back into the line; she could have spontaneously argued that she had only momentarily left her place. In the end I let her assume what she assumed.

When I finally get to the cashier he is upbeat and asks if I'd like my paper bag doubled so it won't tear. He tells me he's exhausted but is looking forward to the gym after work. I smile, nod, thank him; he says, "You know those days when you just want to sit on the couch?" I nod again and smile and he continues, "When it feels like it's too dangerous to even go out the door?" I am still smiling, say, "I guess we could be in Libya." He nods and smiles. There's a short pause before he shakes his head, "Those people man. Amazing..." I agree, thank him for the doubled bag and make my way to the R train. When it starts to drizzle I keep thinking the bags will get wet and tear. Someone next to me, waiting for the streetlight to change, is talking about a brand of dental floss; he keeps repeating, "It's exceptional." I listen, next to him at the light, as he tells his friend it's because the floss is made of "something elastic," and is excited, "It never tears…"

On the packed subway platform I'm with everyone else waiting for a train to Brooklyn. I wonder why I didn't go back to New Jersey, where I sometimes stay with my brother's family. I am especially tired. My daughter, over the phone, asked me to stay the night, cook dinner so we could catch up. We have fleeting conversations between her classes and mine. I sometimes wake up in her apartment to a 4 a.m. Skype conversation she is having with someone in Greece. She'll say she's going to bed soon, that she's finishing a paper, a project. I'll find myself lying awake, listening to her breathing when she lies down next to me.

The myriad thoughts of those early dawn hours are full of rain, sirens, voices from the street, someone drunk, passing cars with the music amped up. One night I listen to a couple having sex in the next apartment. My daughter had the flu. I came in from New Jersey to find her sweating in her bed, her eyes glazed with fever as she kept murmuring that she didn't want any medication. I had some ADVIL sinus tablets, which aren't given over the counter anymore, made a vegetable soup and took it to her upstairs; the world, and her fever, somehow tamed by the vegetable soup. After that I lay awake on the couch downstairs when I hear the couple next door. I notice the pacing of the woman's breathing; the jagged rhythm of it like breath between birth pangs, the man's exclamations, and then—it seemed a long time, they climaxed, his drawn out moan more audible, while her exhausted murmur sounds like she has collapsed. After some minutes a door opens, a car revs up, there's a quick honk. I wonder who they might be; she a secret lover? He returning to a family somewhere else, working a dawn shift in another part of the city?

***

"Are you coming home for dinner?" I call my daughter on her cell phone after making a spinach pasta casserole. The rain is turning into sleet. I've made it to her Brooklyn apartment without tearing the paper bags from Trader Joe's. I hear some background sounds, but can't make out where she is or what she's saying. When she calls me back I hear even less clearly as I boil water for the beets. Then the phone rings again, there's a garbled voice. Someone is crying. I am asking, now emotionally, what the matter is, where she is. I think I hear her say her father's name. I wonder if it has something to do with the day's events in Athens, the strikes, the policeman in flames. "Your father?" I'm nearly hysterical. "I *can't* hear you? What are you saying?" I am now screaming into the phone. "*TELL ME* what the problem is?" I hear the garbled sounds again, and then nothing.

I stare at the spinach casserole, something has happened. Someone has died tragically. Someone we know was hurt in the crossfire of today's demonstrations. It's been a long day. I open the front door to let in the rain turning to sleet. I don't know why I am even in New York. Or I do know. I needed to get away from Athens. I wanted to be closer to my daughter. Living in Athens made me feel like I was dying with the city. The news in Greece always grim, the opposite of the upbeat faces on U.S. television; despite the foreclosures and unemployment, there is always someone who believes the U.S. economy is "back on track" or better, much better than it was in 2008. My brother, who is in banking, makes the simple statement that "the U.S. has the great advantage that it can keep borrowing." Perhaps the future is borrowed, but it is, still, a future to look toward. Greece's bonds have been reduced to "junk," and people are being told the next decade, at least, is looking bad. People have to face it, face the past crushing the future: the new marble banisters of the Panepistimiou metro station in Athens smashed by rioters, the newly polished steps chipped, and chipped again. I turned away, arriving in New York where acquaintances and friends talk about their current projects, where signs and ads give directions and promise cures.

"WHAT?" I am shouting into the phone when I call my daughter back. "WHAT'S WRONG?" there is the garbled sound again I think is sobbing, my daughter overwhelmed by whatever it is she is trying to tell me. I am sure it has to do with her father and what happened today in Athens; history no longer distanced by a TV or computer screen. I hang up again, unhinged. Why had I not gone back to New Jersey—would that have made any of the news any better? At least there, I could hear of it with people I knew. My perspective, if you could even call it that, was devastated. I drank some wine, and hoped my daughter would be home soon.

The sleet hitting against the roof and windowpanes is loud. About an hour later the lock turns in the door. My daughter is furious. "WHAT'S wrong with YOU? I was in the middle of a department meeting and had to leave BECAUSE MY MOTHER IS SCREAMING OVER THE PHONE THAT SHE HAS COOKED ME A MEAL." I stare at her blankly. "What's wrong?" I ask, confused. "Did something happen in Athens?" She looks at me as if she has not heard right or I have lost my mind. "*What?*" She takes off her coat. "Did anything happen to your father in Athens?" I say.

She looks at me like I am crazy, and repeats less loudly but still irritated: "Mom? *What* are you talking about?"

***

I try to keep focused like the many moving so purposefully up and down the city's subway steps. Arrivals, like destinations, never feel less guaranteed than when most possible, the almost-there of the finish line, the essay (this essay? j'essaye) shaping itself out of myriad strands, the body mentally and physically exhausted tries not to give out or give up. Elizabeth wrote, "My health is weaker than most my age. Maybe this is why my will is so much stronger." She gave me an immense smile when I found her after class stretched out on a couch and asked if she was all right. "Mind over matter" she said, explaining to me that she resists painkillers. But the matter of the mind is something else altogether.

I am thinking, "mind over matter" as I travel with the wheeled cart my friend Ella insists I borrow. I am always carrying things, my Net book, books and handouts for class, sometimes a change of clothing, sometimes groceries, too. It helps to take the pressure off my back, but it's cumbersome to lift up steps. I'm climbing up the steps at Penn Station, the cart in my right hand and a bag on my left shoulder, when a woman says, "Excuse me." I try to go faster, but I am wary of tripping with the lifted cart. "Excuse me" she says again, irritated. I try to look back at her, or maybe I glare, and tell her I can't go any faster. In less than a few seconds we're at the top of the steps when she blurts: "You're taking up *two* spaces."

Mind over matter is Ella telling me that she wants to unclutter her living space to free it of matter, lighten her mind. She is adamant that I "don't buy *anything* to eat from the street." I look at her quizzically when she says this. "Most of the food vendors sleep on the streets," she adds. This has never occurred to me. I'm not sure how convinced I am, so Ella goes on, "I've seen it more than once, someone getting up off the pavement to put kebab sticks on the fire." I say maybe the vendor is squatting in a corner to get out of the cold. She shrugs "it's the same unwashed hands cooking the food." Ella's studio, that she generously puts me up in when I am not staying in Brooklyn, is neat. When I am there, Ella gives me my own toothbrush, a towel, explains why she never buys shampoos from organic stores like Whole Foods. She tells me they contain sulfates but I don't know what sulfates are. She explains they clog pores and eventually your hair will fall out as a result, "especially curly hair because it tends to be drier." In fact I should avoid "anything with silicone in it, or with any of the 'cones.'"

I learn other terms from Ella, like dimethicone, polymer (which she explains is a scientific word for plastic), sodium lauryl sulfate, all to be avoided. I tell Ella these are first- world preoccupations, because there are choices. But Ella is matter-of-fact and serious, "No one is looking out for me." Intrusions might be threats, and contaminate. When a man sneezes loudly on the subway, a young woman opposite him moves down two seats. The singular self feels so much more single in this city: the woman behind me at Penn Station was openly irritated that I took up more than my single allotment to get the wheeled cart up the steps. When I sit down at Au Bon Pain in the Port Authority bus terminal, I'm repulsed by the table's sticky surface; crumbs left by an unfamiliar someone. These spaces do not share any common Arendtian principle; this is space that "has lost its power to gather [people] together..." We are un-gathered if together. A man asks if he can use the empty seat next to me. I nod yes. He starts to eat his bagel and continues the conversation he is having on his cell phone.

***

A Jamaican woman on the NJ Transit from Chatham yelling furiously at the people on the train gathered our attention, insisting we focus on a young white woman's insensitivity. She had her laptop on the seat next to hers: "I'm SICK of coming from Morristown and never finding a seat! You put your laptops on these seats, you don't care 'bout no one, you have no DECENCY...." People were looking, some shaking their heads. The young woman, probably a student, removed her laptop but the Jamaican woman kept on, incensed. "You don't want to listen to me because I speak the truth!" Someone quietly laughed. The young woman, now pissed, said, "Take the fucking seat!" The Jamaican woman continued. "Even when I have my son with me there's no respect. In Jamaica they give up a seat for a mother." A woman went to get the conductor. Someone said, "Some-one has to get her off this train." When the ticket collector appeared he had a smile on his face. He is white, and said something to the Jamaican woman that seemed to gather her because she started to speak less loudly, "...it's called freedom of speech" she said, when another ticket collector turned up, he is black. The three of them talked. The woman who said the Jamaican woman should be taken off the train repeated that she should be taken off the train. Both of the ticket collectors seemed at ease, chatting with the Jamaican woman who stayed standing until the train pulled into Penn Station.

Arendt writes, "to destroy individuality is to destroy spontaneity" which leads to "the *murder* of the moral person..." The murder of the moral person is a powerful phrase, who is the murderer? Everywhere on trains, buses, subways, the PA voice suggests that we might be, at any moment, in jeopardy, the murderer in our midst. Politely modulated words remind us, always, to "Protect" our "Personal belongings." They tell us not to "display cell phones and other electronic devices." I assume this means laptops, too. The consequence of this murder is: "ghostly marionettes" (Arendt again) once the destruction of the moral person is complete: "Backpacks and other large packages are subject to random searches by the police." The PA voice always ends its announcements with some polite combination of "Have a good day. Stay Alert. And be Safe." I am bizarrely relieved when the guy at the Trader Joe's cash register asks me, "Do I look like a Michael?" A woman who has just paid, quite out of the blue tells him: "You look like my ex-husband." And he answers, "What was his name?" She answers "Michael." I am suddenly friendly, grateful for this young man's spontaneous question. "I don't know," I say to him with a smile, "What does a Michael look like?"

***

There seem to be more homeless on the streets since the last time I lived in this city; perhaps they are just more visible, huddled together because it is winter. A girl outside Whole Foods at Union Square looks like a student reading, sitting on the pavement on top of a relatively clean backpack. She has a sign in front of her: I'M OUT OF MONEY & DOWN ON LUCK. ANYTHING HELPS. Someone was crouched next to her to, I assume, talk her out of her bad luck. I watch her put the book down and shrug as she says something to him. Another day on my way to class, there is what looks like a middle-aged guy, probably not past forty, lying on the sidewalk against the wall of Dunkin' Donuts. People glance down at him as they pass, but no one pauses. He seems to be asleep, in jeans and a surprisingly cheerful yellow fleece. Maybe he is an out-of-towner sleeping off a bad night.

When I come out of the subway station on the corner of E.14th St. and Union Square, a group of the homeless remind me of the Greek pensioners that gather in the National Gardens off of Syntagma Square in Athens.

They are always immersed in fervid discussions. This group at the corner of E. 14th is shabbily dressed and if I get close I can see some have missing teeth, their appearances are disheveled but they speak with a similar fervor as the Greek pensioners. I hear a reference to a "fucking asshole… there to screw us out of every dime." They slap each other on the back in familiar greeting. I start to think of them as remnants (or is it the consequence?) of a lost Arendtian spontaneity, so opposite of the scripted language I see and hear from shop assistants and salespersons to the large, eerie poster I notice the first day I take the New Jersey transit into Penn Station: "Did you SEE something suspicious commuting to work or grabbing a bite to eat? Then SAY something to the NJ Transit Police to make it right. Report Suspicious Activity. Call: 1-888-TIPS-NJ."

I write to an American friend in Athens who isn't very good at keeping in touch, but maybe, as an American living in Athens, she will under-stand my bereft state in the midst of so much of the impersonal. Perhaps words are less needy when the speaker is more firmly placed in the world. The more confidently modulated the voices over the telephone and PA systems, the more anxious I become. Arendt's words help name these spaces where I find myself. From "The Public and the Private Realm" in *The Human Condition*, there's this reference to "behaviorism" that my daughter has underlined: "the more people there are, the more likely they are to behave and less likely to tolerate non-behavior…. In reality, *deeds* will have less and less chance to stem the tide of behavior, and events will more and more lose their significance, that is, their capacity to illuminate historical time" (my emphasis). I read this one morning on hold, waiting for someone from the Geek Squad at Best Buy to tell me why my Norton Anti-Virus that came with the Net book I bought was inactive. Deeds indeed! I wanted to scream.

I was listening to Best Buy's recordings: "*The easiest way to install some-thing is to let someone else do it.… Can't make it to the Best Buy store nearest you? No problem. You've lost your manual? Hey stuff happens.…*" A real voice introduces himself as Agent Andrew after some twenty minutes. He asks me cheerfully how he can help. I am less cheerful when I ask why I can't activate my Norton Anti-virus. I have the software, and the Norton key code, but it isn't being accepted. Can I hold Agent Andrew wants to know, still cheerful, assuring me that I have reached the right person; he quickly comes back to say that the Norton was not activated upon purchase. I tell him that is why I am calling him. I repeat that I bought the computer with the software. He asks me to hold again and comes back on to apologize for the time it is taking to find out how to solve the problem. Another twenty or so minutes pass, when he asks if I want to hear the good or bad news first. I say, "Give me the bad news." He says that I will have to return the computer to the Best Buy store where I bought it since the cashier didn't activate the Anti-virus upon purchase.

It is Saturday, and I am leaving the city for a research project, which means I will need my Net book. "Actually," I say to Agent Andrew, "I won't be able to get to the store for at least another week." There is a brief pause in which he asks me to hold again, if I don't mind, that he is going to get back to me as soon as possible. I wait. He returns to repeat, "Because the computer was not activated at the cash register...." I interrupt him, "Best Buys should be more careful about what they advertise. You do tell people that they don't have to worry if they have to go out of town. And in fact you can't do anything about a situation like mine." Agent Andrew pauses again then says he is very sincerely sorry. I say I understand, and we hang up. I am tired and realize nothing has been resolved except now I know that I have to go back to the store where I bought the computer. This is not Athens on a strike day, or so much worse, Libya, I am not starved, or being shot at, or physically threatened in any way. I am in New York and quite privileged to be here but I am coming apart.

***

A young couple jump onto the #3 train as it pulls out of the Borough Hall stop when the PA announcement goes on, this time telling us to "Be aware of wallets in back pockets." The guy is flirting with the young woman he is with and their energy has people noticing them. He laughs, then almost slurs, "I don't need no idiot tellin' me bout who's gonna slip their hands into my ass." She giggles swinging close to him as the train jerks to another stop. "*I mean really ... Tellin'* me what hands are gonna get close enough to pull a wallet *outta my ass....*" A man with a straw hat who looks like he's an out-of-towner seems concentrated on staring through the dark subway windows. Station stops flash by, there are Broadway plays and movie posters advertised on the walls, people waiting on the platforms, the screeching sounds of other trains. The couple is giddy, "Hey, I *mean* it" the guy says, then asks the young woman "What you starin' at?" She giggles again, leaning into him, "Tryin' to know you," she says. He smiles "I don't sit still enough for anyone to know me like that."

When I get to Brooklyn my daughter is studying for her midterm on Arendt. She tells me of Arendt's insights in *The Human Condition*, how remarkably she differentiates labor from work, how she emphasizes the plurality of political action. Plural, because one of the disasters of Marxism for Arendt was its assumption that political action "could make people act in certain ways" whereas it is individuals who make, create, "*individuals* together become the opportunity for action," my daughter says, giving emphasis to Arendt's italics. "What Arendt calls the *vita activa*," she explains. I write this down thinking again how to gather the un-gathered strands, essayent. She is suddenly irritated. I explain this helps me understand my resentment of the PA announcements, for example, that are so patronizing. She says, "This is my test mom, not your essay." I put the pen down.

***

I go to visit my brother and sister-in-law in New Jersey. It will do me good to get away from the city and my daughter for a few days. My sister-in-law has the TV on while she cooks. A horrendous-looking father (unshaven, overweight, bloodshot eyes that look mad) has run his car into his daughter and killed her because she dared to leave their house and escape marrying a man he insisted she marry. They are Syrian. The girl's picture flashes over the screen, a smiling dark-eyed beauty. It is the news commentator's tone that keeps me focused, when she says, "Here's a man who believed he had a right to murder his daughter because of gender and religion." I notice the assertiveness of her words; their confidence firmly placed in a world whose values she is very clear about. "There is a part of society that believes this is their right. What we have to say to these people is that here in the United States our laws prevail no matter what your God tells you." Arendt's consequence of destroyed individuality, the "murder of the moral person" is enacted by an old world father's murder of his daughter's new world individuality: his deed of revenge against her refusal to behave. When I get back to the city one of the first things I see is a man sitting outside of Walgreen's with a cardboard sign asking his God for help: DOWN ON LUCK. NO FAMILY. NO SUPPORT. GOD HELP ME.

In the subways' arteries I am given pamphlets announcing the coming Rapture. One titled "The Great Tribulation" begins: "Very briefly, the Great Tribulation according to Dispensational teaching will commence after the rapture of the church. Its vortex will take place in Palestine, and it will entail death and suffering affecting the entire world...." Further down, in bold: "**Truth is one. Truth applies to the whole, and therefore, it cannot contradict itself....**" For some reason I keep the sheet of paper. My essay weaves it in, another truth converging with other truths: the Jamaican woman on the NJ Transit train speaking hers, the Syrian daughter's murdered truth, her father's murderous truth, and this leaflet's rapture of Truth. I had tears in my eyes. There was a large rat in the corner of the subway track. I forgot to ask if this was the right side for downtown trains. I ask a young woman reading a book if the A stops at Union Square, she shakes her head. I decide to go back to Brooklyn.

When I get to the apartment there is no one there. It's midday. My daughter's Arendt notes are on the kitchen table. Among her underlinings in *The Human Condition* is this: "Wherever the relevance of speech is at stake, matters become political by definition, for speech is what makes man a political being." The individual becomes political, part of a body larger than the singular self when it can speak of itself as more than itself, part of (an)other. Does this make motherhood an inherently political state, the body, from pregnancy, tied to its embedded, umbilical, other? In Athens, my daughter was part of a world we were both familiar with. Home was our shared familiarity, where we ate, slept, had conversations and argued. But my daughter has left that world, grown up. Who she is in New York is not someone I always recognize, shaped by what she is experiencing of the world's plurality. I buy more groceries than I need to. She tells me to stop because she ends up throwing out the rotting tomatoes, the browned lettuce she doesn't eat. I get her a packet of Trader Joe's pop-up sponges (these were Ella's suggestion); they are "Made from Natural Vegetable Cellulose"; I get wire drain guards that catch food particles in the sink and let water filter through the drain. An effort to make her space more familial, an essay she tells me she does not want to be in.

Familiarity domesticates the unfamiliar. George Papandreou wanted to find a way to domesticate the disastrous effects of the Greek debt by speaking of it as a family affair; his ministers make statements like "We ate it all together," referring to the EU loans that built the infrastructure for the Olympic games in 2004 and paid for public works. But for some, like the ministers, these borrowings also funded private homes and personal pleasures: *adj* L *familiaris,* fr. *familial*: closely acquainted: INTIMATE <a~ family friend>... **3.a** of or relating to a family <remembering past ~ celebrations> (*Webster's Ninth New Collegiate Dictionary*, 1988). In the

2011 spring issue of *Gulf Coast* there's an interview-essay on six poets' responses to the language used to describe the catastrophic BP oil spill (spill being one of the contested words).

Patricia Smith quotes George Carlin's statement: "Smug, greedy, well-fed white men have invented a language to conceal their sins." If this language of concealment remains unfamiliar to those not invested in the game of hiding, if we feel George Carlin's "greedy, well-fed," or George Papandreou, are not being sincere (after all GP expressed more familial sentiments in the White House than in Greece), we are no longer fed on the same words, even if, as GP's ministers insist, we eat at the same table. When she gets back to the apartment in Brooklyn, my daughter sees me reading *The Human Condition* and reminds me that her education is not my essay. What is it I am trying after all to understand – my letting go of her familiarity, my words that no longer feed her?

***

In the Franklin Avenue subway station the drilling sounds like gunshots. It is early morning. A young black man sees the expression on my face. I have stopped walking, reluctant to go down to the platform. He says, reading my mind, there is construction going on in the tunnels. I'm on my way to the post office to send a gift to someone in Greece. I haven't slept well in my daughter's bed while she slept on the couch downstairs. Someone I know on the Greek island of Patmos wants a HELLO KITTY wristwatch; the postal worker with a neatly combed ponytail speaks English with a Spanish accent. He's efficient and terse but smiles. "Can I tape this some more?" I say, not confident that the priority mail envelope won't open. He says it's secure, "I've glued this down well." I say since it's going to Greece who knows. He interprets this as my being distrustful of Greeks. "If they want to open it they will open it," he continues. I say, "I know but it makes me feel better to tape it." He answers, "That's the most important thing. Do whatever makes you feel better." He wishes me a safe and good day. To speak, and recognize, the language of others builds familiarity. The political person for Arendt is the person who can, above all, articulate a relationship to others: "Thus the language of the Romans, perhaps the most political people we have known, used the words, 'to live' and 'to be among men' (*inter homines esse*) or 'to die' and 'to cease to be among men' (*inter homines esse desinere*) as synonyms." Do I feel, here, among: to live.

***

Images of a destroyed Sendai are on all the TV channels. Elizabeth tells the class she was a study-abroad student in Sendai, and has been trying to contact her Japanese host family; she also tells us the word "Itae" in Japanese means one body. It is a Shinto Buddhist belief that when one considers the self, one simultaneously considers the community; the body is not singled out to be singular. That week the class assignment is to begin a sequence poem. Find the small, telling detail, I say, "Especially when you're dealing with big ideas." Leo, originally from Puerto Rico, writes a poem in which he describes Puerto Rico as one of the last colonies of the world, still called a commonwealth. Someone says the Puerto Ricans have voted for this; the popular majority, by a slim margin, has made this choice, though it enrages Leo. Elizabeth writes about Sendai. She shares a Japanese proverb, "After a great storm you can see more clearly where there is solid ground" and describes the TV image of neatly gathered chopsticks some survivors have whittled from the wood of destroyed homes.

Roberto Bolaño has characters whose teeth are missing, the main character in *Amulet* for example, and another in *The Savage Detectives*; none of his characters are in the best physical shape, yet these imperfections are secondary in importance to his character's larger bodies, the body of Chile, the body of Mexico. During an undergraduate student reading, a student from another class reads of yearning for a neighborhood where "things other than disaster and drugs bring people together." What will gather people—a common value, a common hope, the impending rapture? The Tsunami that turned Japan into a single *us*. In Bolaño's *Amulet,* the protagonist calls herself "the mother of Mexican poetry" because she knows "all the poets and all the poets know me." In Athens' Syntagma Square enraged citizens are peacefully taking over the space in front of the Greek parliament. They call themselves "Indignants" or "αγανακτισμένοι" in Greek, and have grouped together as a body, set up tents in corners of the square. There are now banners from almost every lamp and sign post warning of the encroachments of the three-pronged European Central Bank, IMF, and European Union, known as the troika, the foreign body that has intervened with massive loans to "domesticate" the national debt as George Papandreou wants us to believe, "us" being the Greeks with their body of grievances.

When you are lost any doomsayer is a prophet in the dark. Ella says "I am a nobody" and she means no body is familiar or familial enough to inspire her with what Arendt describes as a shared principle to gather her like Bolaño's "mother of Mexican poetry." The Greeks are wary of George Papandreou's assurances that Greece will be saved by the troika with its own body of interests. When Ella's mother was alive, Ella says "I would hang up on her sometimes," her overprotection suffocating until cancer destroyed her. Ella tells me she still has a hard time accepting that her mother is gone. She keeps the glazed ceramic bowls and cups her mother made, using them regularly for soups and teas. But outside the space of her studio apartment she is sensitive to her body's vulnerability, the kinds of dust and temperatures that cause her allergies, the products that produce skin irritations. I chide her about carrying baby wipes everywhere, cleaning tabletops and seats before she sits down or eats.

In the dark of the subway's arteries the doomsayers treat me with familiarity, handing me pamphlets. There are signs on makeshift stands in the passageways. One advertises a "Published Poet;" another, "Organic Sweets;" one announces "Christ Sent You Here." A local *AmNY.Com* paper reads: SUPREME COURT RULES COPS CAN BURST INTO YOUR HOME IF THEY SUSPECT YOU'RE SMOKING POT AND ARE READING [sic] TO DESTROY THE EVIDENCE. The front page shows a full-length photograph of two policemen in uniform with a background graphics of marijuana leaves. I thank the guy who hands me a copy of the cheaply printed-paper with its garish snaps of "Maria on pg. 2," who says "It's painful" referring to her split with Arnold Schwarzenegger. I see mice darting across the subway tracks. In the distance, someone is playing drums. One woman urges me to keep going straight for the Downtown A, even though the sign above the tunnel says Uptown. She says "You have to go through the tunnel before you see the other sign." I have to trust her.

***

The lecture I attend on "Difference and Self-Determination in a Global World" focuses on how the multicultural origins of the immigrant experience in modern city-states complicate efforts at social cohesion. "How to define cohesion apart from homogeneity?" one speaker asks, since all the way back to Plato's *Republic*, homogeneity and consensus was maintained through exclusions. Andreas Kalyvas phrases it as "egoism at the cost of the other." But the erasure of otherness in modern cities is subtler than it was when Medea and Oedipus brought on catastrophes that reconfigured their worlds. Before I left Athens in January there were ongoing outbursts on the metro and station stops, people frustrated with the strikes, the protestors; some supporting them, others against. One man at the Panepistimiou station kept yelling, "We should remember the Occupation!" He got sympathetic nods. Someone patted him on the back. "We'll relearn what we learned then" he yelled in a confused jumble that included declarations of how people survived the Occupation, how everyone walked everywhere, ate apple cores tossed from windows by Nazi officers, rationed water, chickpeas.

Re-member. This is both the danger and hope. For the Greeks there is a suspicion that re-members what threatens to dis-member, what will un-gather them, the too overt dissonance in the essay, what will unravel the braid, maim the body. Otherness needs to be re-membered as Arendt defines it; to become a consciousness of plurality, "the condition of human action." Elizabeth, who lives every day in a plurality of pain, is continually made conscious of her body's otherness, of the dissonance that, at any point, could dis-member her. But the threat re-members her, too, as she pushes her maimed limbs *essayent,* as she tells me why she makes the effort and resists painkillers.

Arendt writes: "The Greeks, whose city-state was the most individualist and least conformable body politic known to us, were quite aware of the fact that the polis, with its emphasis on action and speech, could survive only if the number of citizens remained restricted." The cost of the other in Kalyvas' phrasing of the politics of antiquity, enforced homogeneity; the ego, refusing to be dismembered by the foreign or estranged, banished its threats from the polis. In today's culture, Zygmunt Bauman writes, we live "by seduction, not normative regulation; ...creating new needs/desire/ wants..."—the kinds of behaviorism Arendt mentions which have reduced the individual "in all its activities, to the level of the conditioned and behaving animal." The energetic salesperson at the entrance of American Eagle for example, asks with enthusiasm: "So what are we shopping for today?" and when I say "Nothing" his smile vanishes and he says, bluntly, "Well then you're in the wrong place."

I am in the wrong place, unsure of how to find my way back to the familiar. Like everyone else, I am given instructions of where to go, suggestions of what to do: the always patiently modulated voices over the PA systems in stores, stations, on trains and subways, tell me and everyone else how we can take care for ourselves; to "please offer" our place "when an elderly, disabled, or pregnant person is next to you," to continually "be aware of" our "surroundings" that are full of instructions and advertisements, sale items that assure us that we can save money: "a FREE pair of underwear with a purchase of three panties"; at the cash register in J.Jill, the women's clothing store, a sign reads: "SALE: *shhh*, it's just between us." But who is "us"? Home Depot; TJ Maxx; Target; Best Buy; Verizon; the billboards all along strips of highway under yellow umbrellas of light remind "us" of how and where we will find the bargains.

"Meet Us In Person" reads one billboard on the Jersey Turnpike, in large black letters, next to a smiling young man and woman who look like well-meaning employees. Underneath their attractive figures in the same black letters is: "('Billboards are so impersonal.')" It is an ad for People's Bank. Like the salesperson in American Eagle, the billboard figures want us to understand that "we" can be a member too, receive a CVS Rewards card, a Gap members' card, "Have you opened a preferred customer account with us?" asks the young woman at Barnes & Nobel. In *The Human Condition*, Arendt writes that a function of "modern privacy" is to "shelter the intimate." The social "we" is never, for Arendt, reflective of a private self, certainly not any part of the "us" in J.Jill or People's Bank. But in this city, intimacy too is for sale: "Don't let IMPOTENCE Ruin Your Sex Life. Call 1-866-866-MALE."

On the R train one evening, I overhear a strand of conversation between two guys I notice, because one of them with his curly blond hair makes me think of the young Art Garfunkel. "Everything was great until it was just the two of us. And that's kind of important." His friend is nodding. "It was so weird that it fell apart when it was only her and me. We worked fantastically together but yeah ... she totally changed when it was just us...." I strain to hear more, but their voices are too low after that. "The intimacy of the heart," Arendt writes, "unlike the private household, has no objective, tangible place in the world." And yet, in this city, the signs and ads and PA voices are there to "localize...with certainty" by making public that which will, Arendt points out, destroy the very nature of subjectivity and individualism. There are numbers to call for anything from debt and family guilt to impotence, gambling and snoring.

What then is intimate, my sponging the sink in my daughter's bathroom to clean away anything unfamiliar? I tell Ella that for some reason I don't do this in Athens. I let the dishes accumulate in the sink; I forget to take out the garbage. Ella tells me I am overcompensating because I am far from Greece, that everything feels unfamiliar, including the dirt. I ask about what she did when she visited Africa two years ago, surrounded by all the dirt there. "I can't imagine you with some endless supply of baby wipes." She laughs and says she went to Africa expecting the dirt, and learned how the Africans lived with it, rationing water, cooking and washing in communal groups; she agrees that these village gatherings are intimate.

The unfamiliar can also be intimate with potential. Potential disaster is also potential. The wheeled cart Ella had given me got caught in the turnstile at the Franklin Avenue stop as I was going quickly through it one of my last days in the city. The handle lodged inside of the metal bar and I couldn't pull it out of its locked-in state. A young man behind me, speaking in Spanish to a young boy with him, immediately grabbed the steel of the turnstile and moved the locked-in pole, what I thought was impossible to budge. "Do you want this pushed frontwards or backwards?" he asked. "Frontwards" I said. He nodded and miraculously pushed the handle from out of the steel-rod clasp.

"Oh God, thank you so much," I heard myself say, relieved almost beyond words. He smiled, holding the hand of the young boy with him. "This was so sweet of you!" This stranger had averted a potentially disastrous moment, as potentially disastrous as the moment I might have fallen down the steps at Penn Station, taking up two spaces. The young Spanish man was beaming. I kept thinking how spontaneous and immediate his gesture had been. Ella described a similar stroke of luck when she had to navigate the subway on crutches. Getting off at a stop her crutch slipped into the gap when a man flew out from the crowd, and lifted her up from under her arms. She said she barely had the chance to thank him; he was gone as fast as he had appeared.

Weeks after the Tsunami there are still images of destroyed towns and villages on TV and now, also, anxious coverage of the nuclear meltdown in Fukushima. My daughter's roommate, who is Japanese, shows me a shirt she bought online in support of the Tsunami victims. I show her the electric blanket I bought on sale for their couch. She thanks me for stocking the refrigerator, cooking, and buying cleaning supplies. I tell her it's my pleasure. When my daughter gets back and sees the economy-sized bottles of shampoo and hair conditioner, a body wash and the electric blanket, she is furious. "My room looks like a store Mom! I now have two bottles of body wash, an extra sponge, three kinds of face cream, sun blocks and acne creams, and a bag of Dunkin' Donut coffee that will last me 3 months. Not cool!" I am amused, but vaguely hurt. "It's the immigrant syndrome," I say, "I don't realize I duplicate things." She is unimpressed, and tells me I am encroaching on her space, and resents "this dependence on things." I answer, "You might need them when you run out of what you have." She is clipped. "Then let me run out. It won't be a disaster."

Because I am going to leave the city in less than a week I find myself thinking of what she might run out of first: toilet paper, olive oil; it is my way of domesticating what is not disaster but uncertainty. My daughter is rarely home during these last days. I'm surprised that I've written "home," another uncertainty. On a page torn at the crease, there's a paragraph from a William Saroyan play pinned to her bulletin board along with receipts, postcards. A character named Kitty says, "I dream of home. Christ, I always dream of home. I've no place. But I always dream of all of us together again. We had a farm in Ohio. There was nothing good about it."

That night I dream my daughter and I are in a large body of water, the sea or lake is washed in spectacular blues and bronze-pinks, the kind of dawn-colored light of northern white nights. I am carrying her. She is perhaps six or seven. I am buoyant as I have her lifted above the water line that is glazed in shades of added gold and azure. We're both transfixed by the colors. Gradually the surface begins to darken and I can feel the water losing its buoyancy. Weeds are making it difficult for me to move. She senses my anxiety and looks tense. I reassure her that I am wading toward the shore and able to carry her. For the first time her weight is a burden. The water has become threatening and very dark but I keep focused on getting us through what has turned into a swamp.

When we make it out of the water, she suddenly stands up, much older. There is another, much younger, child on the shore we've walked onto, a dark-skinned toddler with beautiful eyes sitting by herself. My daughter is impatient, she wants us to get going, but I am exhausted. She tells me to pick up the toddler playing in the sand so we can move on. I shake my head and say, "She's yours."

***

One of the first things I notice when I get out of the Athens subway at Syntagma Square is a man on crutches moving in the middle of the platform. People let him pass, making space. Some are wearing white cloth masks, available at any pharmacy, to protect against the tear gas. Large doses of it are being sprayed above ground in Syntagma. It's the second day, June 29, of the 48-hour national strike organized to protest the Parliament's scheduled vote to pass the first troika loan package worth billions of Euros. The metro is working because the employees decided to call off the strike so transportation was available for protesters to get to Syntagma square. My eyes are tearing and my cheeks sting. The next day on TV channels journalists and news reporters will talk about the criminal amount of tear gas the government allowed to be used. Their aim, among other things, was to break up the protesting groups who have gathered over the past month in Athens' main square.

I am home, but Athens has changed. Familiar shops and landmark stores have closed down. "For Rent" signs are up everywhere. Syntagma (Constitution) Square, has turned into a tent city, occupied by the "Indignants"; they gather every day, and every evening at nine p.m. a list of speakers is drawn up from among them to address the crowd. I think Arendt would have been impressed by this body of people who have chosen quite literally "'to live' ... [and] 'be among men' (*inter homines esse*)." And lay claim to a future.

REFERENCES

Arendt, Hannah. *Essays in Understanding 1930-1954: Formation, Exile, and Totalitarianism.* 1954. Ed. Jerome Kohn. New York: Schocken, Random House, 1994.

Arendt, Hannah. *The Human Condition.* 1958. Chicago: University of Chicago Press, 1998.

Bauman, Zygmunt. "Culture in a Globalised City." *Occupied London.* Web. Accessed June 2011.

Kalyvas, Andreas. "The Right to be Different: Difference and Self-Determination in a Globalized World" April 13, 2011. New York: Onassis Cultural Center. Web. Accessed May 2011.

The New Athenian, Independent Coverage and Analysis of Greece and the Region. Web. Accessed March 2011.

Smith, Patricia. "The Way We Learn to Look: A Cconversation with Nick Flynn, Brenda Hillman, Dorianne Laux, Fred Marchant, Laura Mullen, and Patricia Smith." *Gulf Coast* (Spring 2011): 229-250.

BETSY BOYD

Mars

I stood in the ladies' room at the restaurant and cried when your daddy told me we were leaving Mississippi. I couldn't eat a bite of my fine dinner. New Jersey sounded like Mars. I was thirty-three, but I hadn't been anywhere much, and I feared the thought of Yankees, truly. I expected I'd encounter cold intellectual atheists, who couldn't tell jokes or act half-human to save their lives.

I was depressed at first, though I didn't know what to call it in 1960. Housebound with two kids—none other than your big sister and brother—and no snow tires on the car. We lived in Sparta, New Jersey, on Lake Tomahawk in an attractive cabin that had been winterized. This was a very elite little community: Lake Tomahawk Country Club. They wouldn't let blacks or Jews or Italians move in. A private club could have any restrictions it wanted—they didn't have that law then. I'm sure it's all changed by now, which is right.

Though we were new in the area, Daddy and I were invited to a Christmas party at the home of Robert and Louise Wrigglesby. I wore a pink polka-dot cocktail dress I'd bought in Jackson, a sweet little dress. I reasoned the heat from the party would keep me warm in this skimpy outfit, and it did. But I looked inappropriate.

When Louise opened the door, I said, "Nice to see you," with great gusto, and she said, "Likewise," which put a lump in my throat it sounded so businesslike. As she took my coat, she eyed my strapless dress and smiled condescendingly. But she was so pretty, with olive skin that didn't show any age, though she must have been over forty, and black hair she had colored in a beauty shop. Her teeth were so strong and white.

When Louise handed me a martini that night, she told me to relax. "Why not?" she said, and walked away, her skirt swaying elegantly.

Down the street from us was the O'Farrell family with six children. Bobby, their youngest, always had a runny nose, poor thing. The father Sid, a college teacher, hadn't worked in a long, long time. He was always too delicate, scrawny and tense looking. But Judy, his wife, had fat red cheeks and enough energy to pull him out of himself, I guess.

Sid and Judy loved to cook together. They must have had a lot of personal money issues, but they didn't share trouble with neighbors. They invited Daddy and me for potluck dinner parties, where they'd fix the main entrée, which was always special—barbecue chicken, fried catfish, oriental shrimp, you name it. I don't know how they could afford to feed us so well.

One night, Daddy and I were at the door saying goodbye, when Judy took my arm and said, "You all don't go yet! Come back inside and stay a little longer!" We were so young and foolish—I'm sure she was just being polite—but I tell you what, we accepted her invitation.

Louise Wrigglesby was still inside sitting on the arm of the couch, in her swanlike posture. Smoking a cigarette, she looked like a movie star. When I walked back inside, she looked up and said, "Welcome back," with such warmth I melted.

We chose Lake Tomahawk, not because it was elite or exclusive, but because it seemed like a wholesome place for children. I saved up my Green Stamps and bought a swing set for the kids. I'd invite Louise over, and we'd let the children play in the yard while we drank coffee inside. Or sometimes I'd visit her and we'd try makeup tricks on each other, based on ideas we read in magazines. At her house, Louise always suggested we drink brandy, which made me so sleepy I couldn't take much. It made me yawn and giggle at nothing.

Louise's youngest, Claire, was born with a heart murmur. And she was painfully thin. She'd sit in her mother's lap like a baby half-asleep much of the time. Her lips might be blue—sometimes her whole face would turn blue.

Louise had Indian blood—not that she went around advertising it—and often seemed restless. I sensed she was afraid Claire was going to drop dead. She never said so aloud. But she did gripe—about the weather, about the fact that my car didn't have snow tires therefore I couldn't take us shopping in icy weather. Finally, she started griping about the fact that our husbands liked to go to the bar when they got off the train from New York in the evenings. It hadn't bothered me very much—but when Louise brought it up, I started to think I should feel bothered.

One evening in early springtime, the men ran late, very late. Louise and I served the children peanut butter sandwiches and potato chips, put on leotards and performed yoga with a record, and it got to be close to ten o'clock. By the time your father and Louise's husband got home, they were tipsy, to say the least. And Louise was fuming. She told them we were going shopping for new dresses! They'd have to baby-sit! Even though we knew the department stores would be closed, we climbed into my Buick and drove away in a horrible screeching rush, Louise yelling out the window, "Damn you, Robert, and, Clayton, that goes for you, too!"

I turned to Louise and said, "What do we do now?" And she said, "Drive to the lake." So I did. It was thrilling. I drove us down to the manmade lake and we smoked cigarettes in the car and listened to Nat King Cole and things on the radio, and Louise listed men she'd sleep with in this world, starting with John Kennedy, who was still alive, at this point. She said she liked the way he embraced all kinds but mostly he was just gorgeous. She said she'd even sleep with Martin Luther King because of his good ideas. I just bit my tongue. Then she said she'd cheated on her husband once.

I could tell it bothered her, that she'd done this. It did me.

I put my hand on her shoulder and said, "God bless you, Louise," to which she simply rolled her eyes and laughed—though not in a mean way.

She laughed a lot, as though she was privy to answers she'd sworn never to share and which, if she did, would make everyone feel stupid.

She asked me, "You want to jump in the lake and go for a swim? Wouldn't that serve them right if we came home happy and smiling with wet hair?" In the moonlight, I watched her pull off all her clothes and walk into the lake like she did this every day. I stayed back.

Merlane Welsh lived next door. She couldn't have children, or so I learned from Louise, who swore me to secrecy. Merlane was a good-hearted woman with bad acne and a flabby stomach. Her husband, Ted, was handsome, with light blond hair and a fine, strong jaw. He ran laps around the lake every night. He reported the local newscast on television. At first, to see them together made you wonder, "What does he see in her?" But once you got to know Merlane, you couldn't help but love her. They had a happy marriage. Ted always held Merlane's hand in public and rubbed her back, not for show either, so you could tell their sex life didn't suffer, or that's what Louise and I surmised.

Merlane gave me a marble-base floor lamp I still use. It had been a gift from her mother-in-law, whom she disliked. Oh and Merlane and

Ted had a pond in their backyard with orange and red fishes swimming between big gray rocks. How strange it seemed. Not only this fishpond, they also had a baby lamb on their property and several ducks—I have a great photo of the children feeding the lamb with a bottle. We sat in their yard in the summer and spooned Merlane's homemade ice cream. It was the best tasting stuff. So buttery and silky, and just ice cold. No wonder she had a soft stomach!

Some people looked down on Merlane, you could tell by the way they talked to her—she never would wear a stitch of makeup. How could she with her acne? And never a skirt, always pants. Plus, she'd come from Colorado.

One afternoon, we were all feasting on ice cream when Louise's little daughter Claire began to whimper. She was running a temperature. Something was not right. I think I ran home and got an ice pack and tried to act like everything was fine. But I could tell Louise was shaken. Her husband was away on business and she seemed in a state of confusion, the fever had come on so suddenly.

"Let's take her to the doctor," Merlane said, slapping Louise's back, like to wake her.

We took Merlane's Volkswagen bug to the clinic around the way. And while we waited for the doctor, Louise told us again that she meant to take the child to Houston for an operation that might help greatly.

I said, "Good," rubbing her arm. "You should try to."

"Just do it," Merlane said. "Let nothing stop you."

Years later, she did—I learned by postcard. And I shouted to Daddy, "Hooray!"

Russell Grimes, Daddy's boss at the pharmaceutical company, lived nearby—Russell was very society-minded. He looked a whole lot like Clark Gable. Boy, he loved your father. Said he was the best copywriter he'd ever come across. But there were rumors about Russell. Once or twice, Daddy stayed up late talking shop with him and said Russell made flirtatious gestures. In a half-drunk daze, he rubbed circles on his kneecap. Your father let it go, seeing as he was the boss and, to tell the truth, a likeable fellow.

Russell's wife, Janet, was a Southerner, but I never felt comfortable around her. Her hair was dyed bright gold. She was so perfect and placid it made my heart race. Janet tried to give me casserole recipes—"Expand your horizons," she'd say—but they were too complex and didn't sound good to me. I don't care for cilantro. Russell and Janet used to pick us up on Fridays in their dark green Mercedes and drive us to a nightclub called The Teepee only half a mile away. I remember Russell telling me to stand up straight as he held open the front door. He said, "I want people to think you're my girlfriend." And I said, "Ha, sure thing." He whispered to me, "Don't worry about what you're wearing. Act like you're somebody."

One night we four walked to the club. We wanted to study the fallen leaves on the way there, in the sunset—in New Jersey, big red and gold leaves dropped from the trees and decorated the floor of the woods near Lake Tomahawk. It was a beautiful sight. We shouldn't have walked in the frigid air, but Russell would get an idea and not let go.

Well, on the way out of the club that night, we walked into heavy snowfall. It had come early that year. Something like ten inches, out of nowhere. Every tree was covered in snow. Bare branches like skinny arms in white mink stoles. The world looked so fine. I decided for a moment New Jersey could be a kind of heaven.

We got a cab instead of walking home in the freezing cold. But first Russell and I danced in the snow—his idea. He asked, "Are you my girlfriend?" in front of Daddy and Janet, who were trying their best to dance, but not getting into the spirit. When he asked, "Are you my girlfriend?" I stood up straight and answered back, "I'm your friend, Russell Grimes, always." Then he spun me in a circle.

We lived on Lake Tomahawk until January when Daddy got a high-paid offer to come back south, where you, our surprise baby, would be born. Before we left, Louise threw a blowout New Year's Eve bash/goodbye party for us in her basement. It was a treat. Adults only. Merlane gave me a jade vase—another gift from her rude mother-in-law—for our new house in Texas. The O'Farrells fixed brisket that melted on your tongue. Russell gave Daddy a fine, fine watch, though he was sore at him for leaving. And Louise got drunk on martinis and performed a handstand with perfect balance. Her dress flipped up and she flashed the room her white panties and long muscular legs, to which everyone, even the wives, cheered and clapped. They were something else, that crew. Such talented cooks and entertainers! My street in New Jersey was the only street I ever lived on that threw regular parties. Of course, it's been a while. They're all dead now. But, I tell you what: Lake Tomahawk was party central back then! We lived to socialize. We had ourselves a time.

PAUL SUTHERLAND

In the Back Room with Mom

I was surprised my mom at ninety-six could raise the complaint that forty-one years ago I had left and travelled across the ocean making a new
home. In the midst of her age-inspired amnesia she struck that reality
again. I had thought the subject wouldn't disturb our short time together.
It had shaken the house on my return visits over four decades, but for two
years the conflict hadn't been voiced. My desertion, I believed, had been
forgotten. I breathed a long sigh of respite. Earlier today in the back room,
the most lived in space, she rolled out, not lifting her voice, rolled off her
tongue, "I don't know why you left." It was not so much a cliff-hanging
phrase as an underground river had broken to babble on the surface once
more. I bore the consequent grief that some event so far back could create
unhappiness and some irritation that the past couldn't be absorbed; for
her there was no other perspective then that I had left. This fact stuck out
against her uncertainties such as what day it was, what month, what year. I
was tempted to answer that I left to discover new worlds. We had had tilted
dialogues when she was brainy, mathematical and recalled everything, but
she found no peace in my reply then. I kept quiet now. I looked towards
her so black-blued yellow-red forehead and face, result of recent falls, which
coloured over her wrinkles. Her right eye seemed to look out through a
telescope of contusion. I hoped my gaze was received as compassionate,
not obstinate. She sat in a rocking armchair pointed towards where I
relaxed on the settee on the north side of the back room. The chair she
occupied swayed near the expanse of glass windows which gave views of
the still snow-buried back yard and beyond to the neighbours' gardens.
Each gesture, word spoken or calm meant an overcoming of pain. One
fall had injured a vertebra and a second had cut and bruised her forehead.

The back room was rectangular, a large screen TV at the south end with a book case and chest of drawers along the house side and another chest by the window side, along with pictures on the walls and shelves covered with keepsakes and souvenirs. By the TV on a kitchen-styled chair rose the layers of each day's delivered newspaper, printed matter was profuse on shelves, in drawers or letter racks, some items secreted away. Below a polished sculpture of driftwood, in the north inside corner another set of bookcase shelves carried photograph albums going back to before World War I. Mom had said a few times on this visit that I should look at the pictures of when I was a baby, post-World War II. Each occasion she'd used a manner of saying that I should look tomorrow or the next day, sometime. Certain she would forget, I made no excretion to explore those thick covered, lace-bound, collections on black paper, those dense landscape pages of black and white photos. I let the annuals of the past rest. Today she spoke with immediacy. I was compelled to wade through my baby and boyhood. The back room had been split in half once, with a screened in south side and a walled and windowed room to the north. A cold room perhaps, but also where when a schoolboy I did my home-work at a table, so mom had related sometime, an academic corner and she brought treats to the student now and then. A settee resided there lengthwise along the north wall under more large windows, behind that sofa waves of warmth rose from the hidden baseboard heating in winter. Winter on this visit, squirrels could be observed out the windows gathering dry leaves from where the snow had melted around tree trunks. They were busy gathering material to make their spring nests in hollows in the ancient tree that ascended, limb-shattered and lightning-struck, from our garden. With dancing black tails the squirrels would lose half their load of foliage before they reached their destinations.

I had to open the album that recorded my sprouting years; I didn't de-sire to defy but I knew scanning those old images would lead somewhere; comments would be made which might undermine our placid afternoon sharing. I turned the ebony pages that seemed like stone despite how frail or torn in places. There I was at two with a birthday cake on a small table out in the July garden surrounded by other children, a host of adults looking on. Family bonded into family, neighbours, godparents, grandparents, and their young offsprings and mom stood or stooped young and glamorous among them all. I suggested that I was among so many others when a baby, a toddler. From my mass-observation, historical viewpoint I perceived myself with half strangers, in an extended home, making a political point about dependence versus the nuclear family. She missed my subversions and remarked "You were much loved." All the objects, miniature or large, in the back room, which had come back from all her journeys, amplified this assertion. All of us lifeless things had returned to stay, but not you, they seemed to boast and criticise from their painted earthenware faces or glass-blown lips. Mom's much loved meant I had no reason to run off, you can't claim you were unloved and so left, mom sub-orally declared. She left out my many teenage conflicts, the crimson embarrassments when I challenged her, the rudeness I exhibited, how she was so close to hitting me at times, how I broke the rules, hurt her feelings. I offered no retort. Looked at the photographs, some with serrated borders, some over-exposed or out of focus. A much younger me inhabited a known world. Did I remember that inflated paddling pool, my friends and I splashing each other, and recall that blow-up sea-monster that I used to ride, did I recollect my skin burned by straddling it, the hot sun evaporating the shallow water? I loved that creature. Or had my looking at those images so long, on other occasions, caused them to ooze into memories as if they were real when they were pictures from a camera? I too had fallen into uncertainty. My mom gave no tut of triumph that I couldn't divorce the real from the un-real any more than her. She slumped her discoloured face into her hand, a thinker's posture, but too slumped to speak her thoughts. I wanted to tell her don't touch your bandage covering your head wound, in case it starts bleeding again. I said nothing. Moved on to the next page and arrangement of captured scenes. I noted my growing, the emerging of my anti-social self. Everything predicted, despite the sharing, my separating from the family, from that photogenic love and closeness. I saw my estrangement prefigured in the bare slender-limbed birthday boy of two who doubted every contact except that of a rubber sea-monster with a delicate scale-like pattern on its back.

The back room had changed from its natal season of screen and dumping ground where nevertheless I did my homework at an ordered table, mom looking on, perhaps making the odd over-shoulder comment. She saved all my art I discovered later. The room had matured, made weather-proof, glass replacing mesh, made a place of permanence where the years could gather in collections of objects, in memorabilia. The back had become the front room, but less ornate, more lived in, its transience moulded into a location where mom could relax, her frailty and disablement concealed by familiar things, propped up by them, as if she hadn't aged or become detached from her travels, wasn't housebound. On the marble top of the window side chest of drawers the days of the week were printed in a series of rectangular cards, one on top of the other, changed each day to help mom keep up. I regularly re-wound the wall fastened grandmother clock, its tick-tock beat pleasant to her ears, though for mom the numerals had been smoothed away, calibrations worn down to bumps on an indefinite shore. Someone must change the cards from one day to the next, mom wouldn't be able to make a claim on time, be too exact about when and where to care. I knew it was forty-one years back across waves of transformation from youth to middle age to fringes of old age. That one act washed up among a long list of experiences and encounters, many hopes and disappointments, uncounted loves and hates. My leaving wasn't a door in an empty beachscape, it is one of many doors in a crowded household. In the spaces between photographs someone had written with a silver lead pencil often misspelt names and locations, the briefest captions. I was struck by how beauty spots, lakes, rivers and forests, I thought I discovered in young adulthood or on return visits as if my possessions, were already unbeknown a part of my prehistory when my mom was beautiful and her vivid complexion shone. I could feel her love in a flash-on colloid embrace, her returning splash in airy pools.

She went silent, as I trawled through images, not only to my ears, quiet to consciousness. Fell mute until I forgot she was observing from her swaying armchair and saw myself isolated from filial duties, a man living his life in and out of photographs. Then caught a glance, her hands fighting with the hem of her dark maroon housecoat, her back wincing in pain from her month-old fall. Today she hadn't got dressed, despite a sponge bath from a community care assistant. Easier to stay un-apparelled, less buttons, zips, when making frequent visits to the toilet. Her incontinent pads made to stick to her underpants, so everything stayed in place. Her voice, slow and crying, released a short sentence, not as if it was an introduction but her statement was the whole story, she said, "You made a dent in my life." She referred to my abandoning her love and this back room, this view, family, our language of union. The word "dent" troubled. Had all her life been a putting on of armour?

The photographs of sandy shore lakes, clear-bottomed, the water kissing a square wooden cottage, our quick runs into the waves, or hunting for drift wood: each was a link in her chain mail. I couldn't argue my point, let the inference sink in, had no phrases to parry the distress her words implied. By leaving I had attacked her, making a dent, not breaking, but causing a hollow, a wound. My leaving was an accident, a car crash that broke the streamline of her life, which pitted the big curved fender of a late forties' car like the one that a miniature of me was struggling to wash in another snapshot. Maybe she hinted that she could never fill the space I had left, the onus of being born meant you had to remain, always be there, a companion and reflection to the birth-giver. She had given so much, been altered so much by my birth. My staying could help her endure the hurt of birthing me, nothing else could. I hadn't stayed, had vanished, then started coming and going, off and on, here and not here, trying to compensate.

The back room stood silent, the TV blank. I stared at the photos, hardly raising my head to meet her three spaced comments. I wanted to say that her love had made my wish to explore possible, that she had given me the confidence to leave her behind, and find my destiny. I had described this route before, this backhanded justification, but those viewpoints had ended in her looking bewildered and upset, deepening the creases on her face. I kept my counsel.

In a few days, I would be off again, returning to my home across the ocean, taking flight. She soon, a year or so, maybe longer maybe shorter, would be departing, flying out of life. I wondered what would happen to the memorials in pages, on stained shelves, hanging from hooks, even the plants spreading from pots which should be watered once a week if she remembered or not. I held the back room irreplaceable, alive in the moment, then gone into the darkness and dryness, of whom will inherit. Will they care? Her leave-taking seemed a subtle revenge, like her expensive leather purse in view behind her chair, but empty so she couldn't squirrel away important documents or cards in to secret hiding places. She must be protected from herself. And I knew I wouldn't be able to fill that vacuum she would create. Her riposte to my desertion, death would force me to taste and feel bereaved for her long ago sorrow. Perhaps I already did. Her isolated phrases earlier had opened the wound of misgivings about my departing, second thoughts, my fears. The distance I had tried to scar over. My connection with her, that cord snapped, the photographs will take on new meaning, yet unguessed, but imagined. The back room residents will hand me the stack of history and ask, "Do you want these or not?" Somewhere else, I will ease over, one by one, its more tattered pages to find a more estranged mother and son.

ANJOLI ROY

Leena and the Pepper Tree

A loaf of hard white bread sat on the kitchen counter, a half-empty jar of brown swirled with purple muck beside it. Leena looked down the dark paper throat of an empty lunch bag. *Peanut butter and jelly? Again?*

Hungry people eat what they've got, called her mom as she darted through the kitchen to the driveway. *Make it, quick!*

Leena watched her mother's back, felt as hollow as when she'd spoken the words *divorce* and *moving* to her the night before. They couldn't keep the house, with its sparkly pool, on her mother's nursing salary alone.

Leena thought about the moldy dahl in the back of the fridge, the keechuri that would take too long to thaw from the icebox. Ten years old, she tried to remember the last time she'd seen her dad. Leena's arms searched the cupboard and knocked over the cayenne, which bloomed a small red cloud that clawed the back of her nose. The shelves were empty. Her breakfast belly was empty too.

Leena, come on! her mom hollered from the car.

She shoved the empty paper bag to the bottom of her backpack.

You smell rotten, her mom said when Leena sat down, fanning the smell away from her face. She flinched when Leena slammed the car door on accident. They both rolled down their windows. *What did I tell you about letting the clothes sit in the wash all day? What'll your rich kid friends think?*

Leena knew better than to answer. She smoothed down her scratchy uniform skirt and was happy she wouldn't have to wear one in the fall. Even though starting a new school, a public one, meant making new friends. At least the skirt *looked* clean. Still, she hoped Jane and Sophia wouldn't smell her.

She sat quietly, waited for her mother's car to turn onto Wildrose Avenue.

Mildew rose off her body like a rotten morning mist.

The wrinkled face of the San Gabriel Mountains loomed behind Leena as she walked into the schoolyard, talking to her stomach.

Keep quiet, she said.

She hated how it'd started growling during morning chapel. Hated how the sound of her empty belly rumbled across those old stone tiles like so many demons determined to betray her. Leena didn't believe in this church—she wasn't sure what she believed—but she knew it was rude, what her body was doing. Outing her like that. Her schoolmates giggled whenever the sounds got loud, but some church miracle made it so no one other than her friends, Jane and Sophia, who flanked Leena during the service, knew the sounds were coming from her.

Hey, weirdo, talking to yourself again? Jane called to her from the swing set under the soft branches of the school's pepper tree, its leaves floating in the wind like feathers. Sophia laughed. Jane glared at Sophia with that look of hatred that made her and Sophia best friends. Sophia shut up.

Leena smiled at them fast, pretty sure that Jane was just teasing, that she wasn't actually making fun of her. It was getting harder to tell lately.

Leena chose the open swing with the broad black leather seat between her two friends and started pumping her legs fast. The spring sun climbed higher in the morning sky. She hung her head back to look up at the branches of the pepper tree.

Leena wasn't sure why she loved this tree so much. Bushy and wild, the tree looked funny with the other evergreens in the yard that had better posture and trimmer trunks whose bark didn't gnarl and peel away in long strips like paper. But she liked how it looked like the tree could go on forever, like its branches could stretch and hang anywhere they wanted, just as the tree was happily rooted right where it was. Its small pink berries bunched here and there made Leena feel optimistic. Even though she heard the teachers complain about how messy the tree was, how the berries would polka-dot the walkways, make them slippery and wet, Leena loved this tree and the soft shadows it threw on the yard they played in. She saw a drawing in a picture book once that looked like it, but Leena remembered that the story said something about that tree weeping. *A tree that weeps?* Leena knew the school's pepper tree couldn't be that. With its long leaves blowing in the wind, the pepper tree looked like it would always be happy. It would always be just fine.

Leena swung her legs faster on the swing until she felt long lines of sweat racing down her calves. She blocked out Jane and Sophia, who were talking behind their hands from the swings on either side of her. She felt how the boys from their grade were clustering nearer, trying to get Jane and Sophia's attentions, like always.

Jane and Sophia were the most beautiful girls in the fourth grade, had that yellow hair, those straight backs, those loud, confident laughs. They wore oversized flannels on top of uniform blouses that hugged their plump girl bodies. Their moms waited at home for them with afternoon snacks: string cheese, apple juice, chocolate chip cookies straight out of the oven. Big pepperoni pizza they ordered through the phone or crispy fried chicken or nachos and taco dinners that dripped mouth-watering, yellow-red grease splotches on their pretty, clean, flower-print pajamas.

Leena had been the sidekick, pet, to Jane and Sophia since pre-school, had been going to their sleepovers every year, when their moms and dads put all the wiggling girls to bed, teased and kissed each other in the kitchen when they thought no kids were looking, told their daughters they loved them. Leena's parents used to let her have sleepovers too, but Leena couldn't do that anymore, not in her empty house with a gone dad who used to cook everything, where now there was hardly anything to eat.

Leena knew Jane and Sophia were annoyed that they hadn't been invited over to swim in her pool since the heat had exhaled like so many hot, smoggy breaths into the valley where they lived. Leena thought she might have heard Jane and Sophia call her a mooch, a snob, on the playground recently, but she wasn't sure, didn't want to believe they'd say that about her.

Leena did wonder sometimes why Jane and Sophia liked her. Once, when their teacher, Mrs. Johnson, was teaching a lesson on ocean animals, Leena's eyes lingered on a picture of a shark and the little fish that hung around it. Maybe Leena was like that. She didn't attract boys' attentions, was just weird enough—with her frizzy black hair, ever-dirty blunt knees, and up until recently her strange curried lunches—not to be a threat. And she wasn't too weird. Maybe that fish, weird as it was, kept the shark company. Maybe they were good friends. Had fun, even though they were so different. Even though one had a million sharp teeth and a whole ocean full of soft fish to bloody, and the other just wanted folks to be with. Leena wondered though—wasn't hanging around a shark dangerous?

Dana was born with a hairy lip, Jane sing-song-called out across the schoolyard from the swings. *That's why the doctors had to make her a new mouth!*

That's why she's so uggggg-uh-lee! Sophia added, pumping her legs and swinging higher and higher.

Leena watched Dana freeze up when Jane and Sophia said this. She was the quiet girl with a funny scar that ran like a fault-line from her upper lip to her left side of her nose. No one could be friends with her because she got made fun of, had tricks played on her. Dana scuttled back to the safety of the classroom, where she stayed until the morning bell rang for chapel.

Leena didn't laugh at Jane and Sophia's taunts. She didn't look at either of them as they laughed hard into each others' bright pink mouths when they saw Dana running away. Leena kept swinging her stick legs, felt for a moment on her own face Dana's throbbing pink scar.

What's that smell? Sophia asked, jerking her thumb in Leena's direction and making a pee-ew face. *It's like sweat and...*

Cheese farts! Jane laughed.

The boys from their grade overheard this from the field where they were playing tag and laughed too.

Leena tried to shake off the wet blades of freshly cut grass that were clinging damply to her white socks. She pumped her legs until all she saw was a blur of sand beneath her, the swing of the clear blue sky above, and a smudge of pretty pepper tree leaves that looked green and happy, like wild hair, like flying, like being far away from everywhere. She swung her legs harder and harder, sure she'd flip over the A-frame swing set if she wanted to. She launched herself out of the seat, expecting to land on her feet as she usually did. She watched the sand of the playground rise up but felt her feet slip out from under her, then the harsh smack of the ground on her bottom.

Sophia and Jane laughed hard at her. The few boys around did too.

Leena dashed to the girls' bathroom to get out of laughing range. She rubbed some of the sharp, lemon-scented hand soap on her dark blue uniform skirt, then stood under the hair dryer in hopes of burning out the smell.

Sophia and Jane kept their distance from Leena for the rest of the morning. During chapel and morning class, they laughed behind their hands, exchanged glances that Leena didn't understand. The boys started prowling around Leena in droves. They made weird growling noises at her and ran off.

Miss Leena, where's your lunch today?

Leena turned to face Mrs. Johnson, whose seventy-year-old hands were now resting on her shoulders, light as birds. Leena felt Mrs. Johnson's nails clawing at her collarbone. The metal picnic table burned Leena's thighs through her scratchy uniform skirt. Her knees shook like rattles. Mrs. Johnson could be mean sometimes. Leena braced herself, held up her empty paper bag. She showed it to Mrs. Johnson. *I ate it already,* she said, smiling.

You sure do eat fast, missy. Mrs. Johnson patted Leena on the head. As she walked away, Leena heard her call out, *The food you brought is the food you eat. Remember, no sharing!*

When Leena turned back to the lunch table, Jane and Sophia made pouty faces at her before Jane pointed at her lunch, said, *You can have some, if you want.*

We're not supposed to share, Leena whispered across the table to her friends. Leena felt Mrs. Johnson pause a few tables down in that way that made all the kids around hold their breaths.

What did I say about trading food? Mrs. Johnson said darkly to a third-grade boy. She clamped her claws on his shoulders and pulled away the small, potbellied boy from his lunch table for a time out by the trashcans. His head hung low.

Jane opened the silver wrapper of her granola bar, the one with the chocolate chips she didn't like. *I know you're hungry,* she said, looking at Leena with concern. *You don't want your stomach to keep making all those noises this afternoon. What if we can't sit next to each other in class?* she said a little quieter, a threat bubbling just beneath the surface of her words.

Leena felt her heart thudding. Jane was right—she needed to eat something to shut her belly up. She wished she'd packed a stupid peanut butter and jelly that morning.

Jane took a bite of the granola, sucked on and extracted the chocolate chips from her mouth like they were pointy fish bones. She piled them on a little white napkin where her mother had written *Mama loves you, Jane!* Jane had wiped her mouth with the napkin, smudged the *e!* after she'd finished her turkey and tomato sandwich on white bread. She hadn't seen the message. Leena had.

The small chocolate mountain was glossy with Jane's spit.

Eat them, Jane said like a dare. She pushed them across the table to Leena. *I won't tell.* Jane smiled a funny smile at Sophia, who made a face that said gross, crumpled up her lunch sack, and ran out to the recess field, leaving Jane and Leena alone.

Mrs. Johnson was talking to the pot-bellied boy, who was rubbing his eyes.

Leena watched Jane finish an apple, a juice box, a fistful of Pringles, and the rest of that chocolate-chip-less granola bar.

Leena curled her body over the metal picnic table, hoping that if she kept her stomach tight, curled up, it wouldn't growl. She hoped that if she focused on the desert-dry dirt swirling under the picnic table, her eyes wouldn't look so vulture-y.

She waited for the rest of the kids to finish their lunches, to leave the picnic tables before she inhaled a thief's breath, looked around fast to see Mrs. Johnson was long gone, breaking up a fight by the monkey bars across the yard, and smashed that tiny, glistening chocolate pile into her mouth before she darted out to the recess field. It tasted sweet and delicious. She held the chocolate in her mouth, let it melt around her teeth before swallowing it all down. That just might last her until school let out.

When the grass field was under her feet, Leena saw Jane standing beneath the pepper tree, near the swing set that they'd played on that morning. Jane whispered something to Sophia who repeated it to the horde of adoring boys who now surrounded them. Jane and Sophia looked at each other, then pointed their sharp girl eyes at Leena. Their pink mouths dropped open like traps. Leena's friends joined in with the boys, who clutched their stomachs, pointed and laughed at Leena.

Rumble Gut! they called her. *Spit Eater!*

Leena's feet squelched in a puddle by a broken sprinkler at the edge of the lawn. She felt cold mud water flooding her ankles and then her heels. It wasn't the boys' laughter that stabbed her, or even Jane's or Sophia's. It was the sound of a lone laugh at the edge of the small grass field that cut like a kitchen knife. It came from Dana, who was huddled alone by the cavernous mouth of their classroom door. She was standing away from everyone, but was with them in their laughter.

Leena looked up at the evergreen pepper tree, blurry in her vision, and saw that it was trapped in that small, mean schoolyard. The tree was weeping too.

JENNIFER KWON DOBBS

Fetish Mothers

For a child adopted as a baby, the cultural heritage of one's birth mother can only be a dead past detached from one's actual lived experience.
—Vincent J. Cheng, *Inauthentic*

To search for Mother's body is to listen with a poet's attention that can rub across the word's surfaces to listen for a pulse, not the shuffling of documents. Mother, you sit across from a social worker—a woman who is your same age—flipping through pages and indicating where you should sign. You're pregnant—heavy with me during your sixth month—leaning slightly backward because your lower back aches. The social worker—maybe a mother, herself—disassociates from the fact that your bodies, sitting so close to each other, can do the same work: Your pen following the social worker's finger indicating where you should leave your mark, your pen pointing to where the social worker flagged for your signature.

Your bodies are so close to each other that they become one body linked through paper—one that gives and one that takes away. Above you, Jesus points to his thorn-crowned heart and looks beyond the frame's plastic edge. On the social worker's desk, a wedding photo and a little boy laughing and running toward the camera. His right hand holds a red-stitched baseball. The social worker, anxious to return home, checks the paperwork and clips it inside a brown folder marked with a case number. She puts her hand on your shoulder to reassure you. You lean against a mother who wants to rush home to her child in Samsong-dong and who doesn't see you as a mother. You blur together—one taking/one giving me away.

What proof do I have that this is your story? I can only see the space. Here's a round black table, a set of gray office chairs upholstered in the

177

Danish functional style. Here's a tissue box, a beige telephone with a red button to place a call on hold. Here are the fluorescent lights. I can hear typing next door. White industrial linoleum flecked with multi-colored chips doesn't muffle noise. Color portraits of joyful adoptive parents show mothers what they can't provide. Tan metal file cabinets. A water cooler dispenses hot and cold. Maxim coffee sticks, styrofoam cups, English tea.

I can see the conversations around this table, the frayed gray fabric, split orange foam, the cooler's cloudy plastic, and water damage stains on the ceiling because the building was hastily constructed (as were all offices during the '70s). You would've been childbearing age—anywhere from eighteen to forty-five—and capable of working in one of many light industrial factories constructed during Park Chung Hee's regime when South Korea engineered its economic miracle on your back leaning over a steady conveyer belt of t-shirts, tennis shoes, toys, tooth brushes, combs, and plastic mirrors crated for export. Your hands rush to keep up with the manufacturing speedway toward South Korea's revolution from an agriculture-based nation to an economic tiger. You're a farmer's daughter from Jeolla-do or Gangwon-do or maybe one of Seoul's own simply wanting to earn some money for family back home still squatting in an unheated room to shower with a hose. So when the social worker asks if you would sign here, you watch your hand move knowing that you will say nothing to your father or mother who take the money to buy food and encourage you to eat well.

You eat in silence that night. You feed us both with your grief.

What am I saying? I can only describe a researched context, a slanted shadow. I can only speculate and dramatize because I can't find you. Is this a fetish or a document of desire? This is not your body. This is not mine. This is my tongue—meat flapping inside my crushed mouth. The military meat that Korea imports from the U.S.—spam/variety meats/mad cow/neo-liberal trade—ends up in *budae jigae*, a stew of scraps.

_____ 님이 가족찾기 하고 있는 중인데 혹시 (입양) 서류를 볼 수 있을까요?

_____ 님이 가족찾기 하고 있는 중이라 자기 서류를 보고 싶은데 갖고 있나요?

Can we see _____ documents? Do you have ___ documents?

I don't want constellations.

Which story is mine? Which story is yours?

178

Mapping and re-centering.

My documents are your documents, aren't they? The words that took me from you had to admit first that I belonged to you—that you're woman's flesh, not a social artifact—even as they erased your name. I don't know your name. I only know this body that came from yours. I only know this page. I try to rewrite this language that took my body away from your body knowing that I will only clear this page of fetishes you would never use for yourself—birth mother, gift giver, social artifact, dead memory, trace, smear, signature, ___, n/a, unknown, even mother. No, Omoni, you wouldn't have been dressed like these, and if I push through your skirts, I find blankness, this smoothness that is not your face.

***

Birth mother, gift giver, social artifact, dead memory, trace, smear, signature, ___, n/a, unknown, even mother. What is the point of calling you such names and pronouncing you a lost or separated part, if not to drain our bodies of blood?

We do not stand across the DMZ at Panmunjeom bussed in for goodwill sunshine—lucky ticket holders drawn from the lottery mass of halmeonideul and harabeojideul who are desperate to see their parents before either one of them dies. To die with some relief, that is not our cause although we're also fighting time. I'm thirty-three years old and still able to bear a child, your grandchild. Can I even speak for you when it comes to our separation, your distance from those who sleep in my body? I can only talk around you overlapping myself. Don't daughters do this when they talk about their mothers?

When my mom was pregnant with me, she didn't have nausea.

My mother's bone marrow matched mine.

It's funny how we both worry about details! Just the other day, mom called—

I see your face—the flicker of you as I have come to know you—in the mothers at Ae Ran Won, the mothers who are heavy and tired walking up the stairwells of Dong Bang. In the footage reels that I have watched of *Achim Madang*, I have witnessed mothers grabbing grown men and pressing their foreheads to their necks—women half the height of the men—and holding their sons with a fierceness that can't be love, and yet it's a feeling that refuses to let go even though the television host interrupts to try to get the mother to separate for the interview. The camera circles to zoom in for the mother's eyes, the man's eyes who do not recognize this woman who is his mother stroking his face and refusing to share this moment for which she has hungered. The camera tightens the shot to document the mother locking her son's face against her chest perhaps in protection. Music. Clapping. Strangers watch, entertained.

Commercial break: 처음 처럼

Sitting around a red plastic table, four students shoot *Chamisul soju*. Hongdae pulses and basses in the background. It's their first time, and they're living it up!

The brown-haired girl in a pale Burberry top will actually fall in love.

How is hope—this blood call—used against us?

What is the difference between this television show and this smear on the page, Omoni? Both of them shame us, yes? Yet you can't read this page, can you? I'm torn from your gaze. What kind of freedom is this not to be able to ask if you're hungry? Or not to ask at all and set down a plate of cut pears that you can find after a good sleep?

***

Omoni, they forced your mind to desert your body—your child to desert your body—and that removal someone else called an act of love. Yet love does not give life away. It gives life a way. It gives, and it gives. Your mind accepted your body as a vacancy, verdant yet razed to clear a way that no one celebrated or wept for. Did they know of your body emptied and discharged from the hospital, your breasts aching with milk to nourish your child, your back carrying your child to the orphanage, or your legs folded underneath your body bent forward in shame? Did they know how good your body was to deliver such a healthy child? (Receiving nations praise Korea for its perfect, beautiful infants.) Did they know of your body ruptured and stitched lying in the hospital bed connected to a monitor? Your body, stretch-marked and sagging where life had grown (where I had grown), climbs Dobongsan, Bukhansan, or Gwanaksan to see this vacancy inside you cupping Seoul bulldozing itself to rebuild as quickly as possible, straining against three mountains. Neon spills, honks, drinks, and advertises global progress: Learn English! Harvard English Institute. The English Language Academy. English Now! Learn forgetfulness: these words whirl, grinding against your arms and face, while across the ocean, someone is holding your child, crying in happiness in a language that your child is scared of. Someone is lighting a candle a year later for your child's adoption day. Your child is laughing. Someone is telling your child that you gave him away because you loved him so much. And you become a "birth mother" who someone says loved so deeply that you gave him to her to love.

***

Even in the act of deconstruction, there's a violence that siphons from your body, which my friend Kit Myers says is "the always becoming sign of 'family' that is instituted by the trace." Even in the word "family" there's your specter breathing through. This slashing away from your signifying body—on your body—constitutes Frederic Jameson's radical break "with another moment of socioeconomic organization and cultural and aesthetic orientation. [Your body] is defined against what it is not, against conditions which no longer prevail or are somehow irrelevant." What is irrelevant, Omoni, and what is not? Who decides context? Who empties the sign draining it of reproductive power rerouted to power some overseas simulacrum? Disney World. It's a small world after all? It's a beautiful child. It's not your child.

Omoni, I was never as strong as you. I was twenty-five years old, in love with a young man who wanted your grandchild but feared providing for him. We were both students. We were poor and young. We named him Juan Alejandro. *Él era tres meses en mi matriz.* I know because—as I laid on my back while the masked doctor pulled off his gloves sighing, "I don't think I got it all," to the nurse who slathered jelly on my stomach and rubbed a paddle across it for the ultrasound—I thought of you letting go of me in the orphanage/shelter/hospital/alley/bedroom. I thought of you lying on your back, your legs spread, and your young body cold on a flat surface.

In that moment, I was your body struggling with its own possibility opened wide for instruments. "No, there's still more. See," said the nurse while AM radio played. (Patients were supposed to be asleep. I drank orange juice that morning not knowing I couldn't take the anesthesia afterward.) She swiveled the monitor toward the doctor who turned away from my parted thighs to see the green pixels pulsing in the black screen. He untied his mask and took a break. The nurse put down the paddle and walked after him. I laid on the table with the image of that vacancy I had chosen and the trace—green static in void—still moving there in my body, and felt that darkness as separation from you, me, him. The three

181

of us lied there together connected by our bodies lost to emptiness only a woman's body can suffer, the three of us connected by loss reaching across three generations.

***

He came back, strapped on his mask, and leaned in siphoning. I wanted him to stop, but I was afraid. I couldn't say no. I said no. I said yes. I couldn't change my mind. I wanted to change my mind. I couldn't stop the machinery, couldn't stop the procedure for which I paid, Omoni.

You never gave money. No one paid you. In Korea, they pay bad women who derail economic progress with shame, not cash. Maybe you were a student, a divorcée with runs in her stockings, an irregular worker punching keys to ring up blue sponges, or a migrant stripping off plastic gloves after the assembly line belt whirrs to a stop. Maybe you were a teenager cramming for a chemistry exam or walking arm and arm with your girlfriends passing Yongsan's *kijichon* where the *yuribang* women lean against glass. Their pink glittery lips pressing hot O, pale arms and legs spreading X.

You definitely were because you gave me life; yet you lie beyond narration though others like to conceptualize you as averted damage, the what-could've-been-had-we-not-chosen-to-adopt, incapable child birthing a helpless child. I was saved from your body. Assimilation begins by fearing your body—my Korean woman's body—by carving trauma on it, a talk-story rerouting our roots toward confusion and shame. Who has the right to imagine your body away from my body? It's not your body, I fear, but this imagination saying to me before I learned how to read:

"You know what a martini is?" says a lieutenant from Akron, Ohio.

"Shaken," my mother giggles, swinging her legs. "No stir."

The lieutenant pinches my mother on the cheek and puts his arm around her. Later that night after last call, he pushes a $10 bill into her hand and licks her ear.

"Stir is better. Let's go."

Mother giggles, rolls the bill up, and then slides it into her shoe.

***

What is this reality that is always a phantom, a ghost that's neither an absence nor presence, neither flesh nor shadow? It's a fiction that haunts where the body should've been, a story that strikes out for a body with memory's force:

182

"Where are you from?" asks my best friend's sister, the basketball team's homecoming queen. She sits down on the den's shag floor and opens her French manicure set.

"My mother's from Korea, and my father is an American soldier," I say.

"Really?" My best friend's sister shakes a jar of angel kiss and applies a thin coat in two thick strokes on her left thumbnail.

"I'm a bastard," I say, trying to copy her technique with Blue #52 on my best friend's toes.

She continues to paint. "That's not true. Only boys can be bastards."

"Korean girls can be bastards." I slide the brush against the bottle's edge.

"Whatever," she says. "That's not Katie's color."

Another attempt:

Surrounded by sons, Mother is dying of cancer and asking for a daughter who she could not afford to keep. Her eldest son holds her hand. She describes walking up the hill to the orphanage's gate, the wet grass and mud, a dull ache in her shoulder as she searched for dry ground on which to set her child down, and her child waking up crying as if she knew that Mother was leaving her in the best way Mother knew how.

Switch off the cameras / Burn the scripts / Unplug / Blackout

What are these stories except tight shot reiterations looping with fresh props, wheeled-in sets, makeup, and redesigned lighting? A dubbed voice chases after a flamingo. What of the players who peel off your face—almond skin floating in saline solution, holes where breath and sight pierce through? Towels stained with flesh-colored cream, eyelashes dropped in a wastebasket—all these are a technology of story re-inventing and re-inventing. No wonder the Material Girl adopted twice from Malawi, though the second time she fought a higher court to overturn child protection laws so that she could take Chifundo away from her father, James Kambewa, a domestic worker living in Blantyre, who learned from the media blitz that his daughter was alive.

***

"This 1.1 birth rate is our revenge," says Ji-Young, "because we're treated so badly."

***

At Duri Home, Omoni, you're taught to ritualize loss by sewing selvages and pleating skirts for first birthday clothes to accompany your baby overseas.

This is not a gift to the adopters. It's your gift to your child so that she will remember you. I asked the mothers, and that's what they said about their labor. This body, this child, of work belongs to you. It's a struggle to own what is yours beyond, as Hagen Koo says, "the dominant image of Asian female factory workers," which "is one of docility, passivity, transitory commitment to industrial work, and lack of interest in union activism." You're imagined as filial daughters/filial workers measuring blue cloth for *hanbok*: "Young female workers in the export sector" who are "controlled not only by the capitalist system but also by the patriarchal culture that had been reproduced in the industrial organization." Young women lean over gray Singer sewing machines pumping trundles with their left feet, feed red pant legs under the presser foot. This is also a language—love shows in details—measuring trim, hemming jackets for crisp collars and green sleeves. The rusted bobbin catches, and you pause to rethread, licking the edge to spear through the needle's eye. You whisper to the other omonideul that you're tired. (They've heard this before.) You can't work much longer. (They've heard this before.) Loss is a labor that's taking your child. The omonideul pause, listening.

Omonideul, what if you stood up like you did at Dongil Y.H. Company on July 25th with only your bodies against the dark blue uniforms and full riot gear? What if you link arms together to form a line between women carrying briefcases and your babies lying in plastic crates? What if before such violence, you remove your clothes and begin singing, your bodies swaying back and forth, salt and sweat, hair and wrinkles, your legs and arms wrapped together as one large embrace? To take your babies is to lay hands on your bodies and to pull apart your singing. What if you refuse to work and so force the dark uniforms to manhandle your bodies to show the violence that they ask you to do to yourselves? They use your love against you to take your children. As one omoni said to me, "They tell us we aren't good enough to raise our children. We can't provide them with private English lessons. How will our children grow up to succeed?"

***

Omoni arm / 어머니의 팔 / Omoni legs / 어머니의 다리 / Omoni wrists / 어머니의 손목 / Omoni palms and shoulders / 어머니의 손바닥과 어깨뼈 / Omoni back and waist / 어머니의 등과 허리 / Omoni thumb, cheek, ears, and breasts / 어머니의 엄지 손가락, 볼, 귀와

가슴 / Omoni hipbone, eyes, and neck / 어머니의 관골, 눈과 목 / Omoni feet / 어머니의 발 / Omoni lips / 어머니의 입술

***

Your name is Shin Sun Mee, Lee Eun Hae, Kim Ok Shim, Kwon Joo Ae. Your name is Truth, Beauty, Goodness, Grace, and Hopeful Justice. I can recite your name's shape, which is not your name or its context. I can listen around, above, and below it to draw an outline to hold in my mouth.

Is this a word—sand sliding through a sieve?

Is this your body—sand assuming a vase's shape?

A mother's fate is in her child's body. As her child matures, a mother ages. Sand pours from one glass to another to measure an hour; one empties while another contains more possibility. A body emerges from another, so a body might emerge from it. A body gives, so another may give. This is how narrative works: Time organized by causality's inner logic. Yet we were torn from one another, Omoni. I hear scraping whenever I say what's not your name.

I hear tanks rumble when I mispronounce Korean. I hear strafing when my eyes stop and fall mid-sentence, shocked and unable to get up. I see your mud-caked hand cover my hand as I steady the Korean language book. Your face coughs in the mirror as I attempt to mimic the shape: 어머니의 입술 grimaces, sucks in its breath, and looks away.

***

How to be a good daughter to a mother who is not a ghost? If you were dead, I would know what to do: Lay out a chesa table with soju, fruit, and rice cakes. Stay up for three days drinking and singing with relatives. Make sure you never go hungry. Make sure you don't wander begging strangers for food.

***

Who are these strangers who tell me I have no right to my omoni's body? These unashamed strangers who know their mothers' names and begrudge me mine?

***

Omoni, are you allowed to imagine me, or must you also turn to context out of need? Perhaps all you're allowed is me so that fear limits context—

the day I was born, the memory of my body sliding out of yours, pink scars and lines my body wrote on yours that time fades? What sections of your memory do guards preside over, holding a nickel flashlight and a set of keys, opening bins and tossing files? The rattling in your head warns. I hear it too in the slow churn of helicopters preparing to take off, telephone line to headquarters crackling, underground drills boring for passageways that infantry could march through, police stacking shields for bus transport, basement pipes knocking while an ajossi buckles yet refuses to provide intelligence, the KCIA applying techniques learned from the CIA to compel an alleged traitor's conversion, a Parker pen drops on to tile, a map shudders, an *omoni* begs her eldest아들 to confess because she and his younger brother are hungry, their stomachs knock and quiver, batons bang against bars to wake inmates who have been imprisoned on suspicion, and we're not supposed to know this, are we?

We're not supposed to recognize each another as family, yet this identification is embedded in our language. When we call out to strangers—*unni, nuna, ajossi, halmeoni* and *harabeoji,* we're one family/one Korea despite distance, difference in blood ties, and destruction of geographies and names. They say네 n recognition, continuing their work without pause. An ajossi hands me change as I gather my bags and leave his cab. An unni nods toward where the napkins are, her fingers rolling kim bap and dotting the kim with water. Yet these are names for strangers/distant relatives. Omoni, what of the ruptured intimacy between us? What paper has disfigured our language such that we're unable to summon each other with our proper names from across a great divide? How must I break English so that you might recognize me? What parallel latitude cuts across our imaginations beginning with our bodies and what we can embody? If I never know your name, I will at least know the name that as your daughter I should call you—엄마, not mother, not my mother—because I have learned this name for myself. I am 내 딸, not somebody's daughter nor a gift that someone gave away.

To know this name is to embody relationships from which I have been estranged, to deregulate loves that I've been institutionally prevented from knowing and inheriting. This is another name for adoption if I look for bodies connected through your body, 엄마, which cluster together in my limbs, hair, nails and teeth, my *ip* and *ko*. This mouth is *wae-harabeoji.* This nose is *jin-halmeoni.* These eyes are yours. This forehead is *samchon.* These ears are shared by *nam dongsaeng* and *unni.* These words are our silences and speak only for me, and yet on this page, I can press my body to the ground in five directions with my body as the center. I can reach across distances that nations insist border us from each other. I can embrace you in forms that no one has imagined before or said because of shame. Hear this rattle? It's the call of bones to bones, muscles and tendons thrumming, the work of intestines and liver purifying the words to their cleanest elements to carry our singing across time and space. It's love. It's possibility. It's our most intimate speech.

Thank you to Dr. Richard Boas, Mads Them Nielsen, Korean Unwed Mothers and Families Association, and KoRoot for their support during the writing of this essay. A generous grant provided by the Korean Unwed Mothers Support Network enabled the research on which parts of this essay is based.

REFERENCES

Cheng, Vincent. *Inauthentic: The Anxiety Over Culture and Identity.* New Brunswick: Rutgers University Press, 2004. Print.

Crapanzano, Vincent. "The Postmodern Crisis: Discourse, Parody, Memory." *Rereading Cultural Anthropology.* Ed. George E. Marcus. Raleigh-Durham: Duke University Press, 2000. 87-102. Print.

Dobbs, Jennifer Kwon. "Real Support for Unwed Moms." *The Korea Times* (digital edition), 30 October 2009.

Koo, Hagen. *Korean Workers: The Culture and Politics of Class Formation.* Ithaca: Cornell University Press, 2001. Print.

Myers, Kit. "Love and Violence in Transracial/national Adoption." American Studies Association Annual Meeting, November 2009, Washington, DC.

MARJORIE TESSER

Like Mexico

The hotel is all right, as those things go, a tall tower next to a pair of lower flat-roofed buildings with terraces facing out to the sea. But it doesn't feel like Mexico.

Annie and Matt each had visited Mexico before they met, years ago when they were young. The summer she was eighteen, Annie had traveled with her friend Sofia down the central spine of the country, speaking high-school Spanish, riding third-class busses with families, farmers, chickens, and even a goat. And Matt, in his twenties, had wound up in Oaxaca—a long story—where, taken in by a local master weaver, he'd spent a week sipping home-made mescal (eating the worm!) and learning the secrets of weaving fine decorative textiles; the Pineapple God he'd seen created back then still hangs in Annie and Matt's finished basement, where he's presided over play-dates and birthday parties, and more recently, Jake's band practices.

When Matt's parents offered to watch the kids and let Annie and Matt go away for their twentieth anniversary, they were tempted. After this year, they needed a break. Their middle child, Skyler, a seventh grader, had been diagnosed with Type 1 diabetes earlier in the year, a gut punch out of nowhere. They'd had to change his diet, monitor his levels, and learn to administer insulin; Annie was grateful Matt didn't shy away from that part of it. They'd gone into coping mode, and had done a great job of being matter-of-fact about all of it so as not to alarm Sky or the other kids. Sky seemed to be managing. But the possibilities, the long-term implications, were daunting.

And now Jake, the eldest and easiest child, always mature and reasonable, had become, in his junior year of high school, sullen and obstructive.

Usually a good student, he was getting behind in his classwork. His band, together since freshman year, had forsaken their moony, good-natured pop punk, and now played ear-splitting fusillades of drum and bass slashed with hectoring guitars and intermittent harangues of barked vocals.

Jake, who had talked at eight months, who was always glad to sit down and chat with adults, wowing his uncles with mature observations, who had, as the oldest child, spent the most one-on-one time with his mother, her little pal, now avoided interaction, other than to mock Annie and Matt's moderate liberalism as "hippy crap" or to espouse anarchy or at least some extreme libertarianism. His views on gun control alone—Annie couldn't even talk to him. He hardly ever appeared at home without one of his band mates, skinny boys with mountain-man hair and scruffy beards, wearing black t-shirts with images of skulls and band logos in intricate unreadable fonts. They conversed only with each other, *sotto voce* snickering communications in one or two word shorthand. Annie found no opportunity to start a serious conversation with Jake; she felt she was being denied access to him, as if cult elders were keeping a vulnerable new member from family contact. Or more like Jake was a rock star or politician using a phalanx of aides to screen himself from pesky fans. Matt told Annie to relax. Hadn't they both gone through the same phase as kids, referencing song lyrics and such with friends in front of mystified adults? But this was different. Annie hardly knew what to say to Jake that wouldn't set off a slammed door or a barrage of sarcasm. She wished she could find some magic words that would resonate with her son, if not in his brain then at some more fundamental level, just vibration, maybe, and he'd be restored to his correct harmonic frequency. Otherwise, their communication would continue to fade out, like fainter and fainter calls across a fast-widening divergence of paths that had once run parallel.

A week before the trip, Annie had come into the kitchen to find Jake making a sandwich. She'd felt a small flush of pride at his self-sufficiency, even as she noticed the explosion of breadcrumbs and goopy knife on the marble counter.

"Hey," she'd said, "How's it going?" Her voice sounded annoying, full of forced joviality, even to herself. He shrugged and said, "PB," waving his dripping sandwich. But he didn't do that little wince he sometimes did when she spoke to him and she was encouraged.

"Looks good," she said, choosing not to start a fight by telling him to clean up after himself. "Have a seat?" He sat.

"What are you up to today?"

"Going over Kevin's."

Her least favorite, Kevin, who believed in the destruction of government.

"Jake," Annie said slowly, "I know Kevin's been your friend for a long time. But lately, doesn't he seem...." The corners of his mouth tightened, but then his phone buzzed. He glanced at the text and replied, tapping the screen with one thumb as he slid out of his seat. He pocketed the phone, grabbed the sandwich, said, "I'm out," and went.

"But what about SAT prep," Annie couldn't help calling after him. "Also, I saw Mr. Bartlett in the ShopRite and he mentioned you were late on your essay." But he was already gone; the only thing left of him a couple of globs of jelly on the floor in the hallway. Annie realized if she wanted to have any relationship with him at all, she'd have to learn to hold her tongue. *His schoolwork should be his responsibility,* she reminded herself. *You have to give him room.*

All the conflict seemed to be affecting the younger kids as well. Skyler, at best of times scattered, had become more and more hyper. And the youngest, ten-year-old Celia, was even quieter.

Annie found it difficult to share her concerns with her husband. Matt had been working late almost every night since the promotion. The last thing he needed was to hear about Annie's getting a call from the school nurse about Skyler's sudden fatigue or episode of vomiting. If Annie brought any of that up, Matt would rake his still longish hair and look so overwhelmed and miserable that she felt guilty. And if she blurted her concerns about Jake, he'd just say, "He's a kid, Annie, it will work out." Matt had gone through his own rebellious phase as a teenager, so he thought of it as normal, while Annie was unsure whether to figure it as growing pains or possibly inklings of a real depression. She had seen marks on Jake's buddy Kevin's arms that might have been signs of cutting. Or not.

So Annie hesitated to go away and leave the kids, but when Matt was actually able to get time off from work, he pressed for it. "Mexico," he coaxed. Twenty years earlier, the discovery they'd each taken a seminal trip there had seemed an amazing confluence that, along with other shared enthusiasms (John Fowles, Pink Floyd, Preston Sturges) had sparked their rapid segue from work associates, to a couple, to married. She knew it was escapist, but Annie was secretly relieved that Grandma and Grandpa would be the ones to monitor the children for a week. Matt's parents were upbeat and unflappable; his mother Bette, a retired nurse, was pragmatic about things like shots and band practices. Annie could get a respite, perspective. A cheap deal for Cancun, which neither Annie nor Matt had visited before, sounded perfect—novel, easy, close-ish, warm.

In the plane there are little screens embedded in the seatbacks. Matt watches a movie, a spy thriller they'd both read, but Annie doesn't have the attention span for it, is too burnt out to even muster the energy to turn off the screen-saver, where a loop of resort ads circles. The day before they left, Skyler had come home devastated; he'd been told that because of his diabetes, he wouldn't be allowed to play basketball. Sky, a busy, fidgety kid, lived for the game; though he was smallest on the team, he made up for it in speed. Of course Annie had called the school, but the administrator was adamant that they couldn't risk the liability. She failed to find the argument that could penetrate his bulwark of official-speak. And now no sports, when they were the highlight of Skyler's day. How will Sky manage the constraints of school without that release? She turns to Matt, but he gestures to his headphones, his screen, where a thin man in black is bludgeoning a chubby guy in a suit.

In front of Annie, the screen-saver still cycles, and Annie realizes that for each hotel, whether in Maui, Bermuda, the Virgin Islands, or Tenerife, the photos are the same, a spacious lobby, a guestroom with a well-appointed bed, a pool with a swim-up bar and neat troops of empty lounge chairs. A woman in a pink uniform rubs hot stones on the back of a supine woman in a pavilion overlooking the sea. A flame flares around a nice hunk of steak or tuna on a grill, and then the meat, garnished artistically, is served to an attractive young couple, perhaps honeymooners, who smile at each other with mutual congratulation. A golden beach, a green-blue sea. How generic. Annie is glad they are heading for Mexico, for more of an adventure.

The hotel they arrive at is not reminiscent of either of their earlier Mexican trips. It is *kind of* like the places in the ads on the plane, but somewhat less; the elements are there, the rudiments of "resort hotel": a lobby, a pool, a small curved beach. It could be any vacation spot. The only clue that they are in Mexico is that while they wait for their rooms (an opportunity for the hotel to try to sell add-on "adventures," a pirate-themed boat ride to a deserted island, jet-skis, ATVs, a zip line, etc.), the complimentary welcome drink is a Margarita. Annie looks up at the popcorn ceiling, down at the mustard shag carpet, at Matt. "Relax," he says, "We're on vacation."

So here they are, in a chain hotel, a link in a chain of similar resorts stretching up and down the long narrow strip. They shouldn't have booked a package deal; it isn't the type of vacation either of them likes, but with work and the kids they hadn't had time to do a big research job, had been lucky they'd gotten it together to book anything at all. They're on the second floor of one of the low buildings, in the middle level of three rows of terraces looking out over a pool with a thatch-roofed tiki bar and, farther down, a little beach. Their room is simple: bed, dresser, a painting of a non-specific field. Matt's phone beeps to announce an email. "Your parents?" Annie asks. Matt glances at it. "Work." "Should we check in with them?" she persists. Matt looks annoyed. "I'm sure everything is fine, Annie." She collapses on the nubby beige bedspread and shuts her eyes "for two seconds" while Matt quickly unpacks. She tries to find a better argument she can make so they'll let Skyler play. She hopes Jake's dealing with school. Matt shuts the last drawer, stows the suitcases in the closet, sits next to Annie on the bed and puts a hopeful hand on her thigh. Instead of relaxing into the caress she rolls away and onto her feet.

Matt locks up and hands Annie the key and she takes custody of it. He holds out his paperback, sunscreen, and baseball hat with an inquiring look and she wordlessly accepts them and stows them in her bulging beach bag. They make their way down the walkway to the little poolside café. The menu is in English, salads, hamburgers and burritos; nothing local, nothing you couldn't find stateside at a burger joint or Taco Bell. Matt orders in his best accent, "*Tacos de pescado, por favor.*" "Fish tacos, you got it, boss," the waiter snaps back. Matt's phone beeps three more email alarms and he scans them quickly, and then, with a rebellious shrug that reminds Annie of Jake, shuts it off. After lackluster guac and tacos that taste like they were made with little Celia's favorite Gorton's fish sticks, they head over to the pool.

All of the lounge chairs have been dragged to cluster at the far corner, where a large boisterous group of sunburned beefy men and a few slender women with stiffish hairdos are drinking and loudly yukking it up. "Are there any other chairs?" Matt asks the man at the towel shack, who wears the nametag "Sonny." "*Los tejanoatejanas*, the Texans," says Sonny. The group is there on a corporate team-building retreat. The Texans have a system, explains Sonny. "All night they are drinking in the bar. The last one to bed puts towels on all the lounge chairs, to save them for the next day. So…," Sonny adds, with a shrug. They shouldn't allow that, thinks Annie. "What about that one," Matt insists, indicating a lounge with just a facedown paperback on it, next to a pugnacious-looking sunburned man with a bushy mustache and a huge belly, like florid walrus. "I'll just take the book off." But Annie holds his arm. The Macarena blares over the loudspeaker and a hyperactive activities director in a bright ruffled costume is dragging some of the Texans out to a space poolside; there is to be a dance lesson. She beckons to Annie and Matt, but they smile and shake their heads. They have always been more beach people, anyway.

On the beach, on the third day, they huddle under an umbrella; Matt, to shield his pale skin, Annie, in her mid-forties, newly conscious of the possibility of sun damage, huddling with him instead of basking. From this remote vantage, the vibrations of her internal antennae, finely calibrated to pick up any hint of trouble with her children, have been muted, but some residual worries slow-simmer, about Skyler, and Jake, and even Celia, who seems to be a happy little girl, but who knew, clearly, you can never know. One minute Sky was fine and the next shackled with lifelong illness.

Annie can't believe she and Matt have become one of those couples they used to make fun of in restaurants, sitting opposite each other, nothing to say. But she just can't think of anything. She won't ask him about work; it's the last thing he'd want to talk about now that he's finally on vacation. Annie's job, writing advertorials and taking photos for a little local newspaper, doesn't bear discussion. She doesn't think her last subject, a hair salon, would be of interest.

"How's your book?" Annie asks about the crime thriller facedown in Matt's lap.

"I'm not really into it," Matt confesses. The first two days, they'd just collapsed; they'd needed the rest. But now, sitting side by side in silence, they feel like they're nowhere.

"Should we check out the pool?" Annie asks, as a shout of "*No hablo!*" followed by a salvo of drunken laughter wafts over from the Texans' vicinity.

Suddenly Matt throws down the paperback, and flashes Annie a conspiratorial grin. "Hey baby," he says, in a movie tough-guy voice, "Whaddaya say we blow this place?" Annie is confused. "Leave the strip. Go check out the town!" He looks so pleased with his idea, so hopeful, that Annie smiles back. They get directions to the bus from the front desk, smugly declining when the girl asks if they'd rather have a taxi. They skirt the cluster of cabs flocked about the hotel front, hoof it three blocks down, past a Sheraton, a Hilton, and a Hyatt, to the bus stop, where they wait for half an hour. The throbbing sun is so intense it's like a heavy object they have to hold up, like Atlas is supposed to carry the earth. Annie bears it, while Matt finds shelter underneath a scraggly palm. At last the bus arrives and they climb on. Their fellow riders are workers at local hotels—each wears a uniform in two tones, black and white, blue and green, maroon and gold. Annie and Matt sit quietly, thighs touching, while the hotel workers get off one by one and then the bus picks up speed, crossing a causeway to another world.

Annie considers her trip when she was eighteen as one of the major adventures of her life. Riding a bus all night through muscular mountains of rough alien scrub, staring out the window at black skies with the hugest white stars, the only human awake save the driver. Arriving in a tiny mountain town at the first gray of dawn and walking deserted streets to the ancient stone hotel set in terraces of bright blooms, just as the sun infused the sky with pink. The deep coolness and beauty of the church interiors, the mosaics of ancient Aztecs, the murals of oppression and rebellion, hill towns and mountain towns and their little pink Hotel Los Flamingoes perched on a cliff overlooking the beach at Acapulco. The man with the bear on a leash in Puebla. Parades of primly-dressed girls promenading under the watchful eyes of their families in the *zocalo*; the mariachis that serenaded Annie and her friend Sofia with "Cuando Calienta El Sol." Hanging back while Sofia, whose Spanish was better, haggled with vendors in the colorful open-air *mercados* for melon or broiled chickens or silver or weavings or tourist trinkets. She'd returned to college a *traveler*, wearing the colorful embroidered clothes she'd bought, pronouncing her name *Ana*, as they had in Mexico.

Thinking back on it, Annie can't believe her mother had let her go at eighteen—Annie would certainly be reluctant to let Jake go at almost that age—backpacks and no reservations, just a map and "Mexico on $5 a Day." Annie guesses her mom had thought it was okay because she'd planned to go with Sofia, a year older, and a stellar student. But Sofia was eager for adventure, her first time away from her protective Italian-American family. The two of them, clomping along the cobblestone streets in platform sandals, skimpy tanks, and cut-offs, had thought the Mexican guys so friendly, with their shouted greetings of *Ay, mamacita*, accompanied by little kissing sounds. Annie remembers with wonder her naiveté. If someone asked them to go somewhere, and he was young and cute, they'd gone. Out to a rooftop bar with two apparent sophisticates, Rolando and Arturo, in retrospect a pair of lounge lizards who hung out in the hotel district looking to hook up with tourist girls, or to a park in

Mexico City with a group of nice younger guys who'd shared some sweet wine, told jokes, and taught them rude words in Spanish.

In Guanajuato, a hilltop city known for its mummified remains, every shop boasted a display of candy skeletons. The two boys who'd met them coming off the bus and offered to take them to the highest point in the city to show them the view had seemed too pushy to Annie, but she'd ignored that qualm, like a worm curled in the pit of her stomach. Sofia seemed to think it was fine, and Annie didn't want the boys to think her a snobbish American. The four climbed though almost deserted cobbled streets flanked with blank-faced colonial-era buildings to a rough area near a large domed church high above the city, houses tumbling down the hillside below them. The boys got grabby, then more insistent. They'd had to shove them away, hard, Sofia brandishing the butter knife she carried around to cut fruits purchased in the market, and stumble away as fast as they could downhill, their platform shoes treacherous on the cobblestones. Around a corner they luckily spotted a policeman, and as they galloped toward him the boys slipped away. But the cop was busy smoking a joint, so they hadn't reported the incident, just returned to their hotel, packed up, and caught the next bus to Cuernavaca, onto their next adventure.

On the other side of the causeway, laborers in white shirts and broad hats are working construction. The road is full of dusty pickup trucks, motorbikes, even a man on horseback. The signs are in Spanish; the houses and stores, cheap furniture, taco restaurants, convenience stores they pass are squat and low and painted in sunbaked pinks and greens and golds. In a vacant lot between buildings, funny animals that resemble giant rats or miniature kangaroos hop in the short tough grass. At last they stop and get out in front of a huge warehouse of a store, MEGA emblazoned in red along the side.

Annie and Matt enter and smile at each other like they're on the same team again; this is more like what they'd wanted. The place is full of color, like the rustic *mercados* of Annie's former trip. At a central kiosk, a woman slaps fresh tortillas on a baking stone. The produce section is replete with bumpy green rounds and mysterious brown gourd-like things, vegetables and fruits with spikes, even fur. Annie and Matt separate and wander, he to check out the liquor section, she in search of a cheap sundress to wear to the beach.

Annie is deep in the clothing section when she sees a stocky, placid-faced woman barely in her teens wheeling a cart with a toddler in it, a dark-eyed girl of one or two, a little beauty; such a long time since Annie's own kids were small. Annie turns back to the sundresses, but looks up as the child starts to fuss, the old mommy radar. There's a rack between them, but Annie thinks she sees the mother reach over to a display and pull off a thin plastic bag, like the ones you get from a dry cleaner, and hand it to the child to play with. The little girl grabs for it.

Annie edges closer, and watches with growing concern. She should say something. The child could suffocate. Would I be seen as interfering, Annie thinks, a pushy North American? But look! The child is palpating the plastic bag with her fingers, raising it up over her head. How long before she brings it to her mouth, inhales?

Annie trails the two out of the clothing area and into a hardware aisle, trying to catch the mother's eye, to think of how to express it, she's hardly spoken the language in thirty years. *Perdóneme,* "Pardon me," she guesses first, politeness the key. *Dangeroso,* she thinks is right. Or is it just adding "o" to an English word, like the Texans at the bar last night, yelling "*Tip-o no incluso!*" as they slapped down a couple of extra pesos? What was "to breathe?" "To be able to" was *poder,* but Annie isn't sure of the conjugation, gets stuck on the conditional. Is *podría* right or is she making it up?

She's been tailing the little mother and child for maybe ten minutes, trying to find the words, when Matt sees her and waves her over; he's found some authentic mescal, worm and all, some yogurts in fun tropical flavors not available at home. Annie looks around for the mother with the cart but she has vanished. She tells Matt about it in hopes he'll help her search. "It's their lives, Annie," he says, wearily. Annie gives it one last look, but can't spot them. Nothing to do but catch the bus back.

They settle in, after that, make friends with a new couple from Louisiana at the pool, buy bead necklaces from some little boys, beach vendors—they even go for a couples massage. But throughout the week and on the plane, and even years later, it still nags at Annie, and at odd times she finds herself re-translating, rehearsing words she hadn't been able to say.

NICOLE COOLEY

In the Dollhouse Nursery

Painted sea foam green, the nursery you arrange on the top floor of your dollhouse has enough space for a gallery of beds—single cots with sheets stretched tight, wrought iron cribs, satin-quilted bassinets. So many babies.

Think Hospital. Think Orphanage.

In this world, you don't have a body, but you can have as many children as you want. No one will grow up.

Tuck your daughters inside the comforters you made from cotton in a ring box.

Hide your smallest baby in a walnut shell for safekeeping.

This is your dream space, your pleasure, your site of pure delight.

You possess and yet you do not.

Tell yourself a lie:

You are the mother. You are the author of this miniature house.

Chicago, 1951

"Swallow the medicine without spitting it out, and I'll give you a dollhouse dresser," Uncle Eddie tells my mother and her sister.

Jacki and Janice have chickenpox. Eddie sits between their beds on the rug, in the bedroom they share with their grandmother, holding the bottle of bitter medicine that neither girl wants to take. Seven and five, the girls are confined to bed.

"Four times a day, if you take this medicine, you can pick dollhouse furniture from the box," Eddie says. He holds a box of miniatures from Marshall Fields Department Store, downtown, on his lap. The girls are under quarantine, not allowed to leave the house, not allowed to get out of bed. But they are given dollhouse furniture as a cure.

For years, the story of Eddie and the dollhouse furniture is my favorite story my mother tells me about her childhood. I would beg her to repeat it.

A medicine bottle, a tiny three-drawer dresser, a pink wing chair, a trundle bed.

"Good girl," Eddie says and sets a spoon in each sister's mouth, and when she obediently swallows, moves the box closer so that she can choose. One piece at a time.

The dollhouse furniture is irresistible, my mother tells me, and each day, she and Janice obediently swallow the chicken pox medicine because they want their reward. Everything in the dollhouse box is shiny plastic. A sink. A yellow-frosted cake, sliced into tiny, perfect quarters. A clock. Their dollhouses—two matching houses—sit on a table across the room though they are not allowed to get out of bed and play with them while they are sick. But they set up imaginary houses on the sheets and chenille spreads that cover their beds.

Later, when she tells me this story, my mother will complain to me about the plastic. "I never wanted you to have *plastic* for your dollhouse. I wanted you to have only wood, real materials." But in the fifties plastic was much cheaper. European exports had been cut off post-World War II, and the United States had stepped up its plastic manufacturing. Plastic furniture was what filled most dollhouses children owned.

"Where were your parents when Uncle Eddie gave you the medicine?" I ask my mother once.

"They weren't part of it," my mother says.

I imagine that they are absent from the dollhouse furniture exchange because my grandmother Ahnie is working and my grandfather Arnold is very ill. My mother's family is first-generation American, from Austria, Hungary and Russia. While my grandparents own the house where they live, many relatives live in it with them. My grandmother Ahnie secured her middle class identity by buying the house. Eddie, twenty years younger than my mother's father, who did not buy the house, but who lives with the family, is the one who buys the dollhouses for the girls.

Ahnie is busy working to support the family so they can keep the house. The girls' father Arnold can't climb the stairs to the girls' bedroom to be part of this dollhouse chickenpox exchange. His heart condition, caused by Rheumatic Fever and playing football in high school, which now could be easily fixed, confines him to the first floor. He can't see the girls when they are sick.

His heart: which no one in the house knows will kill him during experimental surgery in three years.

Yet every day he gets up in the morning, dresses in a suit and leaves the house to not work, to go to the local barbershop and gamble in the back room. To go nowhere, he wears a suit.

"I had my own family," my mother used to tell me, and when I was a little girl I thought of course she meant her parents and her sister and her uncles and her grandmother. But she was talking about her dollhouse: mother, father and two children, a middle class 1950s family. The dollhouse daughters do not share a room and sleep in a bed with their grandmother, as my mother and her sister do. No one cooks strudel and goulash and noodle casserole in the dollhouse kitchen. No one whispers prayers over a Croatian Bible at night.

The dollhouse furniture Eddie gives the girls will help them make an entirely new life, one that has nothing to do with their immigrant past.

Here is a green and white Marshall Fields box.

Here is a dining table. Here is a patio chair. Here is a loaf of rubber bread. Swallow it down.

Marriage

"A dollhouse is a house that never leaves you," Barb McGee tells me as we stand at the counter of her store.

I am visiting McGees Miniatures, the dollhouse store that Barb owns, in a half-closed down, nearly empty mall at the edge of St. Louis.

I have several questions I don't ask: How could a house leave a person? A house can't walk out on you. Wouldn't a person leave a house?

When I don't say anything because I am not sure how to respond, Barb continues. "If your husband doesn't like your dollhouse, if it comes down to the house or the man, the dollhouse stays, and the man can move out."

I want to know why a husband would not like a wife's dollhouse. Would a husband be jealous of his wife's escape into the fantasy world of a dollhouse, an escape in which he has no part? Why can't a husband enter a dollhouse world?

What does a dollhouse offer a wife that a husband can't?

Barb's ideas about dollhouses have nothing to do with children. A dollhouse in this equation—and it is an equation—is not a toy.

What is the solution? Subtract the husband from the house? Remove the dollhouse away from the husband's gaze?

Why do I like the idea of a dollhouse as hidden, as illicit, as clandestine? As wrong?

The Day of the Dead Birth Scene, Merida, Mexico

In the hospital room, the walls are painted sky blue. Four figures, skeletons, all from the Day of the Dead: a doctor, a nurse, a mother and a baby. A bald skeleton doctor and a nurse with blacked out eyes, dressed in surgical scrubs, are in charge. A naked woman lies on a table, legs spread, her body half-covered by a piece of ripped-up paper towel. From between her legs a tiny skeleton baby half emerges, head first, surrounded by deep red painted blood.

The scene is the size of a soup can. I bought the miniature birth scene at the Miniatura Folklorica in Merida, Mexico in the Yucatan. The shop was a single, dusty room. I was teaching a poetry workshop for a week, and I went to the store by myself every afternoon after my class, loving it more than any of the museums or Mayan ruins we visited.

Nothing is idealized in the Miniatura Folklorica, where Day of the Day icons populate the landscape of the store's small objects. The shop is crammed with Dead of the Dead sugar skulls and skeletons, and with shelf after shelf of glass-boxed miniature scenes, all showing Death approaching.

Instead of the way we so often depict birth in the U.S., as a joyful event, here birth is a scene of horror.

I was riveted by the birth scenes on display at the back of the shop. I could not stop studying them from all angles.

I had to bring one home, set it on my desk in my study, keep it with me.

The births of my own daughters were frightening beyond what I understood childbirth could be. Instead of drug-free labors and joyous early days with my babies, I was alone and scared in a hospital room for days without them, while my husband accompanied them for medical tests. My first birth was an emergency C-section following hours of labor, followed by complications, and brain and heart tests performed on a newborn I had seen and never held; the second was a C-section with more complications, my second daughter taken away to the NICU so that I did not see her for twenty-four hours after the birth. Both experiences felt far less like magically bringing a new life into the world than being part of invasive medical experiences where people nearly died.

I loved that the miniature birth scenes told the truth about what birth was like.

But years had passed since these experiences, and the memory was not the only reason I was so drawn to the miniature birth scenes.

The tiny glass boxes captured a moment I had not seen revealed before: the exact moment before motherhood starts. Or the moment when motherhood will never begin.

Is this the best moment of motherhood? Made miniature, made small enough to fit in a box? A baby born yet not born. Forever and ever, the baby stays half emerging, connected to its skeleton mother and yet not. Born and yet never.

Henri Bendel's New York City Holiday Windows, 2013

In the department store window on Fifth Avenue, a red-headed girl is texting.

She is five inches tall.

Reclining on her bed, with a look of intense concentration, she furiously types a tiny, invisible message into her phone. Except for her tiny size, she looks very much like my thirteen- year-old daughter and her friends, or perhaps my thirteen-year-old daughter's fantasy of life as a New York City twenty-something girl.

Another doll lies in a bathtub full of glass water. Two more dolls watch TV. The windows show the inside of six apartments, each its own dollhouse, with city backgrounds made by pop-up artist Robert Sabuda: a sky scape view of the Brooklyn Bridge, fleets of miniature taxis rushing by.

Standing in front of Bendel's, a store where I could never afford to shop, a store I've never entered, the power of the miniature world is enormous. The shock that the mannequins are dollhouse size. The feeling when I study the dolls that I could enter the scene.

I am suddenly the perfect size. I become a dollhouse girl in the Bendel's window. I am beautifully tiny, impossibly compact, forever in my twenties.

Now I'm late to get home from work, I've missed my train, my husband and children are waiting, my bag is heavy with papers to grade tonight, I'm hungry, I'm tired, and all I want is to slip inside this magic dollhouse world in the window.

I want to dissolve, to turn into this girl with her small silver phone, or this girl lounging in a bath, in my own studio apartment, to tumble down a rabbit hole into a glamorous New York City life I've never lived. As soon as I moved to New York, I had a baby. Babies have no place in Bendel's windows.

Neither do real life-sized women. All my life I've struggled to shrink my body. I have always wanted to be smaller. I've counted all my calories, added and subtracted each day and always found myself wanting. I've exercised too much. I've measured myself with a tape measure from the hardware store and secretly recorded the statistics on my body, width of arm and wrist and waist. I've listed everything I ate each day and added it up.

But a dollhouse—and this particular dollhouse world on the late afternoon, snow-filled, icy streets of New York City— transports me to a place where I am instantly and effortlessly tiny—and thin—and perfect.

The seduction for me—and for many other women, I suspect—is the ability to become small.

As a teenager, I lay awake at night and recounted my calories for the day, the number always too high, vowing to be better the next day, to be the ideal girl who kept herself thin for the rest of the week, the month, the year, my life. I set my palm on my stomach and sucked in my breath, hoping it would be flat enough so that I could let myself go to sleep instead of rising from bed to do another set of sit ups on my bedroom floor or smoke a cigarette at the window to keep from eating.

As an adult, being weighed every two weeks during my first pregnancy, I always asked not to know my weight, refused to hear the number, closed my eyes while I stood on the scale in the doctor's office, until finally the nurse snapped at me, "You're pregnant, not fat!"

And in front of Bendel's windows, on this winter evening, if I stand here watching, if I stand here perfectly still, if I stand here long enough, maybe I don't have to have a body at all.

Ruin, 1978

"Stay upstairs," my mother told my sister and me. "The water's too dangerous. Take care of your sister."

Inch by inch, foot by foot, floodwater rose in the basement of our house. Rain lashed the house.

Galvez Street brimmed with water because the drainage pumps failed. Heavy rain, which had fallen for days, would not stop. The city shut down, filled with dirty water.

Alissa and I stood in the kitchen, at the top of the basement stairs, watching the dollhouse. Water rose up to the table where I kept my dollhouse, swirled around the contact paper cobblestone path that circled the house, around the electric light boxes on the sides of the house, but the interior of the house, all six rooms that my mother had decorated, painted shiny enameled pink, miraculously stayed dry and safe.

In the basement, the water was a foot deep – I knew my mother couldn't be worried that we would drown—but like all floodwater it was a toxic stew of chemicals and run-off from the street. Alissa and I sat in the living room and waited for news of our dollhouse.

For three days, rain had drenched the city, and its force was enough to flood the lower-lying neighborhoods like ours, in the Broadmoor district. We lived far from the river, but the city routinely filled to the brim with water whenever there was a bad storm. The flood ruined my family's possessions we had stored there, our suitcases, our boxes of books, photographs and papers. For a week, my parents stayed up late in the basement every night, throwing away soaked cardboard boxes and piling our ruined possessions into garbage bags. The dollhouse was the only object in our basement on Galvez Street to survive the flood.

The 1978 flood was nothing like the flood that would come later, the flood-post Hurricane Katrina that would drown New Orleans in August 2005, leaving the whole city underwater. This was just a storm, like so many in New Orleans, a city located six to ten feet below sea level. This time, after days of rain, water rose in the city faster than the drainage pumps could work, water rose on the street where we lived, and filled our ground-floor basement, destroying everything my family kept there.

The levees did not break, and the river did not crack the floodwalls. I can now imagine what these days were like for my parents, doing the grim work of mopping and cleaning a basement in a house that did not belong to them, while realizing their own belongings that they thought were safe in boxes and on shelves were destroyed. But at the time all I cared about, with typical childhood selfishness, was my dollhouse.

Nothing could be saved.

Except the dollhouse.

To me, the dollhouse surviving dry and intact was proof of its magic. And of my mother's magic and her ability to control the world: she'd built me my own house, which I believed would never be destroyed. My mother made me a perfect miniature universe that stayed safe when the rest of the world collapsed.

MATEA KULIĆ

Return, No Return

Part 1: Return

the apartment—'golden years'—a connection—remembering—the fall—war—blood ties—my mother's mother—a container—nostalgia—full circle—the centre

—

The apartment was a relic from another time, a faded memory. The only person who had hung on to it since we moved to Canada was my mother. She continued to fly back for brief court hearings after privatization, to petition for the property to stay in our name. While the apartment fell into a state of disrepair, lost its market value and middle-class neighbourhood appeal— she awaited the court's decision. Nearly a decade and a-half-dozen trips later, she was vindicated: the apartment was ours. It was a one bedroom flat in a tall cinder block building, the standard model, hastily constructed with a postwar, burgeoning population in mind. It stood near the open *platz* market on a boulevard, that no longer bears the same name, in the center of a city, Beograd, that is no longer the capitol, of the country formerly known as Yugoslavia. The apartment was our origin, my beginning. It was the blank space above the dotted line: place of birth.

—

Ask older folks about the former Yugoslavia and they will speak proudly about the '60s and '70s—"the golden years." Not like other communist dictatorships, they will say; we had passports, open borders. You could work and study abroad, as my parents did. Dubravka Ugresić recalls that Yugoslavs enjoyed many benefits during this period: "Free schooling, education and self-betterment as fundamental values…and the general impression that life was getting better from one year to the next." Funds trickled in via Western powers eager to bolster Tito's regime as an alternative to the stalwart Soviet Union. Even if he was a communist, Tito had said 'No' to Stalin, he liked Hollywood, had starred in a couple of domestic films himself. For a small country, Yugoslavia was considerably renowned. The cultural centres (Belgrade—Zagreb—Sarajevo—Ljubljana) held international festivals of theatre and film. The coastline was known throughout Europe for its pristine waters and unspoiled beaches.

—

In 1976, my grandparents, Baba and Deda we called them, were leaving the capitol for Dubrovnik to live out their own golden years. Deda had been a WWII Partisan and fought among Tito's ranks. He worked his way up to become the manager of an industrial parts factory and, at 59, was retiring with a comfortable pension. Before they left, Deda used his influence to sidestep the wait list and secure us an apartment in the centre. Ask older people what it was like living in the former Yugoslavia and they will speak bitterly about the corruption and nepotism. Instead of a nice car and jewelry, you had a connection.

—

We lived in the apartment as a family. My older sisters, Eva and Nevena, could tell it better: they were already sleeping in a bunk bed; I had just graduated to the little cot. If I can remember one thing it was that Nevena had painted little purple stars on the ceiling of the bedroom. But perhaps I am thinking of another ceiling (the ceiling of our new house in Vancouver?) and perhaps they were yellow stars, the glow in the dark kind. I might be remembering the backdrop of an old childhood photograph. I might not be remembering.

—

After we left, my father, a Croat, said he wanted nothing to do with the place. "That apartment is a hell hole," he would say to me and my sisters, "nothing would make me go back there." It would take me years to understand how his resentment had piled up against the regime. At the age of eighteen, he was forced to leave his birthplace, a small southern village, for mandatory army service. "We were never equals," he would say, "When you're from the coast, you're just a peasant to them, and they let you know right away, mocking your dialect, your mannerism." My father's anger pointed to a greater discontent between regions, between periphery and centre. Despite Tito's efforts to erase differences among the southern

Slavs, to unite the six provinces under a system of "symetrical federalism," old antagonisms restlessly brewed beneath the surface. Slavoj Žižek writes, "Yugoslavia in the seventies and eighties was like the proverbial cat in the cartoon who continues to walk above the precipice—he only falls down when, finally, he looks down and becomes aware that there is no firm ground beneath his legs." It was 1990. The Berlin Wall was rubble, Tito was dead, and with American monetary funds withdrawn, the Yugoslav economy was in tatters. The Croatian Parliament set to announce its independence and sever all remaining ties with Yugoslavia. There was nothing left to do, but look down.

———

I wasn't there for the war, plain and simple as that. The summer of '91, Eva and I cut short our visit with Baba and Deda and hurriedly boarded a bus bound for Split. The airstrip just south of Dubrovnik had been hit. One month later, the full bombardment of the city would begin. But like I said I wasn't there. Safe at home, we watched it on TV; later, kids at school would ask me, hey are you from that *Hurtzagovena* place? I listened in on my mom's late night phone calls to Baba and Deda, *there's an extra room here, I'd book the flights…* Their voices resounding through the mouthpiece: *What would we do there?* Deda in particular protested the idea of leaving his homeland. Everything he had fought for, from his Partisan days, the national building projects of his youth, his participation in local committees. So what if Baba was a Serb, he a Croat, they were united, comrades in marriage. But Deda was still thinking along the lines of an old logic. The "golden years" had come to an end and what had been commonplace in Yugoslavia, mixed marriages, mixed families, would soon become suspect.

———

When Eva and I came back to the coast in '95, Croatia was not a "destination" as we know it today. There were no cruise ships in the harbor, no kiosks selling captain hats, no tourists in fisherman striped shirts. Nor was it the Croatia we left merely three years earlier. Packs of strays picked among the rubbish bins and carcasses of the former four-star hotels along the boardwalk. Shrapnel scarred the facades of the Old Town, sections of the red roofs caved in; closer to home you felt deeper, more personal cuts. I asked my oldest childhood friend and confidante why certain kids had up and disappeared from the courtyard. Her voice took on a severe register and it dawned on me that there was already a big difference between us. Somehow she had aged past her eleven-year old self. "It's just the way it is," she shrugged, "we don't go there, and they don't come here." It sounded like a phrase she had overheard from the adults, but nevertheless, an "us" and a "them" was clearly established. Not wanting to be on the wrong side, I kept my distance from the courtyard games. The question of origins weighed on all of us. Eva and I had been instructed to respond briefly, when asked, to call up the *Patria*, using the birthplace of our father and grandfather as proof our heritage was unpolluted. Motherland, the apartment, the birthplace of Baba, my mother, sisters and I, in one stroke: erased.

—

The following year, I got my period, the same year that in my school in Vancouver, B.C. we lined up to get vaccinations. Seemingly unrelated, I became queasy at the sight of blood. Waiting in line for my turn, I fainted, was dragged to the nurse's station, convinced it was just a prick, and given a cookie to calm down. Menstruation laid me out for days at time, my body weak, immobilized in bed. I was quite sensitive, the doctor informed my mother, because of anemia: a weakness in the blood. Perhaps my adolescent body had a knack for internalizing an external conflict; perhaps it had a flare for the dramatic.

—

My baba was superstitious. She was forever fretting about the Northern *bura* that caused the draft, that caused doors to slam shut and the eggs of young women to perish. Cover your kidneys she would say, wrapping a shawl tighter around her waist. She had never travelled outside Yugoslavia; she did not read books. She spent her days cooking, her evenings knitting and every now and then she threw back a little shot of *rakija* before bed. My mother, a "modern woman," had been abroad to study English literature. She wore makeup and loved the Beatles. Needless to say my mother and grandmother did not see eye to eye on most matters. But Baba did share my mother's cosmopolitanism, her desire for "outside," through food. She borrowed what she liked from all corners— *gnocchi, schnitzel, burek, patlican, torta cassata*—and through her cooking told the history of the various regimes—Ottoman, Austrian, Italian—that had at different times ruled the Balkans. In Vancouver, my mother soon adapted her cooking, becoming vegetarian and assimilating elements of a healthy west coast diet. But still, she will drive the forty-five minutes across town to buy a greasy *burek*, or cheese pie, from the Bosnian bakeshop. Nothing tastes so good as the food from home, she tells me. The food our mothers made, the food that brings your senses to life.

—

Summer of sixteen. Rooms accommodating Italians and Germans once again, but the official language no longer accommodating Italianisms and Germanisms. Our street name crossed out and replaced to honour a local military brigade. It's so long people have a hard time getting it out in one breath. Baba no longer sends plum *knedle* and *pomidores* to neighbours, but certain "others" come to her. Inside, at the kitchen table, a cluster of women: a widow, a mother who's lost her son, a Bosnian refugee huddle over Nescafé. People return to the beach, swimming out from the paved shoreline. A few sun chairs and beach umbrellas stationed near the one in-service cafe; for now, there's plenty of room to spread out. Everyone muttering about which foreigners will buy up the hotels now that state ownership is phasing out. A new big box store is moving in where the local committee used to meet.

—

When a place disappears, you create it in different ways. You go there in dreams and in fantasies, through the stories of others that become your own. *Yugonostalgia* is a term specifically designated for those who long for Yugoslavia and keep its memory actual through recalling it, or at least select parts of it. Abrupt change in particular seems to make people long for that time "before" when there was a sense of stability and permanence. In Vancouver, I used to go to these "Balkan Nights" where a bunch of *Yugonostalgics* would gather 'round to drink Slivovica and dance the *kola*. By the night's end, someone would invariably strike up a Serbian or Croatian national song and then a fight would break out. It was strange to me that a second generation, most of whom had never been back to the "motherland," could be so feverish in their devotion. I stopped going to those nights a while ago, even got sick of the music. But perhaps I simply displaced my devotion, swapped singing for writing the motherland. Perhaps everyone needs a container in which to place their longing.

Deda became difficult in his old age. He was forever writing letters of complaint to any addressee available. Fresh-painted bike lanes in the capital now bothered him. More than the sudden collapse of Yugoslavia, my baba's sudden death drained him of his former optimism. The seaside house was boarded up and Deda took up residence in an old folk's home in Zagreb. Along the bay where we swam every summer, condos and villas quickly sprouted up. Dubrovnik, the 'Pearl of the Adriatic,' was fast becoming the playground of jet setters and glitterati. Locals began selling their houses *en masse*, capitalizing on the market and abandoning crowded Old Town to tourist agencies and restaurants. I, too, was a beneficiary of the new economy. I had been hired to lead group tours up and down the coast. UNESCO heritage programs had prompted a steady reconstruction of injured monuments; towns throughout Croatia were being rediscovered. Each year, the local paper "Free Dalmatia," reported on the rising numbers of foreign visitors in a celebratory mood. Increasing tourism also meant a steady relaxation of border controls. I could no longer claim the "us" and "them" mentality was keeping me from my place of birth. I was twenty-nine years old. I had been inland to Bosnia, north to the slopes of Slovenia and south to Montenegro. I had skirted the entire periphery without having crossed into the heartland, to Serbia, to the apartment in Belgrade.

Part 2: No Return

winter—*where are you from?*—soil—your last name—double meaning—faded stars—Mother again—the fainting subject—lost or stolen territory—home—absence—maps—lines on the body—failure—repeat

—

2014 is a historical year. The flight between Zagreb and Belgrade—grounded for twenty-three years—takes off once again. But the girl returning to her place of birth takes the bus. The journey is only 360 kilometers and she prefers overland travel. She has on a thin wool coat and a silk scarf tied around her neck. The wintry landscape is pale and monotonous. She nods off, then is jolted awake by the rev of the engine. The driver turns off the ignition and announces a wait. Up ahead: a chaotic tangle of trucks and cars inch forward slowly, funneling toward a booth in the distance. The passenger sitting opposite notices her straining to look out the window. "It's the Turks," he says, from across the aisle. He moves a finger across an imaginary horizon. "They come one way for the money, and the other way home."

—

She wishes she had taken the flight. The trip was supposed to take six hours, but took eleven instead. The apartment she's rented is outside the city centre. It's as if one part of her wants to keep a distance. Her upper half (the head) laces up her shoes, while her lower half (the gut) sits motionless. It's about a two-kilometer walk to the market *platz*. Spreading the map out over the table, she scans the route, setting it to memory. She tucks the map into her pocket. She wants to pass through discreetly but it's impossible—everything about her: gait, clothing, hairstyle, draws unwanted attention. 'Home,' she realizes is where you can just show up, without appearing out of place.

———

Milan Kundera writes "during the twenty years of Odysseus's absence, the people of Ithaca retained many recollections of him but never felt nostalgia for him. Whereas Odysseus did suffer nostalgia and remembered almost nothing."

———

One foot in front of the other, she traverses the mental route in her head. At the forefront of her mind, x marks the destination and the idea that the past was always there, just waiting to be discovered. She trundles on as if invisible strings were pulling her. In the fairytales she read as a child, the maiden sets out on a journey, prompted by the witch's command: *Go there, I do not know where, and bring me back a thing I lack.*

———

Before long she needs to pull out the map. She recognizes no landmarks to orient herself; even if she knew the street names, the signs are in Cyrillic. Holding her finger to the spot, she asks a woman standing next to a menu for directions. The woman looks up, surprised by her accent, and immediately asks the ubiquitous question of this territory: "Where are you from?" A pause as she considers she's about to say something she's never said before. "I was born here…" It feels like a song. *Where? Here! Where? Here!* She wants to repeat it over and over but the woman is waiting for her to finish the sentence.

———

Author Damir Karakaš says, *once you leave your spot you can be from anywhere. It doesn't matter anymore.* You can dig up a root, you can create a splint—the way her father did when he brought the cuttings of two figs from Dalmatia and planted them in front of their new house in Vancouver—but you can never return that root to the soil. By the time you do, the context will have changed. New leaves will have fallen, turned to mulch, ground that was once acidic, becomes alkaline and so on. Return implies *al revés* something left behind.

—

Out on the boulevard, concrete looms. She ducks into a dimly lit thoroughfare. An old man, he looks like an archetype, stands in front of a pawnshop. "Got everything you need," he asks between a few silver teeth. "Yes," she mumbles pulling her thin coat tighter around her waist. The apartment building is just up ahead. The façade is chipped, a single bulb buzzes attentive over the directory. Her eyes race down the list. *There*—she sucks in a breath—her surname appears like an apparition. Faded, but visible: It hasn't been crossed out, changed, or disappeared. She stills herself and rings the buzzer.

—

Svetlana Boym tells us that "nostalgia" comes from two Greek roots: *nóstos* (return home) and *álgos* (longing). Nostalgia is a sentiment of loss and displacement, a long-distance relationship, a romance with one's own fantasy. The image of nostalgia, she tells us, is always double—home and abroad, past and present, dream and daily life. As soon as we try to force it into a single image, it breaks.

—

A soon as she enters through the door, she has the disorienting sensation of complete unfamiliarity. *This is the apartment?* Nothing in it belongs to her. *What was she looking for exactly?* The tenants don't understand it either. They're anxious the landlady from Canada might have sent her daughter to check up on the state of things. They try to divert her gaze from the stained patches on the walls, the cracked paint, the kitsch decor. "Don't worry," she says as she walks the short length of the apartment, "I won't stay long." Stepping out onto the tiny balcony, she notices purple etches on the wall. Yes, it's possible! They could be the ones Nevena drew when they were young. She moves in for closer inspection when the lady of the house extends a hand, interrupting the momentary excitement to usher her back in: she didn't want to catch a chill now, did she?

—

There comes a point we realize something about Mother. That Mother is not only the country you come from, but is also her own autonomous region: one that existed before you and continues to exist without you, multiple. X: the misshapen scar of what has been crossed out: origin, womb, beginning. Only a fool returns.

—

She has the nervous tic of a thief. While her body stands immobilized her mind races down the stairwell. To the exit, *exit, exit*. She is unsure if she should put her hands at her sides or in her pockets. The woman's son, who had taken her coat when she first entered, now holds it out again. Her shoulders flex like a soldier at attention. "Let your arm hang loose," he says. It's exactly what the nurse would say seconds before pushing the needlepoint into her forearm. She jerks back, places her arms protectively around her midline. It's not clear what she's defending against. Turning back to the door, with her surname on it, she feels a part of her falling away; colour recedes; blood drains out of her face.

—

"Once history holds your hands, it never lets go," say the narrator in Lynn Tillman's "Lust for Lost." She grips the rail. Whenever she's back in Europe she's visiting cemeteries, ruins and places that take her down. The under belly of the apartment is damp and heavy. Motorbikes look like they're in body bags at the morgue. Someone has spray painted the message, *this is hell,* on the wall. Did they mean life here in Serbia? In the apartment? *I can't breathe,* she thinks but of course she can, she is. She steps toward a vent with its cover ripped off. A grey hole darkens into the middle. "I go looking for loss and I always find it," the narrator continues. She narrows her eyes to locate the edge but realizes the hole is unbounded—she can't point out where it begins and ends.

—

Since the apartment cannot have a happy end, it will be a hard fall. It will be hard to hide her disappointment in front of relatives when they ask about her impressions. She'll blame it on her mother (*why didn't you warn me?*), on her own stubborn resolve. Later she will sit down at her desk, attempt to resolve feeling by extracting meaning. But now, outside of the apartment, she finally lets go of her breath. Her stance is hallowed out, emptied of the origin, of maps and meanings. People passing her by look weary. The men wear five o'clock shadows, the women's faces peel from too much concealer. She begins to walk without expectation. Why should she recognize the streets and signs? In her place of birth, she is just another tourist, lost or with nowhere in particular to go.

—

Overland trips extend the anticipation of arrival, that's probably why she prefers them. Yet the bus trip had another purpose she could not have foreseen. At Serbia's exit, the passengers ready their passports, disembark and walk fifty-odd paces to the entry booth on the Croatia side. As she walks this "no man's land" in-between, she can't help but notice her gait. Her toes spread out in her shoes. Her arms are limber, the breathing space in her chest cavity, ample.

—

In the 1970s Yugoslavia observed a rebirth of the avant-garde artistic movement as a new generation rejected traditional canvas and paint for concrete poetry and performance art. Leaving Belgrade for Amsterdam in 1976, Marina Abramović would become the most famed of this generation. Remaining in Serbia, in Novi Sad where he was born, one lesser-known artist of this generation, Andrej Tišma, continued to make art. After the war, he travelled to the border, and at great risk, laid himself out on it. The stills of this performance depict a body split by a superimposed border: Part Croatian/part Serbian, Part perpetrator/part victim, Part self/ part other. Tišma's work forces the split to the surface.

—

Having taken the bus back from Belgrade to Zagreb, she just had one more stopover to make. Her luggage was at her uncle's, and her cousin Tanja was at the door. "I could have picked you up at the station," Tanja remarks after she'd already taken a taxi. "Don't worry about it," she shrugs, "it was easier to come alone." "So when are you coming back?" Tanja asks, narrowing her eyes. For a moment she considers how to respond. Her cousin had a way of listening selectively in order to confirm her own suspicions. Either she didn't come often enough indicating an indifference to family and roots. Or she came back too often in order to show off the privilege of life abroad. "I really don't know," she answers cautiously, "as soon as I can I guess." She takes her suitcase and puts in the back of the cab. Return was something she would do again and again. It was foolish as it was involuntary. "Well, how nice for you," Tanja says stepping back to the curb. "The way you can go back and forth."

PAULINE B. KALDAS

Aunt Helena

There are not millions of deaths. It happens millions of times that someone dies.

—Etel Adnan, *Sitt Marie Rose*

A week after I turned six, the war began. We must have celebrated my birthday with the usual family gathering—an only child and the first of my generation to be born, my birthdays were an occasion to celebrate with aunts, uncles, and grandparents, pulling together our large extended family. I know we went to Groppi's pastry shop to pick out my cake, and I'm sure I selected the most elaborate one with chocolate swirls rising and twisting into a sculpture of confection. A few days later, I might have sensed the pattern of energy changing, the suppressed tones of urgency, the hesitant movements, or perhaps there was nothing but our daily lives until the surprise of that first day when heightened fear entered each house.

What I remember is the way dusk brought the town crier to our street, swinging a lantern and commanding us to turn off our lights. He seemed a comical figure, this man waving a lamp down the street. I peered out the window to catch a glimpse of him, but I know that hands tugged me back inside as footsteps moved more rapidly, and my grandmother's arms gathered us into a circle to sit on the floor in the living room, one stubby candle placed in the middle. The excitement of an event seeped in—we were all there, even my father who was usually away working several jobs, my mother who was often out with friends, my aunt who was still in college, and my grandmother. We held hands, linking ourselves together. Once the droning of airplane engines above us began, someone blew out the candle, and we sat still and silent in pitch black with only our sense of hearing to guide us. When I asked questions, I was shushed with half-whispered answers. The planes above us droned loudly, a heavy monotone of sound breaking through air. As long as we stayed in this deep darkness, they could not see us. And we could not become a target for the bombs they carried. The entire city blanketed itself in the cover of night like a magic trick, so pilots believed they were flying over empty land. For six nights, we repeated our pattern. Fear settled inside me, heightened by what my mind imagined—the loss of any of us, the extinction of our existence. I sat still, listening for pauses in the humming air above us.

When the candle burned down and the air lifted, giving way to clear sky, we emerged to find ourselves shattered by loss.

At family gatherings, I watched my Aunt Helena, my great-grandmother's sister. She sat upright in a chair, her hands folded on her lap, her heavy body without motion like a model posing for an artist's canvas. A statue carved to imitate life. Her eyes stared into the distance to a place beyond the room where we sat, beyond the walls that framed us. Sadness filled her face and she spoke to no one, her lips sealed into a silence that followed her gaze. I tugged at someone's sleeve to ask why she looked like that, and I understood that her son had not returned from the war, that his body could not be found, that she mourned in that space between loss and hope. My Aunt Helena had entered a place from which she could never return. Only her body remained with us as she looked beyond where she sat to see her son, will him home from wherever he had gone missing. Her body carried that loss to her own death.

Her son, my Uncle Wadi, whose name means calm and peaceful, was a doctor who had been called to enter the war like so many young men. My memory recalls only a vague blur of his existence, a brush stroke that suggests a man who carried himself with kindness. I remember him lifting me off the ground for a hug, a gentleness to his embrace. Every family in Egypt lost someone in the war, tearing gaps like open wounds. My uncle's absence became an empty space between his three siblings: my Aunt Alice, my Aunt Vicky, and my Uncle Makram. Two sisters and a brother who inherited their mother's loss. They still speak of him—Wadi, who was lost in the war, whose body was never found, whose mother could never finish mourning, whose success as a doctor was lost. His place in the family remains open as if one day he could still return.

They suspect he was killed by a mine, perhaps in the Sinai desert, his body shattered by the explosion. Aunt Helena continued to hold onto

215

that translucent thread of hope that one day her son might return. Each of his siblings has lived well into their eighties as if he bequeathed his lost years to them. Israel won the six-day war of June 1967, and Egypt's defeat poured into each home, a devastated country losing the Sinai Peninsula, losing the battle to regain the Palestinian homeland, and losing its power as a nation. My parents, like so many others after the war, lost faith in their homeland and looked elsewhere, becoming part of the brain drain that pulled many in Egypt to emigrate and begin new lives in another world. For me, the war of 1967 is marked by the sadness of my Aunt Helena's face, her still body, and her distant gaze, when I understood how far loss can take you, that the living can follow the dead and never return.

H'RINA DETROY

Knot

It wound like a screw grinding its metal threads. Face down, I felt one foot then two as my ribs angled into the floor through the thin foam mattress. Michelle said this was dangerous. I said I'd be fine. My brain was on a slow smolder.

"Alriiight," she said, curling the word and herself out of blame. I couldn't fathom a better idea at the moment. I couldn't fathom much of anything. We were in the guest room of my distant cousin's apartment in Brasilia. Michelle took the bed. I chose the mattress on the floor, craving a plank to stretch the pain balling like hard fruit along my spine.

I was grateful for a bed after forty hours cramped on a freezing bus that cut the ceaseless horizon of Brazil's pampas like a cold bullet. Michelle and I had hopped bus after bus, holed up in hostel after hostel, for the last thirty-five hundred miles since flying from Costa Rica to Caracas a month ago. She was my closest friend, Oregonian, inimitable travel buddy. We had become experts on maximizing travel on a less-than-meager budget, caterpillering in sleeping bags while we hurtled past anonymous stretches of land. We paid for comfier buses with nicer bathrooms, forgoing a real bed for a mobile hostel. Plush seats and air-conditioning hadn't helped however. My head spinning and back aching, sleep had eluded me for over a week.

We were twenty years old, curious, and in search of something—per-spective, enlightenment, freedom, other vague intangibles—but happy enough rambling about wide-eyed, leaving for what was next, movement our constant. Our last stop had been Salvador de Bahia, in the Afro-Bra-zilian state, during the weeklong debauchery of carnaval. We improvised costumes of feathers and baubles, pushed our way through dense crowds, drank, danced and fended off constant demands for *um beijinho* from men who circled Michelle, drawn to the prettiness of her exotic green eyes and fair skin.

"Does that hurt?" Michelle asked, taking careful steps on my back. The knot was wired taut, resisting her entire weight.

"That's good," I said, mouth squished into the mattress and the cool tiled floor pressing against my forehead. Eyes closed, I tried to relax. But the images rushed back: repetitive black lines crawling across a sheet of white, curves and angles growing and retracting, tracing my name. I had tried to explain my strange state to Michelle, but kept it to myself then, afraid to admit I was still trapped in a mental fit, a synaptic fiat. I pushed away the haranguing thought this could be it, that whatever was plaguing me may never come undone.

Our hotel had been a bargain, located on the main drag of the parade where deliriously happy *fogon* music thundered and rattled our room day and night, breaking at seven in the morning only to roar again at noon. In the downtime, Michelle slept but I couldn't, from over-stimulation, insomnia—I didn't know what.

Salvador de Bahia's cobblestone streets charmed us, sloping up esplanades to cliffs overlooking the Atlantic and stretching to infinity. But much of the colonial city hid behind large, ugly wooden planks erected to protect old fountains, churches and municipal buildings from marauders in crowds numbering close to a million. Men watered the planks, their bladders conduits for endless cans of *Brahma*. The stench seared the nostrils. When the thick heat broke, flash floods submerged piss-stained streets faster than they drained. Sudden rivers snaked around our shins. Bahlan kids squealed with laughter, kicking fetid water in our faces.

We were partying so much we didn't realize it wasn't fun. At least I hadn't. Michelle had been freaked out by the crowds, the partying that never ceased, the bat-shit crazy music. She tried to meditate and wanted to retreat to beaches away and empty from the parade. But I was stubborn, on some philosophical bender to embrace chaos, to surrender to the surge of bodies and revelry. To make *carnaval* an action—the *val* of *carne*, a waltz with flesh, to dance with our carnal selves. Salve demons.

I wanted to know my limits, and push beyond them. Then see if I could find my way back. Like a wish granted, I came apart. I stopped drinking when I started slipping, stopped asking where to score ecstasy when I needed not a pill to alter reality. Constantly awake, I felt like I was floating in an endless dream, my head looping images I had spent countless hours drawing in my notebook. Marooned on bus trips or paddling down the Amazon on a riverboat beneath a misting grey-green sky, I practiced a graffiti tag with a black magic marker. I made a motif of my name merging with "rebirth," the word that came to me once in a dream. It was how I survived, I believed, how often I fled and remade myself. The boyfriend I left in Oregon inspired me with his graffiti tag and I carried a sketch he gifted me with, a flurry of arrows, angles and letters that popped three dimensionally. He was loving, artistic, musical, formidably smart and handsome—overwhelmingly perfect.

Inexplicably, my tag stalked me. Fat letters wound round and again in my head, as if demanding completion by jamming all other circuits. The act of thinking had been hijacked: my thoughts—sentences that began as words—concluded in colors, curves and angles, the rest moot, logic scrambled, meaning utterly lost. I started mumbling to myself, then quieted. I couldn't turn it off. *This must be what going insane is like,* the singular idea I could complete from beginning to end.

My back wouldn't give. It was too tight. Michelle was worried. I wanted to shield my cousin Constance from the weirdness I was dealing with. She wanted to tour us around Brasilia, a city built not long ago in the shape of a crucifix. But, a lake made the arms bend like wings, Constance explained, making it resemble more an airplane.

"I'm going to stop now," Michelle sighed. "We can try later." Carefully, she leapt both feet off at once. A loud crack reverberated the length of my spine.

"Oh my god."

"What?! Are you OK?!" she asked, breathless.

I didn't answer. I was in shock. I felt—nothing. I worried immediately that numbness meant something worse. I pushed myself up slowly on my hands, then knees. "I think … it's gone?" I said as I curved my back into an S on one side then the other. "I think it's gone.… It's gone. You did it!"

"Ah, I heard it, too," Michelle said, grinning. "Wow, that was a crack!"

"I can't believe it…" I rose to my feet. I felt the weight of the knot, its wrenching pain, drain away. *Thank you!* I said and hugged her. At that instant, exhaustion swept me. I lowered to the mattress again. Something else was happening: a soothing sensation of warm liquid spread through my neck, shoulders and back. Lying down, my eyelids shuttered.

Fourteen hours of catatonic slumber later, I awoke early on the opposite shore of pain and torment. In post-climatic euphoria, cross-legged on the foam, I watched dust particles swim in a sunbeam as Michelle slept. I was high in a state of bliss and gratitude. I marveled at my father's relatives, how I was safe in Brasilia. They were the German immigrants that went to Chile and Brazil before and after World War II; my Tantes, the sisters of my grandmother with whom she kept regular contact; the families branching out in South America; the daughters and sons, wives and husbands and children that on occasion would make the long flight from the southern hemisphere to visit us in the United States. I was struck with how thousands of miles away, at the mercy of my own undoing, I had family.

And despite the fact that family had been for me a constant source of pain and disappointment. Michelle and I had so many discussions about our families and their secrets. When I talked about my mother, the usual list of offenses hadn't been enough for her. Michelle probed. "But, how can you hate your mother?" she insisted. I was used to explaining away everything, everyone. Somehow I couldn't win this with her and when the conversation slacked, I felt raw.

This was my second time in South America, three years after being a high school exchange student in a small city deep in Argentina—the first salutary taste of distance from family. I returned wanting to see more. In our tiny house in Eugene, days losing their edges to nights softened by shared beers or inexpensive wine, Michelle and I talked about the paradise we'd find in South America. I told myself I was seeking simplicity. Mind humming and lucid, I knew then I had romanticized it all—the cultures, the people and climate. I was seeking more than escape. I craved connection. Basic and umbilical.

I couldn't push away the thought that I had marked for someday, not knowing when or if that someday would arrive: I needed to go to Vietnam, motherland, place of something unspeakable. Maybe I had family there, too, that wanted to know me as much as I needed to know them. That had wondered what came of my mother. Did they know she had two daughters? My mother never mentioned family, our blood on the other side of the globe. Mysteries to me, as with everything else having to do with her. And her mother? My mother believed that she had died, although she didn't say how she knew this. What was my grandmother's name? I scanned my memory—my mother must have told me, right?

How had I lived twenty years and never thought about this family, my relatives who like me, maybe had wondered what happened? I needed to face this. For me. For my mother—*una cascara de mujer*—an empty shell from whom I ran the fastest, her sadness a silent continent. From whom I fled thousands of miles and traced my tag without root, knowing not even my grandmother's name.

Whatever had been dislodged then snapped into place.

TRONI Y. GRANDE

Baba's Pyrogies

Ten years before my mother was born, on the family farm near More-cambe, Alberta, her mother (my Baba) converted with other members of the Ukrainian community to a fundamentalist Protestant church. Baba never learned more than a handful of English phrases during her eighty-one years of life in Canada, neither early on as a settler in the Ukrainian bloc in east-central Alberta; nor later, once Gido (her husband) died and she moved to Edmonton to live with her youngest child, Kalyna (Kathy to us). Baba handed down none of the orthodox traditions—no special dancing, no Easter eggs or pysanka painting, no Christmas feasting in January, no fancy cross-stitched clothing or embroidered linens, no icons or saints to light candles for. Nothing except for maybe the food, whatever was allowable under the Old Testament clean-eating guidelines of her faith. At every family gathering hosted by Auntie Kathy, I came to look for Baba first, found my way into her room beside the kitchen, where she sat curved over her mending or reading her well-worn Bible, blowing out the air with her lips in that peculiar tuneless whistle she had. She would smile when she saw me, hold out her hand, and I would place my finger in her palm for her to cradle there.

Words seldom passed between us, but I knew by heart Baba's two favourite English catch-phrases: *Maybe rain, maybe snow, I dunno*; and *Listen mama, listen dada, God like. No listen, God no like.* The reverent silence surrounding Baba has only deepened through the decades—she died just as I was about to graduate high school. Yet, though I knew her only but slenderly, I have held tight to Baba as my spiritual mentor. Now that I have children of my own, I feel settled enough in my mother's skin to inquire into Baba's story. For it was Baba's spirit that taught us

222

first how to pray, how to suffer, how to love.

After Baba's funeral in Edmonton, before her body was laid to rest in her Beauvallon church cemetery, her surviving offspring gathered in Auntie Kathy's kitchen, a dozen of Baba's children around the big table. My mother was there, with her ashtray and coffee at the end of the table, but she hardly seemed like my mother. At that moment she was Baba's child. Kathy was lying down in Baba's room, finally quiet after hours of tortured keening at the service.

The truth is, I was anxious for some words of wisdom to put closure to this traumatic event, something in keeping with Baba's beliefs. I cannot tell what words of comfort I received then, and what I have created or inherited since, through the layers of myth-making that envelop my grandmother. I want to remember a tribute to Baba, as a scene. I can see myself leaning against the wall with Cousin Ronnie in Auntie Kathy's kitchen, my mom once more a mourning child, the devoted siblings communing around the table. In my wistful memory, Uncle John is about to break into one of his sermons.

"A better woman was never born. Her price above rubies. Christ came to earth to show us God, but she came to show us Christ. Like a sheep before shearers. Always patient, always kind. She hoped all things, endured all things."

Uncle Mike raises his right hand in the air. "You can't believe what she did with those pyrogy," he says. "Remember? A huge batch, she worked all day, she always did, to get them ready. Her fingers to the bone."

"Such a lot of work," says Auntie Zanovia. "It's a really big day."

"I'm telling it," says Uncle Mike, his right hand up again. "I loved pyrogy. But I hated onions. Stinking things, churning my guts inside. That grease she fried them in, that rank smell. Like the stench of the wicked in the nostrils of the Almighty. And Mamo knew, she knew, she always made them for me without onions. My own special pot. Just potatoes, maybe a bit of cheese, never a stinking onion. So that day I came home, and saw, hey, pyrogy! But only one pot, not two, not my own special pot without onions. And then, dear God, forgive me. Remember, how God judged me?"

Everyone's eyes fix on Uncle Mike. He has us now. "The devil entered me," he says. "I took those pyrogy, the ones with onions, the whole steaming pot, marched out the front door, down that little hill beside the chickens where we used to dump the slop, and I poured all of 'em, every single one with every stinking slippery onion, right on the ground."

Everyone is silent, heads bowed. Finally, Uncle Nestor, staring down at the table, breaks the silence. "How many? How many?—did you dump in the slop."

Uncle Mike purses his lips, his large hands clasped together. Uncle Alec shakes his head, answers for Mike. "Maybe a hundred, maybe two hundred, three hundred, maybe more."

"Rolling, pinching, pleating, that tiny kitchen, that hot summer day," Auntie Vicki says, looking as though she would bolt up from the table any minute. "You're lucky you're not my son."

Uncle Mike's nostrils flare.

Cousin Ronnie stiffens beside me, inhales sharply. He pipes up, in a smaller voice than I've ever heard from him, "What did Baba do?"

Uncle Mike lifts his chin. "That's the point, *malenkyy*," he says, "The point of the story. Did you think it was about me? No. It's about your Baba. She watched me in the doorway, saw all those pyrogy pouring down in the slop beside the chickens. Then she just bent her finger for me to come in. I was still boiling, like a wet hen. I took big long strides into the kitchen, pushed that empty pot right at her. She looked at me without one speck of anger, set the pot down. Then do you know what she did? She pointed to the counter behind the stove, and what did I see? A pot, my special pot sitting there, and inside, my own special pyrogy, the way I like 'em. Not one cursed onion. Me like a wet hen, and her just touching my arm, pointing."

I sneak a look at Ronnie. He has bowed his head and is shaking it. "Poor Babka," he says, half under his breath. "Such a hard life." His eyes are pinched tightly shut. Awkwardly, I take his hand and pat it. I don't know what else to say.

Decades later, something about the scene rings false. I still need to know, how it all really happened. What is Baba's portion? Is it really this extravagance, this waste of sacrifice poured out for us beside the chickens?

Late one Sunday evening, I've just closed the kids' bedroom doors, praying my nightly prayer that they will settle down to sleep, and I muster up the energy to return my mother's phone call. This is the way I channel Baba now. Contact with my mother has become more precious, like a key that could open the murky unlocked mystery of all my past lives. I want all the colour and texture of that history, now that it is almost gone. Those Lakustas are a dying breed, only five of them left now. With every funeral, more stories are getting buried forever. But Mom isn't always in the mood to dig up her family again. So I decide to ask her about something more innocuous, the word itself—*Pyrogies*.

I could never in a hundred years learn to make pyrogies like Baba. When Baba was visiting, she'd surprise us. Except we always knew the surprise was coming, and it was the same every time. We'd come home from school, and on the lucky surprise day she'd be waiting for us at the top of the stairs as we opened the back door. Stooped over, leaning on her cane, she wore the tea towel on her head like a crown, covering the silver silk of her hair and signifying Pyrogy Day. My mother could never help make them because she was always at work herself. And she never taught me. She said it took all day to make them, and twenty minutes to eat them, so it wasn't worth it. Not that I blame her. My mother had to work her fingers to the bone to put food on the table for us. We were fine with whatever we could scarf down.

I've searched for Baba's pyrogies all these years. My heart leapt when I first saw the sign for the Ukrainian Co-op here in town. I finally got around to stopping in, in the hope of buying pyrogies like Baba's, maybe even in bulk. Imagine my letdown when all I could find were the frozen ones. "Auntie Kathy's" brand! But practically the same as Cheemo. The old ways are gone, and Cheemo it is. What puzzles me, with my sorry lack of Ukrainian, is that one package says *pyrogy*, and another says *pyrogies*.

So I ask, "What do you say, Mom—*pyrogy* or *pyrogies?* I keep seeing both."

"Oh, I dunno." I can just see her on the other end, pursing her lips and squeezing her eyebrows into the centre of her face, the way she does when she's concentrating.

"Hmmm, Pyrogy, I guess," she finally says. "Or pyrogies. Whichever. We say both. Or *pedahey*, that too." Across the miles I can see her shrug her shoulders, raise her eyebrows. "When the kids were little, we just called them *dumplings*. Remember? Maybe that's easiest."

As usual, she only adds another layer of mystery. I bring up the story of Baba's pyrogies, that scene that I remember, in that mythical way. I ask her, was she actually there; does she remember it that way too?

My mother falls silent. It makes me nervous when she does that. But mothering teenagers has taught me how to persist, angling for some crumb of truth.

"What a hard lot Baba had," I say. "Did she really make all those pyrogies by herself?"

"No-ooo. No, she didn't," my mother replies. "Everybody helped. Whoever was in the kitchen."

"Like an assembly line, you mean, everyone in a row?"

"Well, no, just whoever was there. Some to peel the potatoes, boil them, mash them; some to make the dough, roll it out, cut it in circles with a can. You'd make 'em into little balls and somebody would flatten them all out. Baba sat in the middle, for the final step. She'd take the little circle of dough in her hand with that scoopful of whatever, pinch the dough over it good and tight, and then pinch again, three times back and forth, forth and back, like that, you've got to do that so the filling won't come out."

I picture them all in the kitchen. I smell the sweet onions frying, feel on my teeth and tongue the smooth, warm layers of the pyrogy edges. Then I recall the discarded pyrogies, tumbling down in the slop. Baba's cherished face, so unlike my mother's. Placid, unruffled. Waiting on the front step for the wayward son.

"Was that a true story, the one Uncle Mike told?"

"Yuh, he really dumped them out. The curious thing is that Mom never even got mad. She said, 'I saved some for you. They're in there.'"

"Really!" I'm stumped. "She spoke? For some reason I thought she never spoke."

"Oh no, she spoke. She knew how to speak, believe me. She had no trouble letting us know when we did something wrong."

"But she never got mad, right?"

"Oh she got mad all right. Mad at me, plenty. Just not at the boys. They liked Vicki too, Mom and Dad did. And Kathy. They had their favourites. I left home and no-one really missed me that much. It's kinda done. Each generation tries to do better. Sometimes it turns out very fortunate. You've improved on your parents; if your kids improve on you, well then you've been very very extremely fortunate."

I write down these words from my mother, faithfully fastening on her idioms, like a chain of pearls, for this is the moment now, to fasten on present truth. But where is the truth of Baba's story? I conjure up the image of her on the farm, when awful Uncle Syl was raging. He was the one who drank, who kept her longer on her knees than all her other children. A couple of years ago Auntie Kathy told me that sometimes on the farm Baba bit her own hand—the hand that fed them—when they wouldn't listen to her. This revenge on her own skin, was it Baba's way of heroically marking herself, moving beyond the role of victim? Or was it her way of performing the victim to perfection, folding in on herself to feel every nerve and sinew in the temple of her spirit? The story of Baba keeps building, layer upon layer. Has she risen already, beyond the story of sacrifice?

A few years ago, another layer of truth about Baba surfaced, something none of us could ever have imagined. I didn't learn about it till my mother asked me to take a day, and head up to the farm, just the two of us.

The landscape of history shifts as eerily as the Northern Lights flashing green and purple across the dark summer sky up in this part of the world. The way back is much changed. The thousands of wooden grain elevators are almost extinct, and the very highway itself from Red Deer to Edmonton, like the superhighways down East, is now limited-access, cut off from the towns, cities, and farms that once served as stopping-places on the C and E Trail. In places, you can still glimpse the old highway, built on the Trail, and imagine the railroad carrying settlers like my grandparents up to Fort Edmonton—in summer through windstorms, clouds of dust and mosquitoes; in winter through searing cold and mountains of snow—see them disembarking from the train, weighed down by their sheepskin coats and heavy trunks with all their worldly possessions, a bag of seed from the Old Country in their pocket, as they make their way with wandering steps and slow to the promised land.

We took our time back to the farm, Mom and I, wanting to revisit all the old shrines. There, in Vegreville, was the giant Pysanka, the Easter Egg so alien to my mother's unorthodox traditions, and the restaurant in the middle of town where we used to stop for orange milkshakes and French Fries. There on the main street of Two Hills, with its tiny erstwhile hospital—a museum now—Gido's heart pumped for the last time before its final arrest. There the graves of Baba and Gido, and all the other relatives asleep in the Lord, rest in the Lakusta section of the little Beauvallon Seventh-Day Adventist cemetery, a stone's throw beyond the mustard church where Baba worshipped in the prime of her life.

We stopped in to visit a Ukrainian widow born just a few years after Baba. There on her neighbouring farm, this little woman, bright-eyed and wiry, maintained an immaculate modernized kitchen, and prepared before us a table of cabbage rolls, salad, pickles, thick slices of fresh bread, foamy glasses of milk. And chicken feet, a farm delicacy I've never understood. They look so sad, vulnerable, irretrievably detached, like children's feet that could be walking around but never will again. My mother took one, but I couldn't stomach the idea, much less the sight of them gnawing and nibbling the flesh off the bony digits.

The neighbor and my mother talked in spotty Ukrainian, my mother lapsing into English from time to time, enough so that I could tell they were talking about my grandmother. The widow kept shaking her grey head, pressing her palms together.

"What was that all about?" I asked my mother, after we'd said our goodbyes and got into the car again. My mother sat for a moment with the key in the ignition. Then she said, "Apparently, Baba and Gido were never married."

"What!" I stared at my mother's profile. "What do you mean? They're joined in death as in life! We just saw it at their graves—one stone for both. *Lakusta. Blessed are the pure of heart for they shall see God.*"

"Well, they might have *lived* like they were married, but actually they never were." My mother turned to look at me, her hands on the steering wheel. "Mrs. Elko says everyone knew it, the whole community."

"But they lived together for sixty years or more!"

"Yuh," my mother said, nodding. "They just never got the certificate, the piece of paper. So in the eyes of the government and the church they're not married. The gravestones don't tell the whole story."

My mother backed the car out of the driveway, and proceeded down the narrow road, more like a lane now. Her eyes were fixed on the furrows ahead. The bushes on either side of the road were so overgrown that only a narrow strip remained for cars to drive down. And the ditches were deep, full of tall brush. If another car should chance to meet us, there wouldn't even be room to turn around.

My mother's Taurus was not taking the bumps well. "Well, what *is* the story?" I asked, as I gripped the plastic armrest to steady myself.

"I guess Baba's parents wanted her to marry another guy," my mother said, "A farmer in these parts. That's what Mrs. Elko says. They had it all arranged, but Mom ran away from him, the other one, and then she had to run away from her parents, because they disapproved of Gido. They threatened to disown her. Somehow she never could marry Gido. She must have been too young, underage, and needed their consent. Which they never gave. So she just stayed with him, all those years like that." My mother shrugged.

"But—but—Baba always told us, Listen to your parents. *Listen mama, listen dada, God like. No listen, God no like.* I can't believe she would do that, disobey them like that. Would she?"

"I guess they were in love."

I paused, not knowing what to say. It seemed preposterous. The bends in the road were starting to look more familiar now.

"Not a word, never a word about this. To find out from the neighbours, yet! What a disgrace." My mother set her mouth in a thin line. Now she needed comfort, and I would have to give it.

"Is it really that big a deal?" I ask. "I mean it's a surprise, sure, but these days wouldn't we just call them common-law? They *did* for each other and with each other, so weren't they partners in every sense of the word?"

"Maybe," said my mother, "But not to be married in the eyes of the church—any church—not to have any record of your parents' marriage— Yeah, that's kinda a big deal. What does that make us, their children—not even legitimate. There's a word for that! And the secret. Why keep the secret from us? We thought she was better than that."

Suddenly it all seemed so shaky, all of Baba's life, the sacrifices, Bible-reading, endless hours on her knees, on our knees. And here she is, running into the arms of Gido, another man, not approved. That's a story with no beginning.

I pushed my mother for details. "Do you think that's why she was praying all the time, and trying to be so good? Do you think she felt, like, *guilty,* for this great sin?"

"I dunno," said my mother. "It's a mystery."

"Why would she continually tell us, 'Listen mama, listen dada, God like'?" I wondered. "Sheer hypocrisy!"

"One person's hypocrisy—another person's humanity," my mother said. She can be quite profound at times.

Along the roadway, on our left-hand side, a gap was opening up in the jagged line of bushes. The entrance to the farm, after all these years! How inconspicuous it seemed.

I watched my mother's farm-girl hands grip the steering-wheel, as fierce and coarse as when she used to pull me to her side when we crossed the street in heavy traffic. She steered the Taurus off the gravel road, and we braced ourselves against the shockwaves of overgrown grasses that we knew led back to the Lakusta homestead.

"You know," she said, her hands firmly on the wheel, "I think they really did love each other."

My mind boggled as images of Gido entered me, against my will. Whisky on his breath, hairy and husky as a giant up a beanstalk! My grandfather? Capable of loving, and being loved!

We jostled over the deep ruts in what used to be the road in and out of there. My mother's hands shook as the car ploughed the waist-high grass and came to a standstill in front of the abandoned farmhouse. We sat there for a long time, staring in disbelief.

The house was leaning in on itself like an old woman's mouth. The shingles, stained a rich chestnut brown, had given way to striations of white and black and beige, and like long teeth from ebbing gums had pulled away from the poplar logs underneath. You could see now that the buildings, the house and the sheds beyond, were sticks, pure and simple. Every door, slanted, pushed in on the walls, as the uncultured grassland encroached to occupy the space. The porch was gone. Bushes were growing up in front of the house, as high as the broken windows. The roof was full of lichen, like a sweater unraveling and bunching up to the nub.

Quackgrass, weeds, and clover, with a shock of purple thistle, grew up together in front of the rough-hewn door, still miraculously square on its iron hinges, bearing without bending the mark of all the elements. You could pick out each delicate strand of uncultivated wheat, curling this way and that. Red Fife, it's called, named after a Scotsman; but the Ukrainian settlers, the Galicians who carried the seeds in their pockets from the Old Country, *they* knew it as Halychanka.

No glass remained in the window at the top of the door, just a few stalks growing high enough to peak through the open barrier between inside and outside. The whitewash plaster was disintegrating, pulling away like gnarled fingers from the walls, and the colours underneath appeared in eggshell watercolour—robin's blue, aquamarine green, salmon pink, gold ore. On the wall a calendar, Atlas-like, held up a world that had refused time's ravages—a mountain lake, jagged peaks and looming evergreens, an eagle arrested in mid-flight. Alberta Wheat Pool, September 1967. The page curled brown like the opening clip of our favourite TV show on Sunday evenings when we were kids. *Bonanza.* Phases of the moon marked the page, first to last quarter, new moon. Sundays in green, other days in black. *30 days hath September.*

An old black boot minus its laces, twisted up into a loop, rested on the crumbling windowsill, wide open to the gusts of wind that sweep across these feral pastures.

My mother and I could not bear to stop long inside the house. For one thing, it wasn't safe. The floor was covered with twigs, leaves, debris blown in by the wind; droppings from bird, bat, mouse, and creatures I wouldn't know; odd old papers from God knows where. The furniture in both rooms, now stripped of its function, lay underneath a filthy layer of black dust.

The open door of the window brought a sudden gust barreling into this great room, which was once kitchen, dining room, father's bedroom. We covered our mouths with our sleeves, as flyers and testaments to past lives swirled in front of us. Down where the lane used to be, I could see the sheds open and empty of grain, toppled like rowboats plunged in a turbulent sea of jello. Tall grasses grew halfway up the doors that no longer served as barriers.

There was life here once. The words enter me, not a thought but a tremor, a shaking knowledge, the present truth I have been seeking. These spaces meant something to someone. This was the home where Gido and Baba conceived, delivered, said good-bye to their thirteen children, where they buried one who never made it through the winter.

We stand on the gentle rise just beyond where the chicken coops used to be. "He never stopped wanting her, you know," my mother says. "He used to call for her, from where he slept on the bed in the kitchen. She would be sleeping with us in the other room, and he'd call out in the night, 'Zina, bring me a cup of cold water. Frozina, some water.' She'd get out of bed, go in there, to him. Then we'd hear them, together, late into the night, doing what married folk do."

I shake my head, turning to look at my mother. "What! He *forced* her? Couldn't she say no?"

"It wasn't like that," my mother says. "When I left home, at the beginning, I'd come back sometimes on the weekend. It was just the two of them alone together then. All those kids had cleared out. And you could tell they wanted it that way. She'd be mad at me for coming. You don't have to be a genius to know when you're wanted, and when you're not. She just didn't want me there. Then, into the night, I'd hear them, giggling with each other, wrestling on that ancient bed in the kitchen. But so stupid, when the kids were small, to ask for a cup of cold water. Always—'Zina, bring me some water.' Tsk. We all knew, we could hear them, what they were up to."

I stand there with my mother, both of us looking back at the house, quiet, resting, not knowing what to say. For once, I am seized with relief, that I cannot make sense of it all. *Maybe rain, maybe snow, I dunno.*

Was this love, what happened in that house, with any of them? I am no closer to knowing my grandmother, no closer to knowing myself, than I was in those darkened rooms, with my fingers resting in her cushioned palm.

But when I stretch my arms out to welcome it, the wind comes. Billowing up, touching me, bending me even, into the tall and unkempt grasses, the wild borrowed wheat, the stippled blue of the sky, the earthy tenacity of this sacred place, here and now, at my mother's side.

HEIDI CZERWIEC

My Son's Brother

When I was young, I checked out armfuls of Choose Your Own Adventure books from the library, ten or so at a time. Reading them the way I did required athletic, agile hands. I wanted to keep all options, all avenues open. Every time a choice presented itself, I inserted a finger in that page so I could retrace my steps, follow each narrative path the book offered. The stories, with their endless turns, required every digit I could deploy, and often I'd end up forced to flip pages with my nose or chin. In this garden of forking paths, my fingers were threads I followed back to the plot so I could always take the road not taken. I couldn't stand the idea of a choice, any choice, being closed to me, so I read on with sprained, spraddled fingers.

***

By the time Wyatt has reached six months, I finally lose the feeling that choosing to raise him has been a mistake. I fantasize less about the social worker, at our once-monthly post-placement meetings, snatching Wyatt away from us and declaring me unfit. Less about turning him back in to the agency before the adoption is made formally legal. Less about telling Jodi, who watches Wyatt three afternoons a week, who adores him and is also waiting to adopt, here—take him. *He'd be better off with you.*

I hate myself for writing those things just now. Of course I would never have done any of them. I love Wyatt. When not in the same room with him, I obsess over him, hunger to hold him again. Plus, surrender was not an option—if I had given him back, I couldn't have lived without him, couldn't have lived with myself or the look on my husband's face. So my only choice was the weird, twilight half-life I found myself living.

233

And it was hard, the kind of hard few want mothers to admit to. Months of midnight feedings that bled into the dark days of a North Dakota winter, months of feeling isolated with an infant while my husband got to escape to the adult world of work, months of growing distrust at my nascent mothering skills. Constantly running up- and downstairs and forgetting to eat except in the odd free moment caused me to drop twenty pounds. As a result, on the rare occasion that I was out in public, people would comment that I looked great, that parenting seemed to agree with me—I glared back, sure they were fucking with me. My writer-friends with new babies both had recently-accepted book manuscripts—publications that would help them ride out the dry spell of those early mothering months. My manuscript languished in the lists of eternal semifinalists—always a bridesmaid. And because I wrote no new poems in the meanwhile, I had nothing to send out. Facebook posts of friends' publishing triumphs seemed to gloat, though I tried to muster enthusiasm. But these feelings, dark as they were, were not unusual among new mothers, especially writer-moms. So why was I special?

Because the worst part was all the deliberate choice that went into being Wyatt's mom. One does not accidentally adopt. There are no surprise adoptions. There is the nearly year-long process of interviews and back-ground checks and psych evals and medical checkups and examinations of finances. Weekends of parenting workshops where we reconditioned ourselves away from fraught phrases: not "give up for adoption" but "choose adoption." Not "your birthmother was bad," but "your birthmother made bad choices." Always the emphasis on the choices, made and unmade.

And all that even before we got cleared to appear in The Book: a collection of profiles (both in binders and online) from which birthmothers make their selection. Many of the profiles had a scrapbook-crafty look—fun fonts and pictures with pinked edges mounted on novelty papers—and featured North Dakota couples and their values: mostly sports, hunting, large extended families, pets as surrogate children. Having so many choices can be a burden. How would we stand out? As a couple with five English degrees between us (three in creative writing), we treated the profile like the high-stakes rhetorical assignment it was: we drafted and redrafted, crafting a narrative that emphasized the heroic birthmother ("you") and her brave choices, inviting her to picture her child in the home and life we described. We were empathetic, fun, educated without sounding elitist, even funny. We hired a photographer friend to shoot unphotogenic us looking as comfortable and warm as possible. We submitted the profile and we waited.

As it turns out, we didn't wait long. The average is a year from when a couple enters The Book; we waited three months before a birthmother chose our profile and her social worker contacted us to set up a meeting. The social worker gave us a thumbnail sketch of the birthmother: white, twenty-three years old, single mother of a three-year-old daughter, seventeen weeks pregnant by an unknown father—she believed she'd been roofied at a party. Had not had a drink since discovering she was pregnant, was still trying to stop smoking. Did we want to meet with her? We did. Now, because the father's unknown, it could be a mixed-race baby. Did we have a problem with that? We did not. You sure? We're sure.

We drove to Bismarck, eight hours round-trip across flat, broad swathes of brown farmland stippled green with seedlings under an endless sky of oppressive blue—after Fargo, nothing to punctuate the landscape except the occasional grain elevator, cryptic exit signs with names like "Buffalo/ Alice," and towns a hundred miles apart. In town, we found the building, an odd, squat cylinder that looked like an old paint can, and made our way through the offices, beigely outdated, to a meeting room where we waited, anxious. Then, Kinzey: a sweet and confused girl with huge brown eyes, liquid behind thick glasses, so shy and ashamed she had brought her best friend to do most of the talking. A lapsed Catholic, she couldn't bring herself to get an abortion, though her friend had offered to help pay and to drive her the two hundred miles to the only clinic serving three states. I didn't know what to say—as a feminist, I supported any decision she would have made, but I was so glad she had chosen to carry this baby, maybe for us.

We let the friend ask questions, but addressed our answers to Kinzey. I let fly a well-timed f-bomb calculated to put her at ease, to win her over—her brown eyes widened, and she laughed in surprise. By the end of the meeting, she had chosen us to parent her child—a son, we soon found out, when she invited us to her ultrasound appointment a week later. A son whose birth we would miss, six months later when, just after midnight on New Year's, my phone rang and Kinzey's friend told us *hurry, he's coming fast* and fast we drove but didn't go as far as Fargo before she texted us pictures of our perfect, angry red boy.

So someone specifically chose me: to mother her child, to give him the life she wanted for herself, wanted to give him before she thought *I can't raise this child,* and then gave him by giving him up. I try to live up to the weight of her choice, to deserve her son. Now, after six difficult months of wondering if I could raise him, I begin to believe I can. The warm sun returns to the High Plains, and Wyatt and I spend afternoons on a quilt in the park. I am finally fluent in his cries, his noises, his rudimentary communications. I plan classes for the fall semester, simultaneously ecstatic to be engaging my brain again, and guilt-ridden over Wyatt starting daycare in a month.

When adoption day comes, I can testify, truthfully, in court, that I want to be Wyatt's mother. We have kept texting with Kinzey both in the months before and after his birth (always texting—she's too shy to call and talk), and pay for gas and hotel so that she can be part of the big day. We celebrate with pictures outside the courthouse and brunch downtown.

That fall, with its adjustments to our family schedule, especially me returning to work, is difficult, but we start to make sense of it, to make plans for our future—I apply for sabbatical leave to finish a poetry project, my husband for law school. Kinzey, working full-time and working at an associate's degree, keeps up with us through sporadic texts. One night while clearing up after supper, my phone vibrates with a message from her:

So some unexpected news im pregnant its a real shock.

I respond with alarm and worry, for which she is grateful. More than anything she fears being judged, and I try hard not to do that to her. But I admit it: my first reaction is disappointment. One of the outcomes of us adopting Wyatt is a second chance for her—to stay employed, finish a degree, and get control of her life. Then she texts

Im choosing adoption again after seeing what a gift it was to you. You are the best parents i could have found for my baby. I dont know if i will find anyone like you.

A few texts later, it creepingly occurs to me that she's hoping for us to offer to take on this child as well. My gut seizes up. Another baby? We didn't plan on a second. I've almost made it through the first year with the first. I do some quick math and estimate that she'll be due around March or April—meaning two babies under the age of a year and a half. My insides curl tighter. I text back something like, *Wow, this is a lot to deal with. I'm glad adoption was such a good experience for all of us. I hope the right decision will be obvious. Let us know how you are, and what you choose. We love you.* Then I call my husband into the kitchen, show him my phone, the exchange of messages.

Over the next few days, Evan and I huddle together in bed and over coffee and picked-at meals, our thoughts running back and forth, hard and fast. *We can't take this baby. I barely made it through the last year—I don't know if I can do it again. What about law school? What about the poetry project? We gave away all the baby stuff Wyatt's already outgrown. I bet we could get it back. Where would we even put another baby? I guess the baby would be in our room for a while, but then would have to share a room with Wyatt.* Now we're imagining logistics, picturing the new baby already in our home, in our lives. *But what about our plans? We'll have to put them off by at least a couple years.* We don't need to ask how we'll afford another adoption process—we have enough, a sum we've stockpiled in anticipation of losing Evan's salary when he leaves his job for law school. And because she's choosing us outside the negotiations of the agency, it will be treated as an "identified adoption," where the adoptive parents know the birth-mother, a process more streamlined, fast-tracked, less expensive. Is being in a position to pay a blessing, or an obligation? *But the cost of another child? That's twice the cost for everything. How would another baby affect the life we want to provide for Wyatt? He wouldn't have as many comforts, but then again, he would have a sibling, his sibling. We never planned on adopting another child. This isn't just another child. This is Wyatt's sibling. If we were the ones who had a surprise pregnancy, a second child we weren't planning on, we'd find a way to absorb it. Does that mean we should, that we have to, absorb Kinzey's bad choices? If we don't, how could we explain to him that we had the chance to adopt his sister or brother, but didn't? But our plans, our plans!* Mornings, I take care of Wyatt, picture trying to keep up with his rapidly expanding repertoire of activities, but once again horribly sleep-deprived, newborn in tow.

I send panicky messages to my guru, another adoptive mother and writer with whom I'd bonded over the previous months. *Two kids under a year and a half! I already feel like I'll never get any writing done ever again. And yet, and yet, and yet. Tell me I'm not a horrible person if I don't take on this baby.*

She quickly responds: *Heidi, it sounds like your gut is telling you that you and Evan can't do this, and feel good about what you can give Wyatt. There's a happy medium between wresting babies away from teenage girls like in the '60s and having a person with lifelong problems fall in your lap as an adult, almost like you adopted Kinzey. You did not adopt Kinzey. You are not responsible for her life and her choices.*

The word "choice" has been around since prehistory, but before the Renaissance, it mostly referred to matters of taste, of preference. The sense of weighing alternative courses of action doesn't really come about until humanity had begun to lose its fatalistic worldview, its sense of predestination.

Over the next week, Evan spends a lot of time pacing the back deck, on the phone with his friends. I sit awake in the dark, feeding Wyatt his midnight bottle, wondering how much longer we will use his bottle-warmer, a hand-me-down on its last legs that burns any stray dribbles of formula to fumes of weird chemical caramel. We worry that we can't say no. We worry that we can't say yes. We worry that Kinzey will become too dependent on us, that she'll rely on us as the answer to all her mistakes. Most people regard choice as a good thing, but the weight of choosing, of the fear of regret, can become paralyzing. Over that week, Kinzey continues to text us, her hints becoming broader, becoming pleas.

And here's the hard thing: this choice is really mine. Evan has always rolled with changes —absorbed them, planned around them, moved forward. But since I'm the one who's borne the brunt of childcare, since this will affect me more, Evan defers to me. He's gracious enough to support me, to call my decision ours, but if we're honest, this is my call.

So finally, we circle back to our initial reaction: *We can't raise this baby,* which is a kinder way of admitting *I don't want to.* We slide our fingers from the page, unmark that path, never to follow that narrative. We text Kinzey to say, gently, that we're sure she'll make another set of parents as happy as she's made us. As soon as we send it, we feel relief. As soon as we send it, we feel sad.

Choice can be an illusion: choosing a course does not mean control over that course. And you never choose only your own adventure. Kinzey, who had never been particularly regular in her correspondence, becomes nonresponsive. We guess that she's sad too, probably hurt—we are the latest in a lifetime of rejections. Feeling guilty, not sure how to feel or what right we have to feel it, we don't do as much as we might to keep up communications. We justify the lapse as giving her space to process this new pregnancy and adoption, to allow her time to be wooed by a new adoptive family. Growing up, no one ever praised her or told her she was special—she had positively glowed under the attention we gave her. We hope she's getting that from someone else.

About a week before she gives birth, she surfaces, and starts responding to texts again, dropping what seem like careless little bombs as though she's corresponded with us all along – it's a boy, she's told us that, right? and oh, hasn't she told us the adoptive parents live in the same town as us? And then after the birth, she fades in and out, surfacing at times to request a visit, then canceling as the trip approaches. We feel sadness, relief.

Guilt, curiosity, self-torture—we are dying to know more about this boy, our son's half-brother. We contact our adoption social worker, the woman who checked on us after Wyatt's placement, who handles all placements for our area. We tell her we want to be in communication with his half-brother's family, offer our contact info, request that they keep in touch. She passes along our info, and reports that while the family is willing, they're a bit overwhelmed with a newborn at the moment, and with establishing a relationship with Kinzey, who apparently had waited until late in the pregnancy to choose a family (hoping we would change our minds?). They ask for space.

But over the next few months, every time we're out in public, I look for new babies who resemble Kinzey and Wyatt—in North Dakota, towheads are the norm, so I study the dark-haired infants, search for the characteristic dimples, the softly cleft chin. Around their own adoption day at six months, we send congratulations, with pictures of Wyatt at that age and a description of his personality—his love of books, pickles, tacos, singing surprisingly in tune at the top of his lungs —hoping the comparison will intrigue them. We have yet to hear from them.

We—I—had a choice, and I said no. And my no continues to disturb me. Whom might I have harmed by my choice? Not us. My drought ends: my book is published and I write a new poetry manuscript that excites me. Evan ends his first year of law school at the top of his class and secures a lucrative clerkship. Not the new baby who, no doubt, is happily exploring solid foods and solid footing somewhere in my town.

Wyatt? *What would Wyatt's life have been like with a brother* I wonder, when he tugs on my hand while I'm cooking, desperate for a playmate. When my sister-in-law drops the news that next year, their daughter is going to have a new little sister. When Jodi brings her own adopted son Eli over to play and the boys clamber on the furniture, the stairs, laughing and shoving, ignoring boundaries the way brothers do.

It's said you can't choose your family, but that's not true—ours involved more choice than most. Our son had little say in any of it, but I don't know if or how much this will hurt him. As an adoptive parent, I'm preparing—as much as one can through workshops and roleplaying and readings—for the inevitable questions he will ask us: *Why didn't my mom keep me? How do I know you'll keep me? Who was my father?* And I've tried to collect information for when he asks about other family, for if he chooses to get in touch, to ask them for answers I can't give him. I'm preparing to deal with his hurt.

But Kinzey's hurt is plain. What does it mean that I said *no* to her, a girl who said yes to us in the biggest, most unimaginably beautiful way possible?

I'm grateful for today's model of open adoption, for humane communication to replace the wrenching away of babies from anonymous mothers. But it visits its own hurts. At some point, our love and nurturing of the birthmother is revealed as a sort of performance to gain the agency's approval, to elicit her yes. An illusion exposed by its eventual limits. Open adoptions prolong the contact until new and different disappointments are probable, inevitable. Even under this new system, where it seems the birthmother makes all the choices, pain is still the price she pays for her mistakes—some in the old expected ways, some entirely unanticipated. Some in which I've participated.

Kinzey had choices; Kinzey had babies. She chose us and we said *yes.* Then, we—I—said no. I owe it to her to own it.

MARILYN MORIARTY

Swerves

A pack of runners catches up with me on the sidewalk as I wait for the light in St. Germaine des Prés. They jog in place, a kaleidoscope of black pants and arm bands measuring heartbeats, steps or calories. The light changes. The runners acknowledge my existence only by the swerve my presence puts in their path, moving around me like they were fish and I was a reef. Their swerve brings to mind my cousin Annie's question to me, Annie, the daughter of my mother's sister, Annie who speaks no English, who is my age, who loves to read historical novels about George Sand and the queens of France. I have just come from her home in Orléans.

"What does being half French mean to you?" translated her bilingual husband, Christian. There was a deeper question here. I am adopted. I do not have genes from French parents but my mother (my adoptive mother, the only one I ever knew) was French. Shed blood forms the dark communion wine of French history. "Look here": Annie's genealogical tree traced both sides of the family through the seventeenth century. Several relatives stand out by the legend, "*Mort pour la France.*" Died for their country. Everyone there has been vetted.

My answer: "If our identity has to do with the way we narrate our lives, then being French is central to the way that I narrate my life."

Crap. Lousy answer. Too postmodern chic, even for me.

Now I am walking the streets in Paris trying to understand something about the culture bequeathed to me by a woman long dead and something about the family who accepts me as French, or half-French, or as their American relative.

Andrée died when I was fourteen. She rarely spoke of the prison camps. No document, no identity card, no photograph precedes 1946, the year she married, as if the rest of her history dissolved the day she married an American Army officer. She was twenty when the Germans moved into Paris, twenty-two when caught by the Gestapo, deported to Germany at twenty-three, worked in prisons until she came home at twenty-five. Annie and Christian did not know their aunt went to prison for three years. The living remembered only that Andrée was gone a long, long time. Anyone who knew something is dead.

On the map Paris resembles an *escargot*. Twenty boroughs (*arrondisements*) curl, shell-like, three revolutions inside the external boundary of the Periphérique motorway. The Seine River skewers the snail, creating two banks, one north of the river (Right Bank) and one south (Left Bank). The bull's eye of Paris lies on the island in the Seine, the Île de la Cité, where Notre Dame Cathedral stands. A long time ago, the Île de la Cité and the Île Saint-Louis were inhabited by a river-going people, the Parisii, who used boats to travel. They called their outpost by a (probably) Celtic word meaning "marsh" or "muddy." With Julius Caesar's conquest of Gaul in 53 B.C.E. the area became Romanized. Caesar's *The Gallic Wars* is famous for its famous opening line, "All Gaul is divided into three parts." The Celts, who inhabited the third part, the Romans called Gauls. As the Romans circulated the Parisii toponym "Leuk Tin" in their Roman accent, it became Lutece, or, in French, Lutetia.

Lutetia became Paris in 360 A.D. when the Roman emperor Julian changed the city's name to *Civitas Parisiorum,* City of the Parisii. The originary Celtic name of Paris remains conserved by the Hotel Lutetia, the first luxury hotel in the Left Bank. Like others of its kind, this art deco building resembles a stone, wood and glass Napoleon, not only in its design, but in its siting, with tiers lining up with surrounding buildings. Squatting on a corner with front entrances on two streets, the location made it attractive to the German *Abwehr*, which requisitioned the hotel during the war; and then, with a twist of delicious irony, De Gaulle made the hotel the meeting place for returning refugees after the war.

When Christian asked me, "How did Veale and Andrée meet?" I remembered something about a function organized by the Red Cross.

"*Croix-rouge!*" Annie said. "Hotel Lutetia? Hotel Lutetia!"

"We just saw a movie," Christian explained.

My mother did not die for her county but she went to German prisons for the French resistance. Her life always seemed to me something hollowed by war, a mise en abyme swallowed up in its zero point. She died at the young age of forty-seven. In my own mind and heart, she died for "la France."

"Don't ever leave your country," Andrée told me once, even though she received American citizenship, all of us going to the ceremony and waving small flags on sticks. "I am a citizen," she said, "but if there was a war with France…"—she would go back to fight for France against the *États-Unis* is what she means, in her broken English learned from watching the television. That was my country—*Ay-tah Zuni* is how I heard it.

In the *Aytah-Zuni,* she played opera and Edith Piaf torch songs. She kept her culture alive in a small bag of water like an aquarium fish, and then she died in a Florida bungalow surrounded by kids who ate Reese's Cups, jawbreakers, Sweet Tarts, and drank Coke. She cooked gourmet cuisine for a family that thought Hardees hamburgers were a treat, this woman who lived in times so hard her lunch was a boiled carrot on a piece of bread with mustard. Andrée would fight for France if forced to take sides; of course, she would. Even if she was an American citizen.

She longed for France like a murdered lover.

To be French: it is to take a position. To take a position in language. I know the good names and the bad names: love De Gaulle, hate Hitler. To be French is to be like Paris, the human embodiment of duality: two sides split by a river, two sides joined by bridges.

Is to inhabit the world as a creature of internal differences.

It is to be connected to a war.

I walk days through the streets of Paris, into the twisting alleys of the Latin quarter, down the long tree-lined boulevards designed by Haussmann at the turn of the century, into the corners of the Marais, up and down the caged steps of the Tour Eiffel. Memory and imagination are powered by the same neurons; my legs are mapping a city inside my brain. Perhaps, this way, I can make it mine.

What does it mean to me to be half French? I actually have no idea.

Maybe it behooves me to become a tourist for a day. I take the number sixty-nine bus to the Pere Lachaise cemetery in the twentieth. Rick Steves' travel book Paris gave the secret: enter the cemetery through the back entrance, which opens at the top of the hill. Since it will take two hours to walk through the cemetery—if you visit the famous tombs—you will gladly be going downhill. Seated in front of me are three other Americans, one holding the same book I cradle in my lap.

These other Americans know what I know. They have read the same book. They, like I, like Rick Steves, can narrate the trip, the places, and the routes. They can make a claim to ownership through discourse. How can this be different from me?

Stepping off the bus, we set out at the same pace and then look around for the road that leads to the cemetery. I follow them, we exchange pleasantries, and they turn off with their guide maps and discover other graves—Jim Morrison, Edith Piaf. I head down hill in the cemetery, leaning back to walk forward. I came to see only one grave, that of a pair of lovers buried together.

An off-duty guide directs me to a loop road at the base of the hill. This monument lies behind another grave. I find them this rainy dark October, the twelfth-century lovers Abelard and Heloise. Their torrid love affair fills the letters they sent to each other after they went their separate ways, he to a monastery, she to a convent. The letters tell how Abelard fell in love with Heloise, the girl he was hired to tutor; how they secretly married, and how Heloise's uncle assaulted Abelard at night and castrated him. Now they are boxed up in a white sepulcher, statues of each lying side by side, stone pillows beneath their heads, hands raised in prayer, eyes open. Metal spikes like spears fence the tomb. They are worthy saints. I have read their letters. I know who they are.

My hands grip the fence as I study the twin forms on the top of the sepulcher. Both are portrayed in long robes. His hair is tonsured; she wears a wimple. They are buried looking up to heaven, spirits following sight lines. I think about them and their lives, holding them in my thoughts as in a mental act of resuscitation. Exploiting the homophonic link between *denken* and *danken*, Heidegger once said that thinking is thanking for being. My thought erects a canopy over their dead bodies. Memory invites them under its roof for shelter. We are here—they in the sepulcher and I outside the fence, saying a prayer without a god—because collectively we know that love is worth remembering. Pilgrimage centers pay tribute to divine love, to the places where my god or yours has walked, suffered, rested with a hand in a wall, a hand in a rock commemorating the divine. These lovers were not divine, but their letters strike sparks across time, like static electricity from the bedclothes. It is enough for me to thank them, thinking of them, whose anguish and pain became timeless in their writing. In the strange displacement of heart logic, their memorial answers me.

These lovers in the graveyard remind me how all things end, a most leveling notion. But all beginnings are glorious, figured by the spark, the flame, a Pentecostal holy spirit igniting a chain of events. We love the babe in arms and not the second childhood, the coiled fern not the dried frond. This end curves, the snake gulps the tail behind its head and my mind's eye closes on the sight of the American Major called to the Left Bank. Perhaps he has been invited by the Red Cross to offer his expertise, or perhaps he wants to see how they run their operation, after all he's been dealing with POWs since he's been in France. An afternoon in early autumn, he enters the lobby of Hotel Lutetia, where, outside, fences have been papered with the faces of returning refugees.

The Major takes a seat in the restaurant, where a meal or a tea or brunch or a dance has been organized by the Red Cross—

> now I use the French "*Croix-rouge*" because something really makes
> a difference when you speak a word in a different language; and
> I am pulled into it more and more as the city engulfs me; French
> carries in the language a gesture like a slap, a nod, a raised eyebrow;
> French puts me on a side in the story....

—and a woman asks him for his order. Her blond hair is pinned on the side. Her face carries a Grecian symmetry, this caryatid who has thrown off her architrave; clear blue eyes under tweezed eyebrows make her look perpetually inquisitive. When he speaks to her, her face lights up from within.

She is so lit from within that he cannot make direct eye contact with her for three seconds because he must call back his fled heart. Finally, he asks her, "*Wie heissen Sie?*" *What's your name?* German now is their common language. You can see the irony here, can't you, the way the language inserts itself like a trowel between bricks and joins them the way that bridges of Paris unite two side of the river, divide two sides of the river.

He is handsome, and, let's face it, as wholesome as any of the German youth, with a sculpted face, cleft chin, a radiant smile. With his shirt hanging loose from his shoulders, his belt cinching baggy pants, he gives the impression of a large teen-ager. In their first few words is the beginning. For her it will mean the start of an escape from poverty. For him, it marks the next chapter in the Catholic story of family. Later they will go out, maybe even dance. The Zazous loved American jazz and shouted "Let's swing" as their cry of revolt, but she's not like this, this girl from the country where her grandmother raised the chickens she chopped for the pot. They will listen to Piaf and dance to her torch songs if there is any dancing at all. Perhaps they hold hands as they walk, her skirt flipping up, his head thrown up, and the tongues of nascent lives sparking off them like fire. Love—the beginning of high romance, the glorious cadence of life before the genre changes. It seems right the name she first gives him is both true and false: "Liliane."

Her *nom de guerre* has a life to go with it: she was Norwegian, born in Oslo, she tells him. Her father, too, was Norwegian. They moved to Paris but she won't go back. Her Nordic looks match the story. The camera he bought in Germany blinks on a crowd. In black-and-white photographs illustrated by Parisian landscapes, she stands out like a bullet hole; shot at dusk, shot in fog, her blond hair flares, a votive candle among shadowy blobs.

Maybe something will change for her with this handsome soldier, the Americans different from the Germans. An authentic life roots in her fiction. Andrée grew upon a farm. She knew how things planted and tended can grow. Miracle of life—it comes from nothing—sunshine, water, air. A little clock starts ticking. Something quickens. Out of the inert, a germ. A seed stretches inside its coat, one cell becomes another, until the seed splits. A little green thing puts a foot outside to the earth and holds on; its head rises by increments until a sprout stands erect, the remnants of the seed hanging on a leaf's edge, till the wind blows it off. And then in the heat, the wind, the storm of the storm troopers, how easy it is to die. It is easier to kill something than to kill a memory. Sometimes nothing can kill a memory, not even the doubt of those who maintain it.

MICHELLE ELVY

Between Worlds in Penang

Walking in the park, in Penang. The Malaysian sun beats down. We seek shade at every corner. Here's Fort Cornwallis, built by the British East India Company and named after the eighteenth-century Governor-General in Bengal. Star-shaped fortification with ten-foot walls, shored up during the Napoleonic wars by Indian convict labourers. These days, Cornwallis is most famous for its largest cannon, dating back to 1603. A gift to a Sultan. A symbol of fertility.

Over there, women dressed in *burqas*, gathered under a shady tree. Beside them, a placard—piercing eyes at the top. Something I can't read, but I know one word, cantik: beautiful.

The women beckon. I step closer.

Two women welcome me into the mix, smile.

You want to try?

Hands reach out: animated hands, talking hands, decorated hands. Gold glinting around fingers and wrists. Eyes peering intently.

They are coordinated in blacks and purples and greens. A pin here, a flourish there. Delicate. *So colourful,* I say.

Yes, why not? they say.

Come, try, they say.

My youngest daughter joins me, stands close. She is ten. In no time they have a small burqa over her head and are buttoning up the front. Then the *hijab*, then the *niqāb*.

Cantik! Cantik!

My husband snaps photos—she is beautiful. A group of Muslim men has gathered also, at first on the periphery but now closer. They have cameras, too.

How does it feel? the women ask.

My daughter's eyes flash from the small slit of her *niqāb*. "Surprisingly cool."

The women are enchanted.

Now it's my turn. My vision darkens as they pull large swaths of black over my head, then the hijab. The *niqāb* is carefully tied at the back of my head, leaving only my eyes to take in the world around me.

I see my daughter admiring her outfit. *Snap snap* go Nikons and Canons.

The women smooth the material down my sleeves, tucking here, tugging there. Fussing and cooing. Laughing and whispering. They are completely in the moment, and now it's my turn to feel enchanted.

The material is airy, roomy. Billowing and strangely freeing. I lean into the voices of these women. I forget myself. Where do I go? I am not me but I am wholly me.

And what matters in this moment is the space between these women and me.

***

I am thinking a thousand things at once, wanting to ask a thousand questions. The burqa: flag of fundamentalism or symbol of freedom? Does more covering mean less liberty? Have we got it right or wrong? And what does that even mean—right or wrong? Is that girl in the bikini, riding on the back of her boyfriend's moped, *free?* Is the curve of that woman's tattooed thigh more alluring than these kohled eyes, or the delicate hands dancing so lightly in the air? And that young woman with the sunburnt shoulders, snapping photos of the rugged fortifications of Fort Cornwallis: is she making her own choices? Are these women making theirs? Will my daughters make theirs?

I look from my one daughter to the next, the younger one covered head to toe in a flourish of borrowed clothes, the other covered head to toe, too, in the comfort of well-worn jeans, sleeved shirt and floppy hat pulled low over her eyes. That one there, my teenager: her shy, watchful nature keeping her at the edge next to her father, looking on and making notes to pour into poetry in a later quiet moment. And this one: the effervescent youngster, here, with me, stepping into someone else's costume, if only for a moment, experiencing *this* feeling, whatever it is and however short-lived.

My daughters have grown up largely outside the typical boundaries of government and gender politics, having lived on their sailboat their whole lives and traversing oceans and borders —albeit at a very slow pace. Between Mexico and Hawaii, Alaska and French Polynesia, New Zealand and Thailand, they have lived beyond any fixed framework but skirted the edges of someone else's at every turn. The way they are now—one diving in fully, the other reflecting quietly, is how they live in the world. I wonder how stepping into a *burqa* will impact my young one, how it will stack up against calling to injured gibbons or picking plastic out of an ocean. I wonder what poetry will come from my other daughter's pen after this experience—how, even if she stands apart, she'll sculpt words around these dark eyes and delicate hands, one day. And not for the first time, I wonder at how the lessons my daughters learn never seem to be writ large, but instead arrive quietly, in the smallest points of contact and fleetingest of moments.

***

Their wrists jangle with bracelets. Their eyes sparkle with light.
What do you wear at home? I ask.
Whatever we want—giggles—*sometimes even less than you!*
And in the bedroom? Behind closed doors?
More giggles. *It's the same as for you!*
We laugh a lot. I ask more questions. They delight at my direct nature; they are eager to share. Something here transcends language and culture. We are women under the protection of a shady tree. That's all. In a moment we'll be a million other things again, but for now we are linked.

And now they grow serious, speaking of choice and love and connection. Of the sacred space between a man and a woman. They say, over and over, like mothers addressing daughters, like women knowing a wisdom long forgotten, in a way that tears down the clichés even as they say the simplest words: *you are beautiful* and *beauty is inside.*

Something nags me, of course. I wonder how these women's insistence on choice really works, how their Muslim men, so smiling and friendly there in the shade, would not approve of them stepping into our garments for a half-hour. I struggle with fundamental questions. These are, after all, complete strangers. And this is all very strange.

But despite these questions, they have issued an invitation to look closer.

So I look. And I see a world I know doesn't exist outside this space. Peace. Calm. Generous smiles.

Down to the core. Down to those eyes.

Then, the *niqāb* is untied, the *hijab* pulled up, the *burqa* unbuttoned. My daughter and I step out of their world and back into ours. Before we leave we pause for photos—they want as many as we do. Each woman hugs my daughter and me in a parting gesture: cheek to cheek on either side, one-two. Another: left-right. Again, and again.

The space between us is anything but empty.

Terima kasih, I say.

Terima kasih banyak, my daughter says.

More hands extend towards us. More air kisses, one-two, the thin material of their *niqābs* the only thing between their skin and ours.

Terima kasih, they say to us. *Accepting with love.*

AMINA GAUTIER

A Cup of My Time

The two boys are fighting inside of me. I can feel them doing it, making a commotion, sapping all of my energy. I make it to the bathroom and slap a wet washcloth over my forehead, dragging it down over my eyes and cheeks as I try to do deep breathing. Now I see hollows and shadows in my face where before I only saw beauty. I am worn. Dead skin collects on my face because I have no time to slough it off. Dark circles grow under my eyes in widening rings. It is the fault of these babies, these twins, these embryos, these fetuses—I really do not care what you call them—moving inside of me. According to our doctor, these babies are battling it out inside of my womb ("like Jacob and Esau inside of Rebekah," she said, as if that reference had any meaning for me). Sharing the same placenta, they are fighting within my body, each one trying to appropriate a larger portion of blood and nutrients for himself. Cary doesn't know it, but I have named our fighting twins: Sanjay and Sanjiv. Sanjiv, the larger boy getting most of the blood, is at risk of heart failure, while the smaller Sanjay is starving. Today the pain is worse, making me imagine tiny little fists concealing knives, brass knuckles and nun chucks. I imagine sucker punches and black eyes and all out brawls. These twins are duking it out inside of me, kicking my ass.

Once I return to the living room, I hear Mrs. Majumdar outside on the stoop. I can hear her all the way up here on the second floor. Her voice isn't so much loud as it is thick. It presses all the air out of this living room and surrounds me, closing in like walls. I reach behind me for the arm of the nearest chair and lower myself into it, listening to Mrs. Majumdar as she scolds her husband's cousins. I'd seen the two earlier when I'd staggered up those stairs. They'd been sitting in the same spot all day long, nesting like pigeons. For the past week, they'd been living above me on the third floor of the triplex. "Pradeep! Rohit! You know better than to be lounging around like lazy lazy boys. You're bringing down the value of my property. Tomorrow you go to your uncle's restaurant. We'll put you boys to work. Now upstairs with you."

Mrs. Majumdar's English is followed by a scolding in Punjabi, which I do not understand. My grandparents put it away like so much old luggage when they left Amritsar after the Partition. They never handed it down to my parents who never handed it down to me.

The pain subsides as Mrs. Majumdar talks. Her voice calms the twins inside of me, even though they are hearing it through a sac of viscous liquid, a mound of flesh, and a wall of plaster, sheetrock and brick.

I rise with difficulty, preparing to make my way to the front door.

Cary appears by my side and steadies my elbow. "Need some help?"

"Where did you come from?" Every morning Cary rises at six, the same as when he was going to campus to teach. Now, he locks himself in our other bedroom—the room meant for Sanjay and Sanjiv—which has become Cary's makeshift office, at least until the end of his sabbatical.

"Who can write anything with all of her racket?" he asks.

Living here was his idea. Now that he's on leave and so much underfoot, he notices how vocal Mrs. Majumdar is and how frequent are her visits. She comes upstairs every day to borrow something from me.

Mrs. Majumdar knocks on our door. My husband pleads, "Don't let her in Sona. Not today, all right?"

I am already waddling toward the door. "I have to," I say. "She's our landlord."

"For all the time she spends in our apartment, she should be paying us rent," he says. After the words come out, he smiles at me sideways, trying to pass it off as a joke. He disappears, cloistering himself, before I even reach the door.

I open the door and Mrs. Majumdar comes in, removing her chunni from her hair, letting it drop to her shoulders. "Sonali, did you see those boys? Those lazy urchins I have to call my kin?"

"I saw them earlier when I was outside."

She adjusts her glasses. "Eh? Outside? You should stay in here resting. If you need something and Cary is not around, Pradeep and Rohit will go for you. They don't have anything else to do."

"It sounds like you'll be putting them to work," I say.

"Eh? So you heard? Tomorrow they'll be sorry! Once my husband gets them, they'll never know what it means to be idle." Mrs. Majumdar takes a seat on the couch. Her pajama-like salwars bunch beneath her.

"That should be a good learning experience." They keep the lights low in Kaur and Singh so that you don't see how badly the place is in need of repairs. The ceiling there is made of popcorn stucco and the concrete stalactites hang over the patrons' heads, years and years out of code. "You've been nothing but kind to them."

"Who are you telling? Do you think they appreciate anything? Last night, I went upstairs to check the radiators, and I asked them 'Where else do you think you can get the whole third floor and pay nothing? Nowhere! I could have tenants in that unit and be bringing in some real money, but I give it to you lazy rascals who don't even appreciate. What do you give me? Nothing! You don't even cut the grass out front for me! Winter will come and you probably won't even shovel the snow'."

"That's the least they could do." I set a cup of tea and a platter of biscuits in front of her.

"The very least! The money I could be making. That apartment could have been filled. They don't know how lucky they are to find it vacant. If they had been a week later? Well, who knows?" Mrs. Majumdar says. She pours milk into her tea, bites into the sweet crunchy cookie and brushes crumbs from her kameez.

It wouldn't have mattered if her husband's cousins had come a week or a month later, the upstairs apartment would have been vacant no matter what. Cary and I have been living here since he first began teaching, and the only person I'd ever known to live upstairs for any real length of time had been her daughter Geeta.

"I wonder, Sonali, if I could borrow a cup of sugar?" Mrs. Majumdar asks.

"Certainly."

On Monday it was sea salt. On Tuesday, it was milk. On Wednesday it was cumin. Today it is sugar, but I only have Splenda, sugar substitute. Not that it matters. Mrs. Majumdar has no interest in our meager staples. What she really wants is a cup of my time.

"Is Splenda all right?" I ask, measuring out the sugar substitute in the kitchen.

"Whatever you have will do nicely."

"Have you heard anything from Geeta?"

Mrs. Majumdar makes an exasperated sound, expelling wind past teeth.

"That girl. Do you know how long it has been and I have heard nothing from her? I worry," she says. I barely remember her daughter Geeta. A tall willowy girl with a penchant for blue contact lenses, Jimi Hendrix and Eric Clapton, she'd loop "Purple Haze" or "Layla" and play the one song for three hours without stopping. Like her mother, she was more sound than woman to me, a blistering guitar blaring through my ceiling, bleeding down my walls.

As I search the kitchen cabinets, she recaps all of Geeta's major offenses, lost in her own world of self-pity. To tell the truth, I like Mrs. Majumdar's visits. They keep my mind occupied on someone else's pain. While Mrs. Majumdar complains and demands sympathy, I do not have to think about these babies tearing me apart. Listening to Mrs. Majumdar list Geeta's unjust treatment of her, I don't have to think about the weekly sonograms, or the possibility that without laser surgery to correct the unequal flow of blood, neither baby will survive. I do not have to think about my body and the world of conflict it carries.

With Mrs. Majumdar, I think only in terms of measurements. A half cup of milk, a pinch of sea salt, a tablespoon of cumin, a cup of sugar. These measurements block out the doctor's measurements, her pronouncements on my boys' meager lives, her words pouring out, "Sixty to seventy percent of the time both of the babies will die."

I pour the cupful into a baggie and zip it closed. When I reenter the living room, shaking the small pouch, Mrs. Majumdar is wiping her eyes with her chunni. She reaches up for the baggie, looks at me with red-rimmed eyes. "Soon you will know how it is. A mother always worries."

As soon as she leaves, Cary reemerges from his office. In honor of his sabbatical, he has ceased wearing shoes in the house. Walking around in stockinged feet, he slips into rooms without notice.

"Is she gone yet?" He touches my shoulder, then tries to wrap his arms around me from behind. After two unsuccessful attempts, he walks around to face me. He takes my hands in his, rubbing my palms with his thumbs.

"You know when she leaves down to the second," I say. "The incredible appearing man."

He buries his lips in my neck. "You smell like honey."

I touch his hair, letting my fingers sink into the thick sandy-colored strands. He's been growing his hair long since he's been on leave. Now his hair hangs over his eyes and curls at his ears and neck, thick and unruly. His hair turns up all around the house. I find it in the shower's drain and on our pillowcases. Just the other day, I found one of his hairs curled around a carton of milk in the refrigerator.

"When are you getting a haircut?"

"I hadn't thought about it."

"How about before the next doctor's visit? I want her to think we're a respectable couple."

"Having very respectable babies," he says. "Same time next week?"

I nod. Ever since they discovered my twins were sharing the same placenta, the doctor has been making us come in for weekly sonograms, but Cary always needs reminding.

"So, what did she want this time?"

"Sugar."

"She's got her own damned restaurant. Probably gets shipments of fifty pound bags of sugar and she wants sugar from us." He rubs the nape of my neck, and I lean into him. My stomach tightens and the upper portion of my abdomen fills with a sharp and debilitating pain that eclipses the earlier pain, making it seem merely unpleasant.

I latch onto Cary's arm, gripping it to keep myself upright and steady. "Call the doctor."

Used to the false alarms, Cary does not rush. Every time I have the slightest pain, we go to the hospital. Cary thinks I'm paranoid, but I remind him we have full coverage and excellent health insurance. Within their world inside of me, the boys have their own troubles, fighting for blood. They have their jobs, and I have mine. My fight is a battle of vigilance. Although the surgery that could save them is best done early into the pregnancy, each week the doctor says the boys are in too awkward of a position, that one false firing of the laser could tear their shared placenta and cause the twins to bleed to death. We can only wait and hope for them to move. Each time I feel anything, we come to the hospital.

"You did the right thing by coming in immediately. Your twins appear to have moved," the doctor says. Her voice conveys no emotion, as sterile as her gloved hands. "By tomorrow morning they should be in a favorable enough position for the procedure." She reminds me of the risks involved, tells me that I will only receive local anesthesia. I will have to be awake and still the entire time. She says that many things can go wrong while she attempts to cauterize the blood vessels. Once I am dressed again and about to leave, she says, "I have to prepare you. If the procedure fails to save the fetuses, the two of you will have a tough decision to make. You'll have to choose which one you want to live."

We have known the risks all along. We have known what we might have to do, but hearing it stated aloud in such a dispassionate manner, as if we are being asked to choose between DSL and dial-up, is more than we should have to bear. All the way home from the hospital I am crying. I start as soon as we climb into the cab and I am still crying when I climb into our bed.

Tomorrow, we will have to choose which child will have a chance at life. I think of my doctor's wan face and fantasize about hurting her. I feel power rush into my hands. It feels like I could twist the metal bars of our headboard into a pretzel if I wanted. "Either way, I guess she gets paid!" I cry. "How could she be so heartless?"

Cary defends her. "It was just a formality, Sona. She had to say it."

"How can she expect someone to choose? Why can't she save them both?"

"She'll try."

An emptiness spreads through me. No matter what Cary says to calm me, I cry and cry and cry. Cary tries to soothe me, but I will not let him. I am thinking of all that has been asked of me, all that I have given, all that I have eked out in order to help soothe others. I cry, wishing this cup would pass from me.

After some time, he gives up trying to console me. "Let's just try and get some sleep," he says. "Sona, do you want anything before we lie down? Can I bring you a cold compress or something?" he asks.

"No."

He climbs into the bed beside me. It is too early for sleep, but he turns off the lights and pulls the cover over us.

"You've got to try and take it easy, Sona," he says. "It will be all right."

"How? If we don't choose, both Sanjay and Sanjiv could die."

"They'll both survive," he says. Then, like an afterthought, "I like those names."

"What if they don't?" I ask. "What should we do then?"

Cary rubs my shoulders. "It's your body Sona. It should be your choice." He smiles, pleased with himself for saying what he believes to be the right thing.

I lock a word deep in my throat and my throat grows raw with holding it in. I wonder if my voice will now grow thick like Mrs. Majumdar's. If it will fill up this apartment and coat the walls like paint. If it will seep under the doors and sills and cracks and flow out onto the stoop and all the way to the curb until it has coated the street.

"I'm going to go turn out the lights in the living room. Do you want anything while I'm up?" Cary asks.

"No," I say. I do not care that he is trying to distract himself by being solicitous. I do not care that maybe this is tearing him apart too.

"Fine," he says, exasperated. Then, "Honey, are you sure? Isn't there anything I can do for you?"

How easily he can offer his support, knowing full well that his body won't be carrying a dead twin to term, knowing that when things get unpleasant he can always hide in his office and shut everything out, knowing that he is not a walking reminder of failure. "Pray?"

Cary sighs, smoothing my hair across the pillow. "I haven't prayed in a very long time. Not for anything. Not even that time when I thought you would leave," he says. "I don't know if I remember how."

"Fine," I say and Cary gets out of the bed.

"Fine," I say again even though there is no one to hear me, liking the sound of my own voice. The sound fills up my mouth. It fills up my lungs. It fills up my head. "Fine fine fine fine fine."

I can't hear him walk away from me, but I know he is in the living room double checking everything, making sure that we've locked the door, set the alarm, and that the lights won't burn through the evening and run our electric bill sky high. These are the things he can control. They give him a semblance of normalcy, allowing him to pretend that tonight is an ordinary night and we are an ordinary couple having ordinary babies. As long as he secures us for the night, he can pretend that—like so many other couples—the decisions we make are trivial, altering the lives of no one.

After some time, Cary returns and climbs back into bed beside me. "There's got to be something I can do for you," he says.

I say, "Yes."

"Tell me."

He scoots against me, curving his body into a spoon. His chin digs into my shoulder, his head rests heavy against the side of my face. I do not push him away. Lying beside him, I am preparing for tomorrow. I practice being still. "Sona?"

I say, "Choose."

LAURIE KRUK

Just Across the Border

We were getting ready to cross it: the 49th parallel, or famed "medicine line" of First Nations, that magical border dividing North America which fades away or is dramatically redrawn with shifts in the geo-political climate, turning neighbours and kin into strangers again. We had Canadian passports for me, my husband, our two daughters, with directions and information harvested, from the safe distance of spring, from Google Maps and Wikipedia. But as summer arrived, and the travel plans pencilled-in on the calendar drew near ("Visiting Maxwell and Tyler in Wisconsin!") suddenly, the distance we had to cross seemed too great.

Looking back on my relationship with my husband's son, Maxwell*, I now consider step-mothering a deliberate, and delicate, border-crossing act in itself, daring to care across distances of blood, history, memory. Tenuous and tentative from the start, it is a connection that can be readily dismissed with the accusation, "You're not my REAL mother!" followed by a shrugging off of the many gestures and gifts of building or bridging family ties. If the other mother is still present, as in our case, you end up occupying a parallel space, but without easy access to the role and title of *Mother* … even if you share many of the day-to-day maternal responsibilities and realities, from bills to birthday parties. I know this now, from the inside-out.

When my step-son and I first met, nearly twenty years ago, his father, John, was a soon-to-be divorced man, temporarily sharing quarters with his mother and dying father, and I was introduced to Maxwell as John's "new girlfriend." Oblivious, obtuse, over-earnest single woman that I was, I approached this new role like a camp counsellor or casual babysitter, the only real previous experience I had had with children. Luckily, eight-year-olds are generally inquisitive, open and accepting. When John and I decided to live together, we bought a house on the lake, financed with my new professor's salary and managed with his resourceful ingenuity as full-time writer and "home guy." We moved in that spring, eager to fill out our new home and new family of John, Maxwell (for four days every other week), and me, still learning just to be part of a couple. Our renovated cottage-home was tiny, but boasted a stone fireplace, large deck and, most importantly, waterfront with dock and boathouse. We couldn't wait for the snow to disappear and reveal the sleeping beauty.

The long Victoria Day weekend came, traditionally the "first weekend of summer" to Canadian campers and cottagers. New to northern Ontario, I was determined to take my first swim in "our lake," despite the fact that the ice had probably been off it for a mere three weeks. Maxwell was also game, he said; his father was noncommittal. Saturday morning, we two donned our suits, even though both sky and water remained grey and gloomy-looking. Shedding sneakers and gingerly putting my bare feet on the cool dockboards for the first time, with Maxwell close behind, I dropped my towel, slipped into the water. My splash was probably drowned out by my shriek, as I felt the lake's wintry tentacles clutch my lungs, freeze my bloodflow while jolting my heart into hyperdrive. Maxwell was also wailing as his Dad reached in to pull him out. "Freaking freezing!" was all I could manage, shuddering, fumbling blindly for my towel (I had removed my glasses in blithe anticipation of full immersion). Maxwell was already being re-dressed by John, who had thoughtfully carried down our discarded clothes. I turned to him for comfort and commiseration. Half-laughing at each of us in turn, John shook his head knowingly, while Maxwell and I whimpered pathetically. Above us a bush plane roared, announcing the start of northern Ontario summer—but from a safely dry distance.

As July arrived on our lake, we were able to swim every day, and I delighted to see father and son playing in the water. They had a game where the boy would climb onto his Dad's shoulders, hold his hands, and rise with him as he stood up, Maxwell vaulting off in an attempted somersault back into the water. It was always half-executed, leading to the repeated cry of "One more time, Dad!" Meanwhile, I was in and out of the water, floating on a raft constructed of pool noodles, sometimes shouting encouragement, but with a new motherly note of worry: "Watch the dog!" (Our new Labrador cross was invariably paddling close by, wondering what all the fuss was about.) Or "Don't hit me!" as another human cannonball was launched, just over my head. Mostly ignored, I was glad to be too big, or too old, to be thrown myself. Laughing, they would try again to perfect the stunt, for hours of seemingly endless play. We were at our freest, half-dressed bodies surfacing in sun, submerging again in shadow. In the water, seemingly weightless, we could float—and perhaps, with time, fly. Afterwards, we hung our brightly-coloured beach towels over the balcony, where they fluttered in the breeze like the proud flags of summer.

That first season, John and I, both writers, challenged one another to write in our journals every night, to compose "raw" and unfiltered impressions which we would (rashly) read aloud and share, like the still-unmarried naifs we were. Maxwell insisted on joining us. I kept a copy of one of his entries: "*A good day! I ALMOST made a perfect roll over. Got water up my nose, tho. Buster kept barking at my Dad, after, like he thought I was in trouble. Silly mutt.*" We were in a safely liminal space, it seemed, suspended between land, water and sky, where identities like mother, father, child could be shed simply by moving from one element to another. At one moment, I was Maxwell's rival for his father's attention and the next, his big-sisterly guardian, cheerleader and playmate.

Seeing my partner nurturing, protecting and encouraging his young son made me aware that he already was a good father. That essential tie would always draw him away from me, toward his first marriage, his shadowy earlier life. But their closeness, and my inclusion within this new triangle, also gave me a glimmer that he would be a good father to any future children who would tie us together, too. And indeed, this proved to be true. Two years later, after our first daughter was born, we made our status "legal." Maxwell was Best Man at our simple lakeside wedding, an eleven-year-old performer in top hat and tux who toasted (and teased) us, in the words of TV's Bart Simpson: "Blah-Blah-Blah!" His sisters—half-sisters, technically, but never viewed as partial—arrived when Maxwell was ten and thirteen, one *pre-* and one *post-*nuptials, saving him from "only child" self-absorption and loneliness. The girls looked up to their big brother, who played with them and read them Dr. Seuss, and later they sheltered him, with keen sisterly protectiveness, from my own adult inquisitiveness.

When Maxwell was almost fifteen and living with us half-time on joint custody, we reluctantly left our renovated cottage on the lake and moved into a bigger house closer to downtown, with an extra bedroom and a proper yard for dog and kids. While regretfully giving up the pleasures of living on the lake, we thankfully relinquished its perils: yearly ice damage to boathouse or dock, struggles to keep the old septic system up to code and not contaminate the water, source of our city's drinking supply. And we gained the more conventional advantages of proximity to the girls' new school, my university and Maxwell's mother's home. But now that we were officially a "blended family" of five, the walls between step-mother and step-son went up.

One day, he was dropped off early, by his mother, who remained planted, as usual, faceless behind the wheel of her car. John was cutting his mother's grass; the girls were at her house while I marked final exams. Maxwell's face was dirt-smudged, blotchy; he grabbed a Pepsi from the fridge, muttering to himself. "Anything wrong?" I asked. I knew he wasn't enjoying Grade Ten; his classmates were either "jocks" or "buttholes," while Maxwell was more interested in writing or drawing. He shrugged, "Nothing. School sucks, that's all." And closed the door to his room, turning on his Playstation game system. From my marking desk, I soon heard the synthetic screams of zombies and zombie- killers. I worried he was being bullied for being "different." But more and more often, when I approached Maxwell, I heard "I need to talk to my Dad," the pointed exclusion, as if I couldn't possibly understand or be of help. Sometimes they would talk in Maxwell's room with the door closed, neither looking any happier afterwards. I overheard John say something to his son about "standing up for yourself" and "picking your battles," but to my inquiries, my husband only said I wouldn't understand. Meanwhile, I flashed back to memories of slipping down the back lanes and alleyways of my Don Mills suburb, when I was eleven, to escape my tormentors, surprising cats and delivery men as I tried desperately to disappear. On schooldays with us, a year later, Maxwell would get up early and walk over three miles to school in winter, just to avoid the school bus and its confined chaos. The driver remained grimly oblivious to Maxwell's complaints of rough-housing turned vicious, while the principal John phoned to discuss a school trans- fer seemed wary of getting in the middle of "another cross-town custody battle." Again, avoidance seemed easier than confrontation.

A second wall that went up, when Maxwell was finishing high school, was the digital divide, as he entered the web world, first tentatively then whole-heartedly. This clearly created a generational division, drawing a line between we literary luddites and Maxwell as "millennial" and "screenager." It often seemed to me to draw a line between the genders, too, as Maxwell entered the male-dominated world of violent video games and online role playing. Onscreen, under an alias or "avatar," a geeky, scrawny kid could be a killer, a soldier, a leader. If it separated him from us and his young sisters, it also provided a doorway to new relationships and possibilities beyond our common borders. For the web world allowed him to meet Tyler, just a year older and also from a so-called "broken home," living in the States, whom he first encountered on a Batman fan site. As teenagers separating from their parents, this electronic in-between-space, accessed in dark basements or private bedrooms, allowed them a chance to try on new, bold and mature identities. That fall, Maxwell started, then eventually dropped out of, the university where I taught, leaving me feeling disappointed and (perhaps absurdly) embarrassed. Although he seemed to love reading and writing, as I did, he did not enjoy pursuing these activities for credit in courses on American literature or Shakespeare. After buying some of the books, he skipped class, stayed in his room, and seemed to divide his time between writing stories on his laptop and gaming on his Playstation. When questioned by his father about his future plans, he shrugged: "I don't know. I don't need to be pressurized by school, right now, that's for sure. It's boring. I'm working on my own stuff." Fearing depression and likely blaming himself and the divorce, John backed off, muttering something to me about "delayed adolescence" and "more breathing space." We worried, separately.

Meanwhile, Maxwell's web world grew as he hid in his basement room at our house, at his mother's, and chatted online with Tyler. They shared web-profiles, email handles and eventually, phone numbers. Soon they were instant-messaging daily, trading art and web links as their intimacy grew. They both had a fascination with wolves and exchanged their own anthropomorphic wolf-art. Were we concerned, jealous?—of course. One day, there came a phone call from Tyler's parents, warning of their discovery of pornographic images passed between the boys. By then, Tyler was nineteen, Maxwell eighteen, and John told me that the obligatory parental "Sex Ed talk" had taken place several years ago, including cautions against easy access to internet porn—but probably not addressing this particular direction. Before we knew it, Maxwell and Tyler had planned a summer visit, with Tyler driving "up" in his parents' car. The trip got postponed, then postponed again. John and I figured this was a kind of "pen pal" affair, a temporary infatuation. But while Maxwell was still registered in university classes (if not attending them) and living more and more with his mother, where he didn't have to deal with pestering by his young sisters, or questions from me, we heard that Tyler was "coming up" for a weekend visit. Maxwell's mother had a spare room, and if she wasn't thrilled with the idea, she at least seemed ready to tolerate it, to humour her introverted, reclusive son, and encourage a friendship. Tyler and Maxwell dropped by for a few minutes that Saturday and while standing in the driveway, charmed the girls by teaching Buster Two how to catch a Frisbee. Our invitation to stay for supper was refused. Later, we heard from his agitated mother about an exchange of vows, involving rings and a Wikkan classmates of Maxwell's, conducted in her apartment while she was out getting groceries. Again, we worried, wondering if this was the "difference" Maxwell had been hiding all along. While never giving up on loving his son, John admitted this news was "hard to take."

That was almost ten years ago now. Tyler and Maxwell have not given up on their long-distance, border-crossing relationship, pursuing plans for Maxwell to move across the border to Wisconsin, where Tyler is now employed. During those years, Maxwell's chosen career as writer and self-taught web-page designer was increasingly underground and mysterious to us, but he did manage to produce some income by it, judging from his regular online Amazon orders for games, DVDS, electronic parts for his well-used laptop. We cheered him on in his quest for independence, even if it meant Maxwell had to leave Canada and his family behind. After crossing the border this spring, Maxwell was granted a Visitor's Visa, with six months to grapple with the colossal bureaucracy which authorized Green Cards, on the grounds of either an offer of full-time employment in the States or family reasons, such as marriage to an American citizen. Homeland Security now had him in their sights. Meanwhile, as John reminded him, Maxwell could qualify for Native Status in Canada through his part-Cree grandmother and so claim the treaty right—at least in theory—to cross the border and reside in the States without question. All it took was affiliation with, and approval from, her traditional band up in northern Ontario where she was born. Even his fair-haired, blue-eyed sisters, her granddaughters, were eligible for this entitlement: true "double agents," they would never know the discrimination and abuse that came with the Residential School years and the colonial reservation system. But in the States, I learned, this regaining of lost heritage and tribal membership now depended upon the "Blood Quantum" rules that would permit free passage of the "medicine line" separating Canadian provinces from American states. A more biological or "essential" approach to identity, the American policy insisted upon a certain amount of Native "blood" via his ancestors and their subsequent unions. In a famous example of sexist double standards, Native women marrying White men in Canada had lost their birthright and had to fight for it to be restored in 1985 with Bill C-31; this was the case for both Maxwell's maternal and paternal ancestors. Maxwell decided quickly that the bureaucracy around Native status was even more complicated and unpredictable than that around American residency—better to stay on his current path.

At twenty-seven, Tyler is working as a manager of IT for a large chain of popular family resorts across the States. For the near future at least, Tyler will be the supporting partner. He recently put a down payment on a house in his name, meant to be a shared household. Though they have spent more time online than in person, they are obviously a couple. And after several more visits "up north," Tyler has become more to us than an identity on a screen, or a stranger outside our house. He's a gentle giant with a southern twang who has a good sense of humour and an obvious tolerance for long-distance driving. And he clearly cares for Maxwell. Their new home is in the Republican state of Wisconsin, a farming community, and I worry about their neighbours. Do they carry guns? Do they sport T-shirts or bumper stickers that say God hates fags? Maxwell sent us pictures, via Facebook, of their surprisingly large, spacious house in the countryside, with a large deck and a basketball net. There were five bedrooms, and I had hopeful fantasies about driving down there in the summer, to spend a couple of days as their amazed houseguests, drinking local Spotted Cow Beer and buying the girls yellow Cheesehead hats. Should we bring a house-warming gift? Or a wedding present? Their "Thanks for coming" as they waved good-bye to us, backing out of their driveway, would be answered proudly with "Thanks for having us—" Excited by the pictures, the girls wanted to know if "Max and Ty would get a dog now."

But those blank calendar squares allocated to July and August quickly filled up, as they tend to do, and the trip to Wisconsin was put off, for reasons partly practical (time, money), partly emotional (uncertainty, hesitation). At the end of July, however, we found ourselves in the border town of Sault Ste.-Marie, Ontario—or as "the GPS lady" pronounced it, "*Saltstemmary*"—for my younger daughter's Ringette Camp. The International Bridge beckoned. As we already had our passports, I persuaded my husband to take a day-trip over the border "for practice." We could visit the reconstructed fort in Mackinaw City, site of an infamous surprise attack by the Anishnabe/Ojibway—a rare gaining of the upper-hand over their British colonizers—with the mock *baggatiway* game at Fort Michilimackinac that, like the Greeks' Trojan Horse, allowed them to breach the walls, shed some blood. Rolling across the bridge with the morning commuters, we pulled up to the customs window. Before we could even flash our new passports, we were scolded for not stopping at the correct spot and throwing off the surveillance cameras. Nervous foot, my husband, the driver, apologized. The burly border guard ran through the standard list of prohibitions, peeked into the back of our van, and then asked John the dreaded question, "And what do you *do*?" But today he didn't shy away from the label of "Writer. And poet." The guard grunted, said something about cookbook-writing paying better. We nodded, grateful for a touch of humour or humanness, explained we were only going across for "a quick look." We were cleared to roll forward, yet in my mind, the interrogation continued, as the guard leaned further out his window to lock eyes with me, to demand, "And you, Ma'am, what do you think you're doing here? You claim to be on 'a family visit,' but I don't think you're kin to anyone on our side. Maxwell certainly doesn't want you pretending to be any kind of mother, now that he's twenty-six. He doesn't need you messing in his private affairs, either. Hasn't he made that clear?" But we were already on the I-75, with its miles of summer safety cones cutting into one lane, forcing us to straddle the shoulder while the road workers moved about casually, insouciantly, like obstacles on an extended driving test on *America's Worst Drivers.* Watching one worker throw his arm around another's tank-top-bared shoulders, I recalled that, just this past June 2015, the highest court in America struck down the state-by-state policy on same-sex marriage, and proclaimed it legal across the USA.

At Mackinaw City that day, we enjoyed our quick tour of the fort, the North American history lesson on speed-dial, musket firing demonstration, the female blacksmith bending forks, the restored Catholic chapel, and the breeze off Lake Michigan. Beneath the handsome movie-set reconstruction were the shadowy remains of the actual three-hundred-year old fort, part of an archaeological dig established in the 1960s. Posted signs around fenced-off patches of bare earth referred to this as work in *"stratigraphy."* Looking this word up later, I discovered its relevance was to more than just this authorized, and funded, archaeological uncovering. *Stratigraphy: [Archaeology] "a vertical section [cut] through the earth showing the relative positions of the human artefacts and therefore the chronology of successive levels of occupation*" (*Collins English Dictionary*). Wasn't our blended family history, as I reconstructed it, just such an archaeological window onto "the relative positions of the human artefacts" and their "successive levels of (chronological) occupation"? Layers upon layers were still to be uncovered. But we couldn't linger here, in the strata, as we were scheduled to be back by mid-afternoon to pick up our daughter at the arena. Still, since we were on the American side of the border, under the Mackinaw Bridge—"largest suspension bridge in the Western hemisphere"—John picked up our phone, dialed Maxwell and Tyler's cell, hoping to get voice-to-voice at least. Perhaps our Canadian number on the phone's call display panel was unfamiliar and so, ignored; perhaps they were out; we only got an obscure voicemail greeting that at least *sounded* like Maxwell. "Hey—not in. Uh, catch you later." John hesitated, looked at me, and said. "This is Dad, Maxwell. Sorry we couldn't get any closer than Mackinaw, Michigan. Call us when you get a chance." Then we found our car and turned back to our road north.

As the car rode up the ramp to climb the first of the two bridges that would bring us back to the motherland, I looked down and recalled the expression, *It's all water under the bridge now*.... Seeing Maxwell as a boy, standing on his father's shoulders, rising out of the summer lake, leaping towards the sun. For a few seconds now, it felt like we were flying with the silver-winged gulls rising beside us. Caught between water and sky, remembering climbing from the shadowy strata at the Fort back into the sunshine, where we found ourselves smiling at strangers, I felt a small surge of hope: somehow, sometime, we would return.

*NB: names have been changed.

LAURIE KRUK

Conclusion

Love is this thundering veil, this vast span
with and without precedent.

—A. V. Christie, "Niagara"

So wrote poet A. V. Christie at the threshold of the world-famous water-scape (also honeymoon destination, where many families may well have been started, in the conventional way) of Niagara Falls, which famously borders Canada and the United States of America. This natural wonder, memorialized by artists, photographers, poets who came to the "new land" becomes an apt emblem for the miracle of love and life itself. How do we write the motherland? Is it a place of birth, a cultural heritage, a lost language, a severed connection—or perhaps all of these? While we are all brought into the world through a woman's body, a "mother" in some sense of the word, we rarely stay in one physical or relational environment for very long. In fact, as humans, we have a history of moving, travelling, migrating, escaping, whether due to global crises of war or political rupture, economic catastrophe, familial breakdown, or desire for personal exploration and adventure. New families are thus created out of luck, love, chance, necessity. As a result, we cross borders that are geographic, cultural, linguistic, and willingly or unwillingly, are drawn into confrontations with ourselves, new families and new societies as we meet and mark our particular crossroads.

Mothers are no different. In *Borderlands and Crossroads: Writing the Motherland,* writers struggle with the naming and narrating of mothers who adopt, adopted children who seek their birth-mothers, or mothers and children, daughters and sons, who bravely face the uncanny in the completely "natural" tie. For the motherland is so often unrecognized or unarticulated. In this collection, we see mothering being enacted, or mothers being contemplated, in liminal spaces and unexpected places where past collides dramatically with present. For instance, on a tour of former slave quarters on the West coast of Ghana ... in the German cattle car bearing unknowing Jewish prisoners to the Nazi concentration camps ... in a "MEGA" store in Mexico ... a market square in Penang ... more prosaically, in subways, cars and streetcars ... elevators, back rooms, school yards ... train stations, airport lounges, zoos, bathtubs, beds and even cherished dollhouses. Sometimes the locations are less physical or geographical, but all of these pieces, poetry or prose, bring together history and family in a witnessing to the challenges, gains and losses that mark us all as women and men.

In our Poetry section, which includes thirty-five poems by twenty-six North American poets, we begin within the landscape of a woman's lactating body (Fennelly) and end with an older mother-poet reclaiming her voice by marking the terrain of the page (Dunlop, "Somewhere, a woman is writing a poem"). We hear from the voices of sons as well as daughters, mothers—adoptive or "natural"—of many ages, situations and stages. Children are celebrated, mourned, fought for, fought with, released into their own journeys. Mothers are struggled with, listened to, imitated, questioned, elegized. We move from the flexible mapping of the mindscape that free verse allows (Pelizzon, Neufeldt, Da') to experiments with the restrained intensity of formalist structures such as the villanelle (Taylor, Carstensen), ghazal (Carstensen), maternal elegy (Zawinski, Wheeler, Taylor); experiments with the found poem (Pence, Baumel), postcard or prose poem (McGookey, Czerwiec) and cross-cultural translations of a Thai *khap yani* (Triplett, "Family Spirits).

Our Prose section of twenty-three works formally "crosses the border" between short fiction and creative non-fiction, the old(er) and the new(er), with a strong emphasis on the latter genre, and its focus on the personal voice shaping a story out of its own particular, temporal location. For instance, Sutherland's rueful reflection on a family visit to his ninety-six-year-old mother who, forty years later, still feels abandoned by an adventurous son who retraced the family's roots back to Britain. Reviewing family photograph albums becomes the means to maternal justification: "There I was at two with a birthday cake on a small table out in the July garden surrounded by other children, a host of adults looking on. Family bonded into family …. 'You were much loved.'" The more traditional, well-crafted short fiction presented here offers us another way to leap over cultural or political boundaries, and open ourselves to the voices of women and men, past and present, seeking connections. Gautier's "Taste of Dust" ironically reveals the gap between the foreign woman's desire to touch "Africa" and the local man's confused attraction and mistrust. While refusing to make love to him, as he hopes, this travelling American quotes the Harlem poet Countee Cullen's line, "What is Africa to me?" while caressing his hair, and so turns him into a poem. Edelglass's viscerally-told story of family preservation in the face of horror places the man in the mothering role. Conveyed in the "mother tongue" of Yiddish-inflected English, this story ends with a desperate bid for life even as Abraham realizes, "in this place, there would be no mothers." Hall and Boyd try to fill in the gaps of their lost maternal legacies, Boyd by inviting the mother's imagined confession to her "surprise child" of how the family's many moves brought her into contact with other women, stay-at-home mothers of the 1960s who shared stolen moments of honesty: "We had ourselves a time." Roy's poignant portrait of an outcast girl hungering for more than food at lunch time on the playground points to continuing race and class barriers. The girl finds comfort and inspiration in the playground's pepper tree: "She liked how it looked like the tree could go on forever, like its branches could stretch and hang anywhere they wanted, just as the tree was happily root-ed just where it was." Tesser uses the middle-class "vacation" in Mexico as a "crossroads" to reflect on her heroine's own silences and sadness as a middle-aged woman, trying to trust her own maternal voice as she senses a child is at risk of harm: "Annie trails the two out of the clothing area and into a hardware aisle, trying to catch the mother's eye, to think of how to express it, she's hardly spoken the language in thirty years. *Perdóneme,* "Pardon me," she guesses first, politeness the key…." And "A Cup of My Time," Gautier's second selection, plunges us into the archetypal mother's agony: the choice of which child to let live, which let die. In the end, this contemporary woman refuses her "right to choose" and pushes it back onto her sympathetic yet distant husband.

Borderlands and Crossroads: Writing the Motherland invites us to become the travelling companions of writers who chart journeys of the heart, each writing the motherland as their own personal *terra incognita.*

About the Contributors

Editors:

Jane Satterfield is the recipient of awards in poetry from the National Endowment for the Arts, Maryland Arts Council, *Bellingham Review,* Ledbury Poetry Festival, *Mslexia,* and more. Her essays have received awards from the Pirate's Alley Faulkner Society, *Massachusetts Review, Florida Review,* and the Heekin Foundation, among others. Her books of poetry are *Her Familiars, Assignation at Vanishing Point,* and *Shepherdess with an Automatic.* She is also the author of *Daughters of Empire: A Memoir of a Year in Britain and Beyond* (Demeter Press). Born in England, she teaches at Loyola University Maryland.

Laurie Kruk teaches English at Nipissing University in North Bay, Canada. She has published *The Voice is the Story: Conversations with Canadian Writers of Short Fiction* (Mosaic, 2003) and *Double-Voicing the Canadian Short Story* (Ottawa University Press, 2016). She is also the author of three poetry collections: *Theories of the World* (Netherlandic, 1992), *Loving the Alien* (YSP, 2006), and *My Mother Did Not Tell Stories* (Demeter, 2012). This last collection is described as weaving "tales that powerfully uncover the necessity of vocalizing that which is learned, experienced, and traditionally unshared" (*ARC Poetry Magazine*).

Contributors:

Judith Baumel is Professor of English at Adelphi University and has served as president of The Association of Writers and Writing Programs and director of The Poetry Society of America. Her books of poetry are *The Weight of Numbers,* for which she won The Walt Whitman Award of the Academy of American Poets, *Now,* and *The Kangaroo Girl.*

Betsy Boyd is a faculty member in the Creative Writing and Publishing Arts MFA program at the University of Baltimore and serves as editor-in-chief of Baltimore STYLE Magazine. Her fiction has been published most recently in *Sententia, Shenandoah,* and *Loch Raven Review* and her creative nonfiction appears frequently at *The Huffington Post.* Her short story "Scarecrow" received a Pushcart Prize.

Robin Carstensen's work is recently published or forthcoming in *The Atlanta Review, Connotations Press, Southern Humanities Review,* and *The Tishman Review,* among many others. She teaches and coordinates the Creative Writing program at Texas A&M University in Corpus Christi, and is co-founder and editor of *The Switchgrass Review,* a literary journal of women's health, history, and transformation.

Born in Miami, raised in England and West Virginia, and educated in Texas, **Joy Castro** is the author of *The Truth Book: A Memoir,* the New Orleans literary thrillers *Hell or High Water* and *Nearer Home* (St. Martin's), the essay collection *Island of Bones,* and the short story collection *How Winter Began,* and editor of the essay collection *Family Trouble* (University of Nebraska Press). She lives and works in Lincoln, Nebraska.

A. V. Christie's books are *Nine Skies,* which won the National Poetry Series, and *The Housing,* winner of the McGovern Prize. *The Wonders,* a chapbook-length poem, was an Editor's Selection published by Seven Kitchens Press. Christie received grants from the National Endowment for the Arts, from the Ludwig Vogelstein Foundation, and from the Pennsylvania and Maryland State Arts Councils. Christie died of breast cancer in April 2016.

Nicole Cooley is the author of five books, most recently *Breach* (LSU Press, 2010) and *Milk Dress* (Alice James Books, 2010). She has also published two other collections of poems and a novel. She directs the MFA Program in Creative Writing and Literary Translation at Queens College—CUNY. She lives outside of New York City with her husband and two daughters.

Poet and essayist **Heidi Czerwiec** is the author of two recent chapbooks – *Sweet/Crude: A Bakken Boom Cycle*, and *A Is For A-ke, The Chinese Monster* – and of the forthcoming poetry collection *Maternal Imagination*, and is the editor of *North Dakota Is Everywhere: An Anthology of Contemporary North Dakota Poets*. She lives in Minneapolis.

Laura Da' is a poet and public school teacher. A lifetime resident of the Pacific Northwest, Da' studied creative writing at the University of Washington and The Institute of American Indian Arts. Her first chapbook, *The Tecumseh Motel*, was published in *Effigies II*. The University of Arizona Press recently published her first full-length manuscript, *Tributaries*.

H'Rina DeTroy is a writer living in New York City. Her work has appeared in the *Okayafrica.com*, *The Huffington Post*, *Diacritics*, *Cultural Survival Quarterly*, and *Glimpse Magazine*. She works as a Writing Specialist at the Harlem Children's Zone. In addition to writing, she studies flamenco and often daydreams about polyrhythms.

Jennifer Kwon Dobbs is the author of *Paper Pavilion* (White Pine Press, 2007) and *Notes from a Missing Person* (Essay Press, 2015). Her work has appeared in *Blackbird, Columbia: A Journal of Literature and Art, Crazyhorse, Indiana Review, Solo Novo*, among others. She is associate professor of English and director of Race and Ethnic Studies at St. Olaf College where she teaches Creative Writing and Asian-American literature. She lives in Saint Paul, Minnesota.

Camille T. Dungy has published three books of poetry, most recently *Smith Blue*, three anthologies, and numerous essays. Her honors include an American Book Award, two Northern California Book Awards, a California Book Award silver medal, and fellowships from the Sustainable Arts Foundation and the NEA. Dungy is currently a Professor in the English Department at Colorado State University.

Rishma Dunlop, author of *Lover Through Departure: New and Selected Poems*, received many honors for her work, including the Canada-U.S. Fulbright Research Chair in Creative Writing and the Emily Dickinson Prize for Poetry. Born in India, Dunlop grew up in Beaconsfield, Quebec. Editor of the groundbreaking anthology, *White Ink: Poems on Mother and*

Motherhood (Demeter, 2007), Dunlop was a beloved professor of English and Creative Writing at York University, Toronto. She was named a Fellow of the Royal Society of Canada in 2011 and died after a long battle with cancer in April 2016.

Elizabeth Edelglass's award-winning fiction has appeared in *Michigan Quarterly Review, Lilith, American Literary Review,* and more. She has won a Connecticut Commission on the Arts fellowship, and her work has been nominated for a Pushcart Prize. A portion of the story "As Abraham to Isaac, Bilhah to Benjamin" was a finalist for the *Glimmer Train* Very Short Fiction Award.

Michelle Elvy is a writer, editor and liveaboard sailor, currently in East Africa. She edits at *Flash Frontier* and *Blue Five Notebook* and writes fiction, poetry, travel essays and reviews. She is Assistant Editor of the *Best Small Fictions* series (Queens Ferry Press) and was recently on the editing teams of *Flash Fiction International* and *Voyaging with Kids*. Find out more at http://michelleelvy.com.

Blas Falconer is the author of *Forgive the Body This Failure* (Four Way Books, 2018), *The Foundling Wheel* (Four Way Books, 2012) and *A Question of Gravity and Light* (University of Arizona Press, 2007). He lives in Los Angeles and teaches in the low-residency MFA at Murray State University.

Beth Ann Fennelly directs the MFA Program at Ole Miss where she was named Outstanding Teacher of the Year. She has received grants from the National Endowment for the Arts, the United States Artists, as well as a Fulbright to Brazil. Fennelly has published three books of poetry, a co-written novel, and a book of nonfiction, *Great With Child: Letters to a Young Mother* (W. W. Norton). She lives in Oxford with her husband and their three children.

Jennifer Franklin graduated from Brown and Columbia. Her full-length collection, *Looming*, was published by Elixir Press in 2015. Her poetry has appeared in *Blackbird, Boston Review, Gettysburg Review, Guernica, The Nation, The Paris Review, poets.org, Poetry Daily, Prairie Schooner, Salmagundi, Southwest Review,* and *Verse Daily*. Franklin is co-editor of

Slapering Hol Press and she teaches poetry workshops at The Hudson Valley Writers' Center.

Amina Gautier is the author of three short story collections: A*t-Risk, Now We Will Be Happy* and the *The Loss of All Lost Things. At-Risk* was awarded the Flannery O'Connor Award; *Now We Will Be Happy* was awarded the Prairie Schooner Book Prize in Fiction, and *The Loss of All Lost Things* was awarded the Elixir Press Award in Fiction.

Tanya Grae is the author of the chapbook *Little Wekiva River* (Five Oaks Press), and Yusef Komunyakaa selected her poem "The Line of a Girl" to receive the 2016 Tennessee Williams/New Orleans Literary Festival Poetry Prize. Her poems have appeared *AGNI, The Florida Review, New South, The Los Angeles Review, Fjords Review,* and other places. She is a PhD candidate at Florida State University and holds an MFA from Bennington College.

Troni Y. Grande is an associate professor and the Head of the English Department at University of Regina, where she teaches and writes on Shakespeare, Early-Modern Drama and Eighteenth-Century Drama, and Feminist Theory. Her work-in-progress is a memoir celebrating her ties to the life and spiritual legacy of her Ukrainian grandmother, an early twentieth-century pioneer who helped settle east-central Alberta.

Rachel Hall is the author of the forthcoming story collection, *Heirlooms,* winner of the 2015 G.S. Sharat Chandra book prize (BkMk Press). Hall's recent work appears in *Bellingham Review, Crab Orchard Review,* and *Lilith,* which awarded her the 2015 fiction prize. She teaches Creative Writing and literature at the State University of New York at Geneseo.

Emily Hipchen is a Fulbright scholar who edits Adoption & culture and a/b: Autobiography Studies. Her books include *Coming Apart Together: Fragments from an Adoption* (2005), *Inhabiting La Patria: Identity, Agency, and Antojo in the Works of Julia Alvarez* (SUNY 2013) and *The Routledge Auto\Biography Studies Reader* (2015). Her creative writing has appeared in *Fourth Genre, Northwest Review, Cincinnati Review,* and elsewhere. She is a professor at the University of West Georgia.

Pauline Kaldas is the author of *Egyptian Compass* (poetry), *Letters from*

Cairo (memoir), *The Time Between Places* (short stories), and the co-editor of *Dinarzad's Children*. Kaldas was born in Egypt and immigrated with her parents to the U.S. at the age of eight in 1969. She is Associate Professor of English and Creative Writing at Hollins University in Roanoke, Virginia.

Adrianne Kalfopoulou lives and teaches in Athens, Greece where she directs the writing program at Deree College. She is also on the faculty of Regis University's low residency Mile-High MFA Program. Her work has appeared in *Hotel Amerika, The Harvard Review* online, *BPJ, Superstition Review,* and elsewhere. She is the author, most recently, of *Ruin, Essays in Exilic Living.* Her third collection of poetry, *A History of Too Much* is forthcoming in 2018.

Kirun Kapur is the winner of the Arts & Letters Rumi Prize in Poetry and the Antivenom Poetry Award for her first book, *Visiting Indira Gandhi's Palmist.* Her work has appeared in *AGNI, Poetry International, FIELD, The Christian Science Monitor* and elsewhere. She is director of the New England arts program *The Tannery Series* and serves as poetry editor at *The Drum Literary Magazine.*

Matea Kulić is a writer and educator living in Vancouver, BC. Her cultural background as a Canadian/Serbian/Croatian provides a departure point for her artistic practice; a point which she continually complicates through exploration of language, identity and "the tongue" as a site of transformation. Her work has been published in *The Capilano Review, Dreamland, RicePaper, In/Words Magazine, Impressment Mag* and *The Maynard Review.*

Janet Maher is an associate professor of Fine Arts at Loyola University Maryland, where she directs the Studio program. She works in a wide range of processes and has been a professional exhibiting artist for some forty years.

Kathleen McGookey's most recent book is *Stay* (Press 53). Her book *Heart in a Jar* is forthcoming from White Pine Press in spring 2017. Her work has appeared in journals including *Crazyhorse, Denver Quarterly, Epoch, Field, Ploughshares, Prairie Schooner,* and *Quarterly West.* She has received grants from the French Ministry of Foreign Affairs and the Sustainable Arts Foundation.

Marilyn Moriarty is Professor of English and Creative Writing at Hollins University in Roanoke, Virginia. Her nonfiction has been published in *The Antioch Review* (print and online), *Creative Nonfiction, The Kenyon Review,* and in other journals. *Moses Unchained,* which won the AWP prize in creative nonfiction, was reissued as a paperback in 2012. "Swerves" won the 2014 William Faulkner-William Wisdom Gold Medal for the essay.

Kelly Nelson is the author of the chapbooks *Rivers I Don't Live By* and *Who Was I to Say I Was Alive.* She has lived in nine different states and currently resides in Tempe, Arizona where she teaches Interdisciplinary Studies at Arizona State University. Find more at www.kelly-nelson.com.

Leonard Neufeldt is the author, editor or co-editor of seventeen books, including seven volumes of poetry. His latest poetry collection, *Painting Over Sketches of Anatolia,* was published in April 2015 by Signature Editions. His scholarly work has appeared with Cambridge University Press, Oxford University Press and Princeton University Press, among others. He hails from Yarrow, BC.

January Gill O'Neil is the author of *Misery Islands* (CavanKerry Press, 2014) and *Underlife* (CavanKerry Press, 2009). She is executive director of the Massachusetts Poetry Festival and teaches at Salem State University in Salem, Massachusetts.

V. Penelope Pelizzon's second poetry collection, *Whose Flesh Is Flame, Whose Bone Is Time*, was published in 2014 (Waywiser Press). Her first book, *Nostos* (Ohio University Press, 2000), won the Hollis Summers Prize and the Poetry Society of America's Norma Farber First Book Award.

Charlotte Pence is a professor of English and Creative Writing at Eastern Illinois University. She is also is the author of *Many Small Fires* (Black Lawrence Press, 2015), two award-winning poetry chapbooks, and editor of *The Poetics of American Song Lyrics* (University Press of Mississippi, 2012).

Anjoli Roy is a creative writer and PhD student in the English department at the University of Hawai'i at Mānoa. Her most recent work has appeared in *KUY: Stories and Poems, Kweli, Slink Chunk Press,* and *Spiral Orb.* She looks up to her amazing big sister, who is a free-birther and mother of six, and she is grateful for family, who has always kept her fed. You can read more of her work at www.anjoliroy.com.

Martha Silano is the author of *Reckless Lovely, The Little Office of the Immaculate Conception, Blue Positive, What the Truth Tastes Like,* and, with Kelli Russell Agodon, *The Daily Poet: Day-By-Day Prompts For Your Writing Practice.* Martha edits *Crab Creek Review* and teaches at Bellevue College.

Paul Sutherland emigrated from Canada to the UK in 1973. He has published ten poetry collections and is founding editor of *Dream Catcher* journal. He performs his poems frequently. He turned freelance in 2004, and has been involved in wide-ranging literary projects since, from spoken word, commissions, running workshops to being a private mentor. A *Selected Poems* is due from Valley Press (2016).

Marilyn L. Taylor, former Poet Laureate of the state of Wisconsin (2009 and 2010) and the city of Milwaukee (2004 and 2005), is the author of six poetry collections. Her award-winning poems and essays on poetic craft have appeared in many anthologies and journals, including *Poetry, American Scholar, Able Muse, Light Poetry Journal,* and *Measure.*

Marjorie Tesser is the author of poetry chapbooks *The Important Thing Is* (Firewheel Chapbook Award Winner) and *The Magic Feather* (Finishing Line Press). She co-edited the anthologies *Bowery Women: Poems* and *Estamos Aquí: Poems by Migrant Farmworkers* (Bowery Books). She is the editor of the literary journal *Mom Egg Review.*

Pimone Triplett is the author of *Rumor* (2009), *The Price of Light* (2005), and *Ruining the Picture* (1998). She holds an MFA from the University of Iowa. Currently, she teaches at the University of Washington and the Warren Wilson MFA Program for Writers.

Lesley Wheeler's books of poetry include *Radioland, Heterotopia, Heathen,* and *The Receptionist and Other Tales.* Her poems and essays appear in *Ecotone, Crazyhorse, Poetry,* and other magazines. The Henry S. Fox Professor of English at Washington and Lee University, she lives in Lexington, Virginia and blogs about poetry at lesleywheeler.org.

Andrena Zawinski, Features Editor at *Poetry Magazine.com*, is author of *Traveling in Reflected Light,* a Kenneth Patchen Prize in Poetry; her most recent full collection, *Something About,* is a PEN Oakland Josephine Miles Award recipient. She hails from Pittsburgh, PA but lives and teaches writing in the San Francisco Bay Area where she also runs a Women's Poetry Salon.

Permissions